The Winter of Di

Myth, Memory, and History

STUDIES IN LABOUR HISTORY 4

Studies in Labour History

'...a series which will undoubtedly become an important force in re-invigorating the study of Labour History.' *English Historical Review*

Studies in Labour History provides reassessments of broad themes along with more detailed studies arising from the latest research in the field of labour and working-class history, both in Britain and throughout the world. Most books are single-authored but there are also volumes of essays focussed on key themes and issues, usually emerging from major conferences organized by the British Society for the Study of Labour History. The series includes studies of labour organizations, including international ones, where there is a need for new research or modern reassessment. It is also its objective to extend the breadth of labour history's gaze beyond conventionally organized workers, sometimes to workplace experiences in general, sometimes to industrial relations, but also to working-class lives beyond the immediate realm of work in households and communities.

The Winter of Discontent
Myth, Memory, and History

Tara Martin López

LIVERPOOL UNIVERSITY PRESS

First published 2014 by
Liverpool University Press
4 Cambridge Street
Liverpool
L69 7ZU

This paperback version first published 2018.

Copyright © 2014 Tara Martin López

The right of Tara Martin López to be identified as the author of this book has been asserted by her in accordance with the Copyright, Designs and Patents Act 1988.

All rights reserved. No part of this book may be reproduced, stored in a retrieval system, or transmitted, in any form or by any means, electronic, mechanical, photocopying, recording, or otherwise, without the prior written permission of the publisher.

British Library Cataloguing-in-Publication data
A British Library CIP record is available

ISBN 978-1-78138-029-1 cased
ISBN 978-1-78694-173-2 paperback

Typeset by Carnegie Book Production, Lancaster
Printed and bound by CPI Group (UK) Ltd, Croydon CR0 4YY

Table of Contents

Acknowledgements	vii
Foreword by Sheila Rowbotham	ix
Introduction	1
1. Ghosts of the Past: Myth and the Winter of Discontent	7
2. The Winter of Discontent: Causes and Context	26
3. The Floodgates Open: The Strike at Ford	63
4. 'The Second Stalingrad': The Road Haulage Strikes	86
5. Freezers of Corpses and Sea Burials: The Liverpool Gravediggers' Strike	110
6. Unseemly Behaviour: Women and Local Authority Strikes	129
7. 'Celia's Gate' and the Strikes in the NHS	153
8. Crosscurrents: Myth, Memory, and Counter-Memory	177
Conclusion	205
Bibliography	216
Index	230

To the memory of Mary Jane Martin

Acknowledgements

Many people have helped me in the process of completing this work. First and foremost, I would like to thank Sheila Rowbotham for her insight, patience, and support since I began this project. Neville Kirk, Paul Keleman, Kevin Morgan, Paul Smith, Hilary Wainwright, Mike Richardson, Stephen Williams, Dorothy Sue Cobble, Linda McDowell, Leo Panitch, Pamela Beth Radcliff, Charlie Steen, Gemma Edwards, Mike Savage, Nick Crossley, James Nazroo, and Mark Wickham-Jones are but a few of the crucial individuals who helped to bring this book to fruition.

I would like to also extend my thanks the United Kingdom's 'Overseas Research Student Award Fellowship' and the University of Manchester's 'North American Foundation for the University of Manchester Fellowship,' which provided funding for my PhD thesis, which was the basis of this research. I am also appreciative of the Lipman-Miliband and Barry Amiel and Norman Melburn trusts for their generous support for further development of my research in its later stages.

I want to acknowledge the tireless efforts of all the librarians and archivists at the Labor History and Archive Center, the Bodleian Library, the Modern Records Centre at the University of Warwick, the National Archives at Kew, and the Working Class Movement Library. The Ohio State at Newark library's resources and the great help of librarian John Crissinger were also essential to finishing the manuscript. Also, two anonymous readers at Liverpool University Press offered extremely valuable feedback on my manuscript, and I thank them for their insights. Furthermore, Alison Welsby at Liverpool University Press provided careful and patient guidance in the process of publication, for which I am especially grateful.

This research would not have been possible without the generosity of my interviewees. Each and every one shared their invaluable time and knowledge with me. Although there are too many to name individually, I hope that all of my interviewees are aware of how very appreciative I am of their help.

Finally, during the process of completing this book, my wonderful and dear stepmother, Mary Jane Martin, passed away. Although miles apart geographically and culturally, her feisty and intelligent approach to life was not unlike that of the hard working women I met in the course of my research. Like them, Mary Jane was kind, confident, and fought for what was fair and just. I hope that this book honours those values, and that is why I dedicate this book to her.

Tara Martin López
Port Angeles, Washington, USA, 2014

Foreword
Sheila Rowbotham

'The Winter of Discontent' has assumed a mythic character. According to legend, this was the time when rampant greedy trade unionists held the country to ransom; when the fruits of the capitalist good life withered, to be rescued at the eleventh hour by the election of Margaret Thatcher as Prime Minister. This is the tale invoked in the media whenever trade unions show any signs of resistance.

Tara Martin López provides differing perspectives. She took the sensible course of going directly to workers, women as well as men, to trade union leaders, and to Labour politicians and asking them about their memories of the strikes. While this might appear an obvious way of researching the strikes of the late 1970s, surprisingly few journalists and academics have adopted it. The result is illuminating, poignant, and historically invaluable.

While she makes use of oral material to good effect, she complements the interviews with a large range of written material, from government papers to letters in newspapers. Consequently, this book is steeped in experiential evidence carefully contextualized within the stormy decade of the 1970s.

Both aspects allow her to make sense of the sources for conflict. Those 'greedy' workers were responding to inflation and wage restraint. These, in turn, had their origin in financial and economic crises over which those expected to pay the price had not presided. Their voices testify to grim conditions of work, limited options, and a sense of injustice. Their sin in the eyes of capital was simply that this post-war generation expected more. Only just a little more, it was true, but enough to trouble their employers' profit margins and a Right wing in the Conservative Party, seeking control over unions as a means of reducing inflation. Conflict was stark and overt during the 1970s. It was evident not simply on picket lines, but at management training courses, confidentially headed 'Revenge,' and, as Tara Martin López reveals, in a fierce determination among sections of the Tory Party to rattle Labour's skeletons.

This book documents how an initially precarious Margaret Thatcher fostered the homily of the 'Winter of Discontent' to her advantage; it reminds us of the narrow margin by which the complacent and fatally insensitive James Callaghan was defeated in the Commons; and it traces the way in which the legacy of Thatcher was perpetuated through New Labour as seemingly inevitable. Tara Martin López shows how the notion of an incontestable neo-liberalism has been closely intertwined with the reproduction and maintaining of the 'myth' of the 'Winter of Discontent.'

By 'myth' she means understandings of the past that serve ideological needs of the present, or perhaps we should say of *some* people in the present. Against the prevailing negative picture, Tara Martin López offers interrogatory images, other ways of seeing. Her interviews reveal both the traumatic reworking of memories of the strikes and the resistant survival of counter-memories over time. By digging below the surface, she does what an historian is meant to do: she uncovers what is not immediately evident. For some of her interviewees the strikes marked a setback, the beginning of the end of their hope for an equal society. Among others though, the 'Winter of Discontent' provided new openings; they went on to become active in trade unions, in the Labour Party, or in one of the small revolutionary groups.

One of the most fascinating aspects of this book is the manner in which the startling events of the strikes shifted the pattern of individuals' destinies. This dramatic impact on the trajectories of participants makes the 'Winter of Discontent' comparable to the miners' strike of 1984 to 1985. The miners' dispute also bitterly divided the country, but it gained fervent supporters from many walks of life, who wrote letters in their defence, collected tins of food at supermarkets, drove lorries to Welsh mining villages with provisions, adopted collieries, and signed petitions. I believe this was partially because of the support of women, who implicitly extended the meaning of the workplace rebellion to a threat to communities, ways of life, and values. The strike became a social strike: the miners still were defeated, but they were not to be remembered as bogeymen.

One of the intriguing points to emerge from Tara Martin López's account is that union leaders in the late 1970s put the main emphasis on workers' power to resist. While it is easy to be wise after the event, I believe this to have been a strategic mistake. Collective class opposition to exploitation and solidarity with other workers are vital. But in order to communicate outwards to people who have no immediate empathy with the actuality of work on an assembly line, digging a grave, driving a lorry, handling emergency calls, doing laundry in a hospital, other aspects of tacit class experience need to be spelled out in individual terms. The hidden injuries of class are both physical and psychological. Anger builds up when work is undervalued; when skill is dismissed; when people are regarded with contempt and denied the capacity to define and control their circumstances.

The men and women who went on strike during the 'Winter of Discontent' had briefly glimpsed moderately better times, but during the late 1970s this was being snatched away. Their prospects in life were narrowing. Squeezed on all sides, they erupted into action and have been consistently reviled ever since. Tara Martin López enables the voices of a few of them to be heard. It is to be hoped that her book will encourage more people to come forward with 'counter-memories' to combat the unjust, bullying 'myth' which has portrayed them as selfish wreckers.

In this book, Tara Martin López also brings up several paths not taken, reminding us how, during the 1970s and through the 1980s, alternative propositions to the onslaught on trade unions, the introduction of privatization, the extension of casualization, and the attack on the social wage were very much alive and kicking. Socialist economists were already aware in this period of the global power of multinationals and the inequitable impact of inflation on the poor. They were proposing solutions.

While the alternative economic strategies they were discussing have begun to arouse the interest of researchers, the implications of socialist feminist economic and social thinking in this period have gone relatively unexplored. At a time when more women were entering the paid workforce as well as the trade unions, feminists, as Tara Martin López notes, were challenging a culturally biased definition of 'real workers' as being men in manufacturing *and* asserting the material significance of women's domestic labour in the home. These critiques led to a theoretical engendering of the conception of 'work' and to a practice that conceived the whole-scale transformation of production and reproduction. Socialist feminists within the women's liberation movement of the 1970s were arguing for shorter hours, greater awareness of the toll of work upon the body, and the valuing of care and service to human beings whether it happened to be paid or unpaid. We were also experimenting with new forms of co-operative association in communities, seeking to democratize access to resources controlled by the local and national state, not simply for women, but for those who for whatever reason were dependent.

Moreover, because the women's movement owed its very emergence to a protest against cultural silencing, many socialist feminists saw a political connection not only in the formal assertions of democracy within the Alternative Economic Strategy (AES), but in the practical struggles for direct democracy appearing among the shop stewards' combine committees sprouting in this period. A particularly close link developed with workers involved in the Lucas Aerospace Alternative Plan, when highly skilled men making weapons resisted redundancies by developing their own socially useful prototypes to help people with disabilities and in poor countries. Their respect for tacit knowledge tallied closely with women's liberation's emphasis upon democratizing the processes of knowing.

Socialist feminism was to be a transformative path untaken, even though it affected the lives of many women. However, attempted paths leave traces; these ideas have circulated globally, affecting development discourses and policies. Closer at hand they have had a sustained, though relatively unremarked, impact on women in British trade unions. They feature in Tara Martin López's book and they are a vigorous presence in our contemporary, much battered and besieged trade union movement.

And what of today? There are indeed pressing reasons why Tara Martin López's study of the late 1970s is pertinent. The era initiated by Margaret Thatcher's rule was to leave a legacy of intensified inequality, unregulated financial speculation, highly dangerous working conditions, and a culture that promoted a short-term monetary assessment of cost and value. The capitalism in which we live now is a more brutal, inhuman beast than the derided 'chaos' of the 1970s. But there are some uncanny echoes. In our rich country large numbers of children grow up in poverty and inflation is mounting. Unemployment, especially among the young, is high. Blame is placed not on those who grow wealthy under such a state of affairs, but upon an assortment of those who are badly served; the old, the disabled, the homeless, immigrants, and, of course, trade unionists. There is even talk again of the need to nurture a blue collar Conservatism.

Remembering thwarted past possibilities has, for several decades, been trounced as 'nostalgia.' Yet nostalgia really needs rehabilitating, for within it nestles a profound potency. Tracing a tradition buried within the kind of counter-memories Tara Martin López uncovers prepares ground in which the shoots of hope can be revitalized and recreated in new movements. Her examination of the 'mythologizing' of the 'Winter of Discontent' moreover unlocks one key component in the broader silencing of any fundamental alternative discussion of what might be.

Occasionally, amidst the everyday, people in struggle experience a jolt, an incongruence that makes them look out at the world in a different way and wonder why things remain as they are. One striker in this book graphically describes the world being turned inside out. After some great social upheaval, if the old world comes creeping back, consciousness jerks into place again. But memory remains. This is one of the most elusive aspects of experience for historians – and particularly so when those being regarded are not the winners. History on the whole favours winners, but winners do not constitute the whole story. The ignoble and unknown have gained radical chroniclers, and Tara Martin López joins them in recording neglected aspirations, though her work is also tempered by a democratic awareness of the need to explore the perspectives of a broad range of participants in those Winter strikes who took contradictory and sometimes conflicting paths.

Introduction

In June 2013, Education Secretary Michael Gove criticized striking teachers. 'There are far better ways to secure enhanced working environments for teachers than 70s-style trade union tactics.' Gove's allusion sought to strike a chord with the British public and press. *The Daily Mail* explains, 'Referencing the 1970s will trigger uncomfortable memories of the strikes that shook the country that decade, culminating in the winter of discontent when rubbish was left on streets and bodies went unburied.'[1] The evocation of the Winter of Discontent, a series of strikes over 34 years ago, is still common in British political culture. In 1978–79 workers engaged in a series of strikes in protest against the then Labour government's wage limits. These controls, or incomes policies, were not uncommon in post-war Britain, but for British trade unions, three years of wage restraint, coupled with inflation depressing workers' wages, made the rank-and-file membership increasingly less likely to abide yet another year of such a policy. Towards the end of 1978, Labour Prime Minister James Callaghan's imposition of a 5 per cent wage limit proved particularly galling, and trade unions were in a position to effectively resist the government's efforts. The first rupture came in September 1978, when Ford workers went on strike for an increase of 17 per cent, effectively breaking the income policy.[2] Overtime bans among oil tanker drivers and strikes in road haulage soon ensued. When public sector workers followed with nationally co-ordinated action in January of 1979, some of the most iconic images of these strikes exploded across British newspapers and television with piles of rubbish on the streets because of

---

[1] Andrew Levy, 'Striking Teachers are Using 70s-Style Tactics to Avoid Being Assessed,' *Daily Mail*, June 21, 2013, http://www.dailymail.co.uk/news/article-2346267/Striking-teachers-using-1970s-style-tactics-avoid-assessed-Gove-claims.html.

[2] Ken Coates and Tony Topham, *Trade Unions and Politics* (Oxford: Basil Blackwell, 1986), 198.

striking dustmen, services limited at hospitals by striking domestic cleaners, and, most notoriously, mourners turned away by picketing gravediggers. Such drama prompted the *Sun* editor Larry Lamb to coin this dramatic series of events 'The Winter of Discontent.'[3]

The Conservative Party, under the leadership of Margaret Thatcher, capitalized on these strikes as shining examples of Labour's inability to control its own supporters in the trade union movement. This strategy proved effective, and Thatcher was elected to office on May 3, 1979 with a supposed 'mandate' to 'clip the wings' of trade unions.[4] She made good on her promise for more than a decade, and by the time she left office, 'labour was bludgeoned onto the defensive' with a combination of anti-union legislation, the defeat of the 1984 miners' strike, deindustrialization, and the overall decline of unionization across Britain.[5]

The strikes have also become the stuff of legend. The Winter of Discontent has lingered as a powerful but vague and confused amalgam of negative impressions and, often, historic inaccuracies. When British media scholar James Thomas polled a class of undergraduates almost 25 years later in 2003 about their understanding of the Winter of Discontent, the replies were varied:

> Socialism; mass strikes: rubbish; 1970s *Billy Elliot/Brassed Off* type era; industrial struggle; no fuel; low economy; desperation; 3 day week; street violence; unemployment; rats eating litter on streets; rubbish lining the streets; rioting; Saatchi and Saatchi; Crisis? What Crisis?; country at a complete standstill.[6]

Author Andy Beckett concisely extolls the prevalence of such distortions. 'I have lost track of how many times I have read or heard that the punk revolt of 1976–77 was a "reaction" to the Winter of Discontent of 1978–79.'[7]

The potency of this mix of shared, and often historically inaccurate, rememberings, and its underlying moral narrative of trade union betrayal and Thatcherite redemption, has elevated the Winter of Discontent to something beyond a common memory. As journalist Nigel Fountain observes,

> The Winter persists as myth, folk tale, a Seventies Labour disaster to

---

[3] Quoted in James Thomas, *Popular Newspapers, the Labour Party, and British Politics* (New York: Routledge, 2005), 84.

[4] Thomas, *Popular Newspapers*, 84.

[5] Geoff Eley, *Forging Democracy: The History of the Left in Europe, 1850–2000* (Oxford: Oxford University Press, 2002), 391.

[6] James Thomas, '"Bound in by History": The Winter of Discontent in British Politics, 1979–2004,' *Media, Culture, & Society* 29 (2007): 276, doi: 10.1177/0163443707074257.

[7] Andy Beckett, *When the Lights Went Out: Britain in the Seventies* (London: Faber and Faber, 2009), 2.

cap the Zinoviev letter of the Twenties or the Groundnut Scheme of the Forties. It is the centrepiece of a Conservative triptych flanked by 'the failed spendthrift policies of the Sixties and Seventies' and Beer and Sandwiches at Number 10.[8]

This myth's power has not simply been the fodder of interested journalists, but eventually became an uncomfortable political reality for the Labour Party. The image of an ineffectual government in the face of trade union insurgence so effectively haunted the party that 13 years later, a study exploring Labour's failure in the 1992 general election concluded, 'Labour lost because it was still the party of the winter of discontent; union influence; strikes and inflation; disarmament; Benn and Scargill.'[9]

In *The Winter of Discontent: Myth, Memory, and History*, therefore, I want to move beyond the provocative and one-dimensional representations in order to understand the underlying complexity of the forces that shaped these events. More specifically, I aim to deconstruct the myth that has developed around the Winter of Discontent not merely to debunk misunderstandings, but to penetrate into the depths of *why* it still resonates deeply in popular memory. I then examine the experiences of key actors whose perspectives have been consistently elided from the dominant discourse: local trade union leaders and grassroots activists involved in the strikes. Furthermore, I will interrogate the gender and racially neutral assumptions of class that are intertwined with the dominant narrative. In particular, I want to draw out how social class, which is such a central element in this narrative, is anything but monolithic. Rather, I seek to reincorporate the gender and racial diversity of those individuals who helped to influence industrial relations and politics in the late 1970s. With these essential viewpoints incorporated into a wider investigation, further informed by archival research and the accounts of national trade union and Labour Party leaders, I want to transcend facile characterizations of all the central actors in the narrative to understand the motivating forces and lasting effects of the Winter of Discontent on the contemporary British political landscape and on these individuals' own political identities.

Myth, Memory, and Power

I first learned about the Winter of Discontent in 2003 when discussing politics with a British friend who continually referred to how bad things were in 1979. During the Winter of Discontent, trade unions supposedly

---

[8] Nigel Fountain, 'A Long Hot Winter,' *Guardian* (Weekend), September 19, 1993.
[9] Phillip Gould, *The Unfinished Revolution: How Modernisers Saved the Labour Party* (London: Little, Brown, and Company, 1998), 158.

'were out of control,' and Margaret Thatcher intervened and brought Britain out of a socialist mire. I was amazed not only that a person born in 1980 would have such a powerful memory of the event, but also that it was a touchstone of his conversations decades later. Moreover, as an American, other than the Vietnam War and Watergate, I could not recall any such parallel events from the 1970s that appeared to resonate so acutely as the Winter of Discontent did with my friend. My interest was piqued, so I set out to investigate the history of this series of events myself.

When I began my investigation, my friend's understanding of what had happened appeared vindicated: the trade union movement rejected a fourth year of wage restraint with industrial action that helped to weaken the Labour government and contributed to the rise of Margaret Thatcher. However, as I began my interviews, especially with rank-and-file activists and local trade union leaders, a completely different image of the Winter of Discontent emerged: one of a justified battle against an unresponsive national trade union and Labour Party leadership. Even more intriguing was female activists' depiction of the Winter of Discontent as an invigorating and transformative moment in their lives.

It is the myth, and these key perspectives enshrouded in it, therefore, that will be the focus of my investigation. I will begin with how and why this series of events eventually became so resonant in the British popular imagination. Hence, chapter one will proceed from the immediate end of the Winter of Discontent, at a pivotal time in the development of the ensuing legend. In particular, I will demonstrate how the Conservative Party's election campaign played a key role in shaping the specific contours, images, and narratives that have become entrenched in the dominant understanding of this series of events. I also develop upon James Thomas' assertion that it was the Conservative Party's 're-presentation' of the Winter of Discontent during the 1980s and 1990s that was vital to the crystallization of this myth, the effects of which were very real for both the Conservatives' and Labour's electoral fortunes.

The book's trajectory will then depart from myth and move to history. Chapter two will focus on the historical antecedents to the Winter of Discontent. While international and national political and economic currents will be taken into account, changes in British society will be interwoven into this wider narrative. In particular, the significance of the lives of women, blacks, and Asians will be brought to the fore of this post-war account. Chapter three will detail the rise of the Ford strike in November 1978 by examining the evolving political identities of rank-and-file Ford workers and shop stewards to understand the myriad economic, political, racial, ethnic, and religious forces that shaped their motivation to embark on this first strike of the Winter of Discontent. Chapters four and five will then delve into two of the most controversial forms of industrial action taken in 1978–79: the road haulage and the Liverpool gravediggers' strikes. Not only will these chapters follow the shifting political identities of both national Labour Party and local trade union leaders involved in the disputes, but it will interrogate popular images from these strikes that have comprised the dominant understanding of this series of events. Chapters six and seven will examine strikes among school meals workers and hospital ancillaries in the National Health Service (NHS). In these chapters I will lay specific emphasis on the experiences of the female majority in one of the central unions involved: the National Union of Public Employees (NUPE). These chapters will reveal that seemingly personal experiences, combined with nascent political consciousness and a concerted effort to harness women's energies in 1979 inspired these individuals to take industrial action. Again, a deconstruction of myths about this specific bout of strikes will be compared to the experiences of these participants and empirical research. Chapter eight will tie in the viewpoints of all of these different players, from national Labour politicians to rank-and-file activists, to reveal the different ways these individuals remember the Winter of Discontent and what effect, if any, it had on their political identities in the twenty-first century.

I will argue that much of the popular understanding of the Winter of Discontent has become mythologized and profoundly shaped by the political vicissitudes of the Conservative Party in particular, but also of New Labour. While the hegemonic image of the Winter of Discontent arose out of a very real sense of chaos and crisis, the mythical resonance of these experiences was only developed after the series of strikes had been resolved. Furthermore, I will assert that instead of a fratricidal act, rank-and-file activists and local trade union leaders were engaged in activism that hoped to address declining real wages and shifts in the ideological, gender, and racial composition of the trade union movement and the Labour Party. Although describing the 1970s in the United States, historian Jefferson Cowie helps to frame this dynamic when he writes, 'For working people, the social upheavals associated with the sixties actually took root in most communities in the seventies, which was not simply a different decade but a distinctly less generous economic climate.'[10] Therefore, this series of strikes must be seen in the context of evolving social movements such as the New Left and the Women's Movement. I will also contend that the memories of local trade union leaders and grassroots activists involved in the strikes qualifies the grim and dire implications of the hegemonic understanding of the Winter of Discontent. More specifically, among some of the female

---

[10] Jefferson Cowie, *Stayin' Alive: The 1970s and the Last Days of the Working Class* (New York: The New Press, 2010), 6.

trade unionists, the strikes of 1978–79 provided a transformative inroad into broader activism in the labour movement for years to come. Finally, I will assert that the different rememberings of the Winter of Discontent have distinctly shaped the participants' political identities, delivering a snapshot of the political landscape and opportunities on the Left in the twenty-first century.

1

Ghosts of the Past: Myth and the Winter of Discontent

On January 23, 1979, a concerned Mancunian acerbically addressed British Prime Minister James Callaghan in the *Manchester Evening News*. In the letter 'Hardly all mod cons, but [...] HOW ABOUT A STAY UP HERE JIM?' the author extends a dubious invitation to share the author's view of Manchester's local factories, which are supposedly empty due to strikes.[1] Seizing upon the frigid scene of the city weeks after experiencing its worst blizzard since the First World War,[2] the author warns of ice-covered roads, but sarcastically concedes that, 'I believe we do have a plentiful supply of grit and sand in Manchester – we just can't find anybody to put it down for us,' because of widespread industrial action. The sardonic tone reaches a fever pitch as the writer explains, 'Guests are respectfully requested not to become ill during their stay, as transportation to the hospitals that are open is limited,' again apparently as the result of the industrial disputes.[3]

That same day, 'Working Woman from Wythenshawe,' takes a more optimistic and historic view of the situation. She implores readers to understand the current round of strikes in the context of workers' struggles in the 1870s and '80s. She further encourages readers to remember their forbearers: 'Because of these people [union activists] our kith and kin – we have the right to vote and put our problems to government.'[4] Published on the same day, one letter depicts a Britain steeped in an ungovernable crisis, while the other recounts the same actions as part of a broader arc of noble trade union activism.

---

[1] 'Postbag' (letter to the editor), *Manchester Evening News*, January 23, 1979.
[2] Dominic Sandbrook, *Seasons in the Sun: The Battle for Britain, 1974–1979* (London: Allen Lane, 2012), 723.
[3] 'Postbag' (letter to the editor), *Manchester Evening News*, January 23, 1979.
[4] 'Working Woman from Wythenshawe,' 'Postbag' (letter to the editor), *Manchester Evening News*, January 23, 1979.

Almost a decade later, perspectives on this series of strikes were similarly bifurcated. In her 1985 speech to the Conservative Party Conference, Margaret Thatcher evoked a dismal spectre of the Winter of Discontent:

> Do you remember the Labour Britain of 1979? It was a Britain – in which union leaders held their members and our country to ransom; – A Britain that still went to international conferences but was no longer taken seriously; – A Britain that was known as the sick man of Europe; – And which spoke of the language of compassion but which suffered the winter of discontent.[5]

Regional NUPE officer Frank Huff and NUPE shop steward Jamie Morris, however, summon up a memory of the Winter of Discontent in an entirely different light. For Huff, 'The winter of discontent was worth it. It aroused the political awareness of our members and showed them the need for solidarity.' Morris is more effusive, 'I supposed I enjoyed the winter of discontent. I certainly don't regret it.'[6]

Although conflicting, these impressions apparently transcend individual recollection and have been indelibly impressed upon people on a broader scale. Maurice Halbwachs' concept of 'collective memory' elucidates the contours of this phenomenon. In the early twentieth century, Halbwachs disputed the idea of memory as simply an inert and undisturbed entity 'lodged in an individual's mind.'[7] Instead, he argued that 'the framework of collective memory confines and binds our most intimate remembrances to each other.'[8] Furthermore, according to Halbwachs, this shared remembering facilitates a sense of identity and belonging to a wider group, a phenomenon that will be apparent in the contrasting memories and subsequently divergent political identities forged during the Winter of Discontent.[9]

Beyond memory, the Winter of Discontent has also developed into a

---

[5] Speech to Conservative Party Conference, October 11, 1985. Margaret Thatcher Foundation, http://www.margaretthatcher.org/document/106145.

[6] Maurice Chittenden, 'Year That Put Labour on Ice; Trade Unions,' *Sunday Times*, January 22, 1989. *Academic OneFile*, accessed April 23, 2013, http://go.galegroup.com/ps/i.do?id=GALE%7CA117543208&v=2.1&u=cp;i44332&it=r&p=AONE&sw=w.

[7] Maurice Halbwachs, *On Collective Memory*, trans. and ed. Lewis Coser (Chicago: The University of Chicago Press, 1992), 52–53; Geoffrey Cubitt, *History and Memory* (Manchester: Manchester University Press, 2007), 58. The work on collective memory is extensive. Some key texts include: Paul Connerton, *How Societies Remember* (Cambridge: Cambridge University Press, 1989); James Fentress and Chris Wickham, *Social Memory: New Perspectives on the Past* (Oxford: West Blackwell, 1992); Katherine Hodgkin and Susannah Radstone, eds., Introduction to *Contested Pasts: The Politics of Memory* (London: Routledge, 2003).

[8] Halbwachs, *On Collective Memory*, 53.

[9] Halbwachs, *On Collective Memory*, 70.

salient myth. As historian Nick Tiratsoo illustrates, the process of this myth's evolution is often compounded with that of the 1970s.

> The taste of fear and insecurity lingered on. Thatcher and her colleagues knew what this was all about and above all explained it. Over time, recollection and myth gradually fused to form a new 'truth.' Britain *had* been collapsing in the 1970s; Labour and the unions *were* to blame; and Thatcher *was* the saviour. This is the version which still holds sway in some quarters today.[10]

This observation has its counterpart in the popular culture, too. In the documentary *Filth and the Fury* (2000) on the Sex Pistols, band members Steve Jones and John Lydon narrate their impressions of the 1970s, explicitly indicting the Winter of Discontent for the grim nature of this decade:

> It was cold and miserable, no-one had any jobs, you couldn't get a job. Total social chaos. There was rioting all over the place, strikes on every kind of amenity you could think of. The TV channels would go on and off randomly [...] there was also a garbage strike that went on for years and years and years and there was trash piled ten foot high.[11]

The broader resilience of this myth became all the more apparent in an undergraduate course I taught at the University of Manchester when one student wanted to know the subject of my PhD thesis. I merely answered with, 'the Winter of Discontent.' Another student immediately interrupted with, 'Oh that was when the miners marched down to London!' When I said 'no,' he persisted. 'Oh, then it was the miners' strike.' 'Not exactly.' 'Then it was the 3-day week!'

The lasting effect of this confused but redemptive narrative, therefore, conforms to George Lipsitz's definition of myth, which he asserts is 'one form of storytelling that goes beyond verifiable evidence to providing unifying symbols and rituals that enable people to interpret common experiences. [...] In many ways myths supersede history in contemporary popular consciousness.'[12] Images of rubbish piled in Leicester Square, striking gravediggers, and picketed hospitals eventually became trenchant symbols that would embody the chaos of an entire decade. The embeddedness of a memory infused with a mix of errors, political fact, and evocative images is

---

[10] Nick Tiratsoo, '"You've Never Had It So Bad": Britain in the 1970s,' in *From Blitz to Blair: A New History of Britain Since 1939*, ed. Nick Tiratsoo (London: Weidenfeld & Nicolson, 1997), 189–190.

[11] *The Filth and the Fury* (2000) Quoted in Thomas, 'Bound in by History,' 268.

[12] George Lipsitz, *Time Passages: Collective Memory and American Popular Culture* (1990; Minneapolis: University of Minnesota Press, 2000), 216.

particularly interesting in understanding the Winter of Discontent because it intimates the broader historical significance of this series of events.

What is also distinctive about this legend is its intention and scope. As Peter Burke argues, myths are distinguished by their conflation of the past with the present, the 'unintended consequences [...] turned into conscious aims.'[13] The effects of the Winter of Discontent, most specifically the rise of Thatcherism, accordingly appear deliberate and justified elements of the narrative.[14] Nevertheless, someone has to set such an account in motion, and historian Paul Cohen refers to these individuals as 'mythologizers.' He asserts that they have a conception of the past that they believe to be correct, but their purpose is not to broaden our understanding of the past. Instead, they seek to '[...] serve the political, ideological, rhetorical, and/or emotional needs of the present.'[15] Colin Hay's theorization of the 'collective mythology' specifically of the Winter of Discontent underlines the politicization of memory that Cohen illustrates. Hay argues that the media largely constructed the Winter of Discontent as a moment of crisis that called for the New Right's 'particular type of decisive intervention.' Consequently, the enduring legacy of Thatcherism 'has been the new political lexicon of crisis, siege, and subterfuge born of the winter of discontent.'[16] Cohen and Hay's insights, therefore, re-position our focus not merely on the intricacies of the legend, but onto those who sought to fashion and gain from promulgating a specific version of history to bolster contemporary ideological arrangements. In particular, it allows us to eventually understand how the shared understanding of the Winter of Discontent has been shaped by the Conservative Party and later appropriated by New Labour.

If one were to merely challenge the popular myth, its resonance with people is ignored. As Michael Schudson explains, 'Myths necessarily have multiple meanings; in fancier terms, they are "polysemic." They do not tell

---

[13] Peter Burke, 'History as Social Memory,' in *The Collective Memory Reader*, ed. Jeffrey K. Olick, Vered Vinitzky-Seroussi, and Daniel Levy (Oxford: Oxford University Press, 2011), 192.

[14] The following two works effectively analyse the myth of the Winter of Discontent and the crucial role it plays in understanding the subsequent rise of Thatcherism in Britain. Kevin Jefferys, *Finest and Darkest Hours: The Decisive Events in British Politics from Churchill to Blair* (London: Atlantic Books, 2002) and Tiratsoo, 'You've Never Had It So Bad,' 163–90.

[15] Paul A. Cohen, *History in Three Keys: The Boxers as Event, Experience, and Myth* (New York: Columbia University Press, 1997), 213.

[16] Colin Hay, 'Narrating Crisis: The Discursive Construction of the 'Winter of Discontent,' *Sociology* 30, no. 2 (1996): 253, doi: 10.1177/0038038596030002004. See also: Colin Hay, 'The Winter of Discontent Thirty Years On,' *The Political Quarterly* 80, no. 4 (2009): 545–552; Colin Hay, 'Chronicles of a Death Foretold: The Winter of Discontent and Construction of the Crisis of British Keynesianism,' *Parliamentary Affairs* 63, No. 3 (2010): 446–470.

a culture's simple truths as much as they explore its central dilemmas.'[17] As both Kevin Jefferys and Nick Tiratsoo rightly observe, while the myth of the Winter of Discontent is riddled with constructed inaccuracies, it is essential to understand *why* this version of events strikes a chord with the British public.[18] This awareness, therefore, must be balanced with an analysis of the Conservative Party's well-developed media savvy and political stratagem. Just as one must be careful not to condescend to the British public, neither should we patronize the Conservative Party of the late 1970s by ignoring their proficient and thorough planning during the general election of 1979.

Nevertheless, the legacy of the Winter of Discontent has gone relatively unchallenged in popular literature of the time. In several books recently published on the history of the 1970s, many of the authors frame the Winter of Discontent as the culmination of a decade considered a pale, and in many ways embarrassing, comparison to the dazzling 1960s.[19] Against the backdrop of the 1960s, the 1970s represented '[...] the sickly, neglected, disappointing stepsister to that brash, bruising blockbuster of a decade [1960s].'[20] Howard Sounes reflects:

> There was a consensus among journalists and other pundits that the decade was somehow a rather stupid, indeed vulgar, one – certainly when compared to the ever-glamorous 1960s – but amusingly stupid and vulgar: a time of endearingly foolish fashions, embarrassingly bad (so bad it is good) music and deliciously trashy TV and films.[21]

Nick Tiratsoo and Colin Hay provide the most focused academic investigations of the mythology of the Winter of Discontent. Tiratsoo, first of all, provides a point-by-point refutation of the common misconceptions about the Winter of Discontent. More importantly, he effectively rejects the assertion that the Callaghan government mismanaged the British economy and emphasizes key economic improvements after 1976.[22] While Tiratsoo

---

[17] Michael Schudson, *Watergate in American Memory: How We Remember, Forget, and Reconstruct the Past*, rev. ed. (New York: Basic Books, 1993), 124.

[18] Jefferys, *Finest and Darkest Hours* and Tiratsoo, 'You've Never Had It So Bad,' 163–190.

[19] See Howard Sounes, *Seventies: The Sights, Sounds, and Ideas of a Brilliant Decade* (London: Simon & Schuster, 2006); Christopher Booker, *The Seventies: Portrait of a Decade* (London: Allen Lane, 1980); Alwyn W. Turner, *Crisis? What Crisis?: Britain in the 1970s* (London: Aurum Press, 2008). Andy Beckett takes a much more critical approach to the negative image of the 1970s in *When the Lights Went Out*. Mark Garnett argues that a form of 'retrospective relish' or nostalgia has developed about the 1970s in *From Anger to Apathy: The British Experience since 1975* (London: Jonathan Cape, 2007).

[20] Bruce Schulman, *The Seventies: The Great Shift in American Culture, Society, and Politics* (Cambridge: Da Capo Press, 2001), 1.

[21] Sounes, *Seventies*, 1.

[22] Tiratsoo, 'You've Never Had It So Bad,' 189–190.

touches upon the media messaging during the Winter of Discontent, this subject is of primary focus for Colin Hay. More specifically, Hay unpacks the media representation and argues that such imagery reveals that the Callaghan government was not especially crisis-ridden due to the inherit flaws in the Keynesian model; rather, the Winter of Discontent was largely a 'manufactured crisis.' From the outset it was an unsympathetic media that framed this series of events.[23] These two works will provide a key foundation upon which my own analysis will develop.

Other accounts have attempted to redress the bad image given to the decade of the '70s as a whole, and debunk key misunderstandings about the Winter of Discontent, but they reaffirm that the grim image of this decade continues to be pervasive throughout British society:

> I have been hearing what was wrong with Britain and British politics in the seventies all my adult life. No other political theme has been as relenting. The seventies were grim. The seventies were the hangover from the sixties. The seventies were violent. The seventies were a dead end. Above all: We don't want to go back to the seventies.[24]

What is apparent is that the Winter of Discontent is embedded in a wider mosaic of British post-war history. To interrupt this chronology would, consequently, dislodge the adjoining historical understandings of preceding and subsequent events.[25] Such chronological rearrangements can be profoundly disorientating. By challenging a myth, authors would be posed with the uncomfortable task of questioning the contemporary ideological and political order. Paul Cohen articulates the disquieting effects when he states, 'The dismantling of the mythologized past [...] is seldom pain-free: It entails a loss, often irreversible [...] that can be severely disturbing and may, because of this, be stubbornly resisted.'[26]

This resonant 'pain' to which Cohen refers also helps to also explain why historians sympathetic to trade unions have not provided focused accounts of these strikes in 1978–79. Seeing this series of events as the beginning of a 'dark period of trade union defeat and decline,' some scholars have avoided bringing additional attention to this point in history.[27] Ralph Darlington

---

[23] Hay, 'Narrating Crisis,' 253–277; Hay, 'The Winter of Discontent Thirty Years On,' 545–552; Hay, 'Chronicles of a Death Foretold,' 446–470.

[24] Beckett, *When the Lights Went Out*, 2. See also Jefferys, *Finest and Darkest Hours*; Tiratsoo, 'You've Never Had It So Bad,' 189–190.

[25] Hodgkin and Radstone, Introduction to *Contested Pasts*, 1–21.

[26] Cohen, *History in Three Keys*, 211.

[27] Richard Hyman, review of *Glorious Summer: Class Struggle in 1972 Britain*, by Ralph Darlington and David Lyddon, *International Labor and Working Class History* 64 (October 2003): 187.

and David Lyddon's *Glorious Summer: Class Struggle in 1972 Britain* best exemplifies this trajectory. In both the title and thrust of the work, the authors intentionally shift from what is seen as preponderant attention given to the Winter of Discontent to the 'glorious summer' of strikes of 1972.[28]

This series of strikes has also been broadly framed by the 'dealignment thesis.' British historian Eric Hobsbawm most notably elaborates on this theory in a series of highly influential speeches called *The Forward March of Labour Halted*. Hobsbawm argues that soon after the Second World War the 'common style' of British working-class life, prevalent in the nineteenth century, began to dissolve. Two culprits emerge in perpetrating such disillusion: consumerism and 'economist militancy.' The strikes of the late '60s and '70s, where groups of workers were pitted against one another in order to attain higher wages, would exemplify such 'economist militancy.'[29] In a similar vein, labour historian Robert Taylor explicitly singles out the Winter of Discontent when he writes, 'This was no historic struggle of labour against capital, but a harsh internecine conflict within the working class itself.'[30] Therefore, a reluctance to examine this series of strikes is rooted in the sense that the strikes were an ignoble devolution of working-class political consciousness that easily played into the hands of the Conservative Party.

Absent from these accounts, however, are those perspectives that contest this dominant narrative and provide a more nuanced understanding of class. My analysis, based on more than 60 interviews with participants and corresponding archival material, therefore, will illuminate the perspective of striking workers seen as irrationally working against their own interests in 1978 and 1979. In the process a current of memory that challenges the dominant narrative, a counter-memory, will emerge. George Lipsitz's definition of 'counter-memory,' first of all, helps to understand the memories of both grassroots activists and national leaders whose accounts challenge

---

[28] Ralph Darlington and David Lyddon, *Glorious Summer: Class Struggle in 1972 Britain* (London: Bookmarks, 2001).

[29] Eric Hobsbawm, 'The Forward March of Labour Halted? (1978)' and 'The Debate on "The Forward March of Labour Halted?" (1981),' in *Politics for a Rational Left* (London: Verso, 1989), 9–28 and 29–41. See also Paul Foot, *The Vote: How It Was Won and How It Was Undermined* (London: Viking, 2005) and Robert Taylor, 'The Rise and Fall of the Social Contract,' in *New Labour, Old Labour: The Wilson and Callaghan Governments, 1974–79*, ed. Anthony Seldon and Kevin Hickson (London: Routledge, 2004), 70–104.

[30] Taylor, 'The Rise and Fall of the Social Contract,' 96. Exclusive historical investigation into the Winter of Discontent exists; however, others that echo Taylor's view include: Denis Healey, *The Time of My Life* (London: Penguin Books, 1989): Kenneth Morgan, *Callaghan: A Life* (Oxford: Oxford University Press, 1997); Bernard Donoughue, *Prime Minister: The Conduct of Policy under Harold Wilson and James Callaghan* (London: Cape, 1987).

this prevalent legend. In addition to shedding light on the lives of those previously ignored, counter-memory also textures our broader understanding of the history of the Winter of Discontent:

> Counter-memory looks to the past for the hidden histories excluded from dominant narratives. But unlike myths that seek to detach events and actions from the fabric of any larger history, counter-memory forces a revision of existing histories by supplying new perspectives about the past.[31]

Lipsitz reveals the importance of excavating these counter-memories, not with the purpose of simply seeing them as isolated and distinct experiences, but of understanding their connection to broader historical trends.

Nevertheless, forces of counter-memory must undergo the same rigorous interrogation as that of the hegemonic remembering of the Winter of Discontent. In the process of analysing the 60 interviews gathered during my research, some of the interviewees were inaccurate about details of their memory. While archival research was essential to corroborating their accounts, these errors can provide insight, too. Italian oral historian Alessandro Portelli, for instance, has noted that despite interviewees' factual mistakes, the 'errors, inventions, and myths' that arise 'lead us through and beyond facts to their meanings.'[32]

In addition to meaning, identity can also emerge from these accounts. Charlotte Linde defines 'life stories' both as a medium through which identity is expressed and as a means of defining one's identity in relation to others. Linde observes that life stories indicate how people define their values, beliefs, and their overall membership in a group.[33] Historian Daniel James put this concept into practice in an exploration of the life and political identity of the Argentinean trade unionist Doña María Roldán covering a span of several years. He notes that rather than seeing Roldán as 'simply a repository of more or less coherent, more or less available historical data,' he came to understand that 'Doña María was narrating, telling me a story of her life, reconstructing her past in a selective way that would both legitimize

---

[31] Lipsitz, *Time Passages*, 213. While Michel Foucault's understanding of counter-memory precedes that of Lipsitz, the latter's specific definition of counter-memory will frame my argument here. Michel Foucault, *Language, Counter-Memory, Practice: Selected Essays and Interviews* (Ithaca: Cornell University Press, 1977).

[32] Alessandro Portelli, *The Death of Luigi Trastulli and Other Stories: Form and Meaning in Oral History* (Albany: State of New York Press, 1991), 2. See also Fentress and Wickham, *Social Memory*.

[33] Charlotte Linde, *Life Stories: The Creation of Coherence* (New York: Oxford University Press, 1993), 3.

it to me and make sense of it to herself.'[34] Hence, a critical deconstruction of interviewees' 'counter-myths' will not only be challenged, but utilized for the inaccuracies that lead to deeper insights about the Winter of Discontent. Moreover, interviewees' omissions and nostalgia provide unique insight into how people interpret and understand not simply the events, but their role and effect on individuals' political identities.

The dynamism of participants' accounts and identities, consequently, necessitates a much broader understanding of social class. E.P. Thompson's emphasis, for instance, on the critical role, not only of work and economy, but also of the social and cultural forces shaping class, creates a more encompassing conceptualization that frames my analysis. He suggests that people are not helpless in relation to these forces, but are, in fact, active agents. He writes:

> Class happens when some men, as a result of common experiences (inherited or shared), feel and articulate the identity of their interests as between themselves, and as against other men whose interests are different from (and usually opposed to) theirs.[35]

Thompson's definition moves beyond the idea of class as a structure, presenting instead a fluid set of shared experiences in which individuals continually fashion and refashion a collective identity. He therefore not only challenges us to understand the agency involved in creating class, but also inspires us to look beyond economics for other signifiers of class, such as gender and race.

Feminist historians have been especially attuned to the complexity of class and have criticized the tendency of labour historians to continue to 'refer to "workers" and the "working class" when they are really writing about male workers.'[36] The effort to 'write' working women into the larger narrative of labour history has not simply entailed acknowledging the efforts of such women; it has involved a broader critique of how women have been often disregarded as a depoliticizing and/or a conservative force in politics.[37] As Ava Baron observes, there is no realm that goes untouched by gender. Rather

---

[34] Daniel James, *Doña María's Story: Life History, Memory and Political Identity* (Durham: Duke University Press, 2000), 123.

[35] E.P. Thompson, *The Making of the English Working Class* (1963; repr. New York: Vintage Books, 1966), 9–10.

[36] Ava Baron, 'Gender and Labor History: Learning from the Past, Looking to the Future,' in *Work Engendered: Towards a New History of American Labor*, ed. Ava Baron (Ithaca: Cornell University Press, 1991), 4; Sheila Rowbotham, *A Century of Women: The History of Women in Britain and the United States in the Twentieth Century* (London: Penguin, 1997).

[37] Baron, 'Gender and Labor History,' 7–8.

than being at the periphery of labour struggles, gender is an intrinsic element in working-class life.

> As a social process, we need to think of *gender* not only as a noun but also a verb. The study of gendering is concerned with how understandings of sexual difference shape institutions, practices, and relationships.
>
> A gender analysis of work and economy means going beyond the study of women workers and women's work to study how gender affects and is affected by capitalist development and class formation. When we study the gendering of work, we look at how gender becomes a property of activities and institutions as well as of individuals.[38]

Part of this process has redefined the sphere of politicization. Historians Laura Frader and Sonya O. Rose argue the need 'to dissolve the oppositional categories of public and private [sphere]' in an effort to better understand the political role of women in labour history.[39]

Literature on trade unions has also paid scant, if any, specific attention to constructions of race. More specifically, they have tended to ignore white, West Indian, and Asian identities and instead subsumed such racialized experiences into class. Sociologist Paul Gilroy highlights the problem with such a methodological approach:

> Conflicts around 'race', nation and ethnicity must be examined in the light of these other divisions where the unity of a single 'working class' cannot be assumed but remains to be created. [...] The concept is useful to the extent that it ties political struggles to the goal of reappropriating the material structures of production but the antagonisms which form around 'race' and racism are not limited by that aim.[40]

Gilroy argues that while West Indian and Asian workers do share experiences based on class with white working-class people, race and racism are distinct elements of their daily lives, so to privilege a working-class identity over that of a West Indian or Asian identity ignores powerful forces that distinctly shape their lives. Such insights help to reposition my focus as I seek to understand the dynamics of class, gender, and race at this time.[41]

My investigation thus seeks to fill in the voids and omissions by system-

---

[38] Baron, 'Gender and Labor History,' 36–37.

[39] Laura Frader and Sonya O. Rose, 'Introduction: Gender and the Reconstruction of European Working-Class History,' in *Gender and Class in Modern Europe*, ed. Laura Frader and Sonya O. Rose (Ithaca: Cornell University Press, 1996), 23.

[40] Paul Gilroy, *There Ain't No West Indian in the Union Jack*, rev. ed. (1987; Milton Park: Routledge, 2006), 9. For an additional insight into the issues of race, gender, and class in British history see: Laura Tabili, *'We Ask for British Justice': Workers and Racial Difference in Later Imperial Britain* (Ithaca: Cornell University Press, 1994).

[41] A key work that incorporates a broader understanding of working-class politics and

atically analysing the myth, the memory, and the history of the Winter of Discontent with particular attention given to the classed, gendered, and racialized forces at play during this crucial moment in history. Therefore, in this chapter I will briefly trace the beginnings of this myth during the general election campaign of 1979 and then chart how politicians revisited and helped to fuel the salience of this legend on through the 1980s and 1990s. Finally, with an understanding of this dominant narrative firmly established, I will embark upon my investigation of the history and counter-memory of this series of strikes in the twilight of the 1970s, providing a textured juxtaposition to this mythic backdrop.[42]

Media and Myth

With a click on the BBC Archive Hour's online slideshow of 'The Winter of Discontent: Thirty Years On,' a Conservative campaign poster, not a photograph of strikes, initially appears.[43] The famous Saatchi & Saatchi advertisement released in August 1978 pictures a seemingly never-ending queue of people, snaking away from a sign, 'Unemployment Office.' The ominous 'Labour Isn't Working' towers above these people, and the small, but hopeful copy in the right hand corner declares, 'Britain's Better Off With The Conservatives.'[44]

The ubiquity of this poster in Winter of Discontent remembrances helps to locate the source of this myth in the general election campaign of 1979. In particular, it can also be a window into the distinctive process of mythologization the Winter of Discontent has undergone. First, while the intention of the poster was to highlight the rising unemployment rate under Labour, the queue pictured was in fact a group of Young Conservatives from South Hendon, not desperate Britons on the dole.[45] Second, when the Labour

---

counter-memory in the American context is Penny Lewis, *Hardhats, Hippies, and Hawks: The Vietnam Antiwar Movement as Myth and Memory* (Ithaca: ILR Press, 2013).

[42] Paul Cohen provides an insightful use of 'juxtaposition' in this context: 'But like photographs, which always leave out far more than they include, the kind of truth they ("mythic representations") convey is fundamentally ahistorical-subjective, one-sided, egregiously incomplete. It is not until contending mythologizations are drawn together, juxtaposed in such a way that they begin to temper and qualify one another, raising questions instead of dismissing them, that we move in the direction of a more historical understanding of the past.' *History in Three Keys*, 214.

[43] 'Winter of Discontent: 30 Years On,' *BBC News* online, accessed May 20, 2013, http://news.bbc.co.uk/2/hi/7598647.stm.

[44] Figure 2.1 in Tim Bell, 'The Conservatives' Advertising Campaign,' in *Political Communications: The General Election Campaign of 1979*, ed. Robert Worcester and Martin Harrop (London: George Allen, & Unwin, 1982), 16.

[45] Bell, 'The Conservatives' Advertising Campaign,' 16. See also: David Butler and

Party challenged the veracity of the poster, the Conservative campaign was delighted by the added publicity, which was, according to one Conservative official, 'Worth £2 million to us.'[46] Finally, Tim Bell, who led the advertising campaign for the Conservative Party in 1979, stated that the use of such advertisements was emblematic of 'communications techniques' that were used with the goal of 'transforming a vague dislike of the circumstances in which people were living into a burning issue for them.'[47]

Just like the misleading queue of Young Conservatives standing in for the unemployed, the history of the Winter of Discontent has often been maligned with emotionally powerful images that upon closer inspection obfuscate a more complex and sometimes blatantly contradictory reality. Moreover, in line with the political leanings of the poster, political motivations, on both Right and Left, have helped to direct and shape the course of this emotional residue and salience in British collective memory today. In those distortions, however, the concrete discontent of the British public can be located in this 'vague dislike of circumstances.'

Since the media is so integral to the dominant narrative of the Winter of Discontent, it makes logical sense that it should be our first point of investigation. The media symbolism, imagery, and dominant frames of understanding can be found in the general election campaign of 1979. By the end of March of that year, most of the strikes had been settled between the Labour government and unions; however, a vote of no confidence in Parliament forced the call of an election. With the Winter of Discontent providing the Tories with 'the opportunity to heighten public dissatisfaction with the government,' the Conservative election campaign was poised to deftly use industrial unrest to their advantage.[48] Their skilled manoeuvring not only brought the Conservatives an electoral majority in May, but they injected enduring images and themes that eventually became permanent fixtures in the dominant narrative of the Winter of Discontent.

Three key changes that preceded the Winter of Discontent bolstered the Conservatives' ability to use these electoral memories and helped propel them to power in 1979. First of all, as will be explored in more detail later in the book, the Conservatives by 1977 had developed a 'Stepping Stones' strategy that featured the media as the central tool in overcoming what they

---

Dennis Kavanagh, 'Central Preparations,' in *The British General Election of 1979*, ed. David Butler and Dennis Kavanagh (London: Macmillan Press Ltd., 1980), 140. '"Epoch-Making" Poster Was Clever Fake,' *BBC News* online, March 16, 2001, http://news.bbc.co.uk/2/hi/uk_news/1222326.stm.

[46] Bell, 'The Conservatives' Advertising Campaign,' 16. See also: Butler and Kavanagh, 'Central Preparations,' 140.

[47] Bell, 'The Conservatives' Advertising Campaign,' 12.

[48] Bell, 'The Conservatives' Advertising Campaign,' 12.

saw as 'the major obstacle to national revitalization: trade unions.'[49] This detailed policy paper, authored by John Hoskyns, outlined a communications strategy to disseminate a 'symbolic policy' that would force voters to see that the Tories were not just attacking unions in the defence of class privilege, but rather they were the party 'resolute' enough to stand up to this formidable threat.[50] More specifically, this deft and disciplined use of images and messages would exploit fissures already present in the labour movement. As the paper emphasized,

> Drag every skeleton out of the union cupboard, linking it to Labour [...] The aim should be to make the Labour Right wing and the union leadership close ranks, while the rift between the latter and their rank-and-file begins to open. All must be done in the most friendly and reasonable way – simply seeking the truth, ensuring that all are informed.[51]

Second, the 'Stepping Stones' strategy was taken seriously. This was most apparent in the Conservative Party's employment of Saatchi & Saatchi in March 1978 to run the party's advertising campaign.[52] It now had the necessary media skills and resources to seize upon the emotional residue of the Winter of Discontent to cast Labour as unable to grapple with the chaos and crisis of that winter.

Finally, the Conservatives were aided by a 'marked shift to the Right' that had occurred in the British press by the 1970s.[53] One of the most important aspects of this shift occurred in July 1978 when Britain's most popular daily, the *Sun*, switched its political affiliation from Labour to Conservative. This affiliation developed into an enduring and intimate relationship. During that time, Tim Bell, the Director of the Conservative Campaign, and Thatcher's publicity agent, Gordon Reece, frequently met with *Sun* editor Larry Lamb:

> Lubricated by large quantities of champagne, they would 'discuss each other's plans and seek advice' and Lamb would be rewarded for his support with access to inside political information and gossip as well as praise for his allegedly unique insights into public opinion.[54]

---

[49] '"Stepping Stones" Report (Final Text).' November 14, 1977. Archive (Thatcher MSS). Margaret Thatcher Foundation. Source: THCR 2/6/1248, http://www.margaretthatcher.org/document/111771. For an overall view of the Conservative Party's relationship with British trade unions see: Andrew Taylor, 'The Conservative Party and the Trade Unions,' in *British Trade Unions and Industrial Politics: The High Tide of Trade Unionism, 1964–79*, ed. John McIlroy, Nina Fishman, and Alan Campbell (Aldershot: Ashgate, 1999), 151–186.

[50] '"Stepping Stones" Report (Final Text),' 40.

[51] '"Stepping Stones" Report (Final Text),' 42.

[52] Butler and Kavanagh, *The British General Election of 1979*, 138.

[53] Thomas, *Popular Newspapers*, 61.

[54] Thomas, *Popular Newspapers*, 76–77.

Even amongst the more left-wing press, many were dissatisfied with the Callaghan government. *Daily Mirror* journalist Geoffrey Goodman describes how in April 1979 Sir Alex Jarratt, chairman of Reed International, held a private dinner party with the editors of Reed's newspapers, such as the *Daily Mirror*, *Sunday Mirror*, and the *People*. Goodman recounts:

> With great candour [Jarratt] declared that he wanted to see an end of the Callaghan Government. No 'ifs and buts' or 'on the one hand this [...]' etc. [...] He, and the Reed organization, had had quite enough of this Labour Government. He made no bones about the fact that he regarded the Callaghan Government as a complete disaster.[55]

Explicit campaign electioneering complemented this media shift. Only four days after the call of the general election, Thatcher emphasized the Winter's central role in her campaign, and immediately situated key images to represent the Winter of Discontent, which would shape the contours of the eventual myth:

> We have just had a devastating winter of industrial strife – perhaps the worst in living memory, certainly the worst in mine. We saw the sick refused admission to hospital. We saw people unable to bury their dead. We saw children virtually locked out of their schools. We saw the country virtually at the mercy of secondary pickets and strike committees and we saw a government apparently hapless to do anything about it [...] I think we all know in our hearts it is time for a change.[56]

Her colleague Conservative Lord Hailsham offered a similar narrative:

> Do they really think we have forgotten the last winter? We have seen the gravediggers refusing to bury their dead. We have seen the refuse accumulating in the streets. [...] We have seen cancer patients having to postpone their operations because hospital laundry is not done, floors not swept, or meals cooked [...] I could go on indefinitely. These are facts. What is theirs but the law of the jungle?[57]

Like a poignant and well-written novel, the campaign ended on the same note upon which it began. In the April 23 Conservative Political Election Broadcast (PEB), the narrator asks, 'It hasn't been a lot of fun living in Britain these last years, has it? And what a winter!'[58] Shots of rubbish

---

[55] Geoffrey Goodman, *From Bevan to Blair: Fifty Years' Reporting from the Political Front Line* (London: Pluto Press, 2003), 234–235.

[56] Reprinted in Butler and Kavanagh, *The British General Election of 1979*, 167–168.

[57] Butler and Kavanagh, *The British General Election of 1979*, 189–190.

[58] Reprinted in Appendix 1: Extracts from Conservative Party Political Broadcasts in *Political Communications: The General Election Campaign of 1979*, ed. Robert Worcester and Martin Harrop (London: George Allen & Unwin, 1982), 172.

in the streets, supermarkets empty, graves undug, hospitals picketed, and airports closed emerged on the screen as the narrator followed, 'Labour policies make workers bitter. Skilled workers, firemen, nurses suffering.'[59] This narrative is rooted in what Barbie Zeilzer would term 'synecdoche,' or a 'narrative strategy by which the part "stands in" for the whole.'[60] The 'synedochic' images the Conservatives most often used were the images of piles of rubbish strewn about the streets of Britain, striking gravediggers, and hospital pickets (and most often in this order). The Conservatives spotlighted the strikes' effects to 'stand in' for the chaos and the supposed 'snarling envy and motiveless hostility' to which Britain had supposedly succumbed, facilitating the development of a vivid and evocative legend.[61]

The *Sun*'s support made this feeling of suffering and despair all the more acute. On the day before the election, *Sun* editor Larry Lamb headlined the phrase 'Winter of Discontent' over a centre-page spread, paying homage to the importance of memory. 'Lest we forget those long cold months of industrial chaos that brought Britain to its knees.'[62] The alternative to this bleak picture became obvious on election day as the *Sun* declared: 'Vote Tory to Stop the Rot.'[63] Like the Saatchi & Saatchi poster, a media construction tempered by political bias became a central symbol of the Winter of Discontent.

Even when the Labour Party's campaign began to gain momentum by attacking the Conservatives' tax policy, one Labour MP admitted, 'We have nullified the Conservatives' tax pledge but not the image of a hearse being turned away from a graveyard of a NUPE picket.'[64] Therefore, the strategic use of memory of the Winter of Discontent sought to have voters reject Labour and position the Tories as an alternative that could bring a new beginning to a Britain engulfed in supposed anarchy and decay.

Throughout the 1980s and 1990s, Conservatives continued to employ the Winter of Discontent as a spectre of decline and chaos. On the campaign trail in 1983 and 1987, Thatcher's 'most frequent request' was 'for copies of the newspaper headlines from the Winter of Discontent, which she would then hold up as a warning of the consequences of voting Labour.'[65] The theme re-emerged in a 1987 Conservative PEB, when the narrator grimly asserted:

[59] Reprinted in Michael Pilsworth, 'Balanced Broadcasting,' in *The British General Election of 1979*, ed. David Butler and Dennis Kavanagh (London: Macmillan Press Ltd., 1980), 224.
[60] Barbie Zelizer, *Covering the Body: The Kennedy Assassination, the Media, and the Shaping of Collective Memory* (Chicago: The University of Chicago, 1992), 37.
[61] Margaret Thatcher, *The Downing Street Years* (London: HarperCollins, 1993), 8.
[62] Thomas, *Popular Newspapers*, 84.
[63] Thomas, *Popular Newspapers*, 85.
[64] Butler and Kavanagh, *The British General Election of 1979*, 326.
[65] John Whittingale quoted in Thomas, 'Bound in by History,' 274–275.

> Under the last Labour government more than fifty million days were lost in Britain through industrial strikes. The Labour government was brought down by its own unions after a winter of discontent in which strikes left rubbish piled in the streets, the dead were left unburied and cancer patients turned back from hospital.[66]

The reiteration of this narrative reveals that subsequent general elections became 'commemorative ceremonies'[67] where the narrative of 'rubbish piled in the streets, the dead left unburied, and cancer patients turned away from hospital' were revisited and refreshed in collective memory. In the vacuum the Tories deftly inserted ideas such as 'a shareowning/homeowning democracy,' 'popular capitalism,' and 'enterprise culture.'[68]

Most devastating for the Labour Party was the ascendancy of the political thinking enshrined in the Conservative sound bite 'There is no alternative.'[69] According to James Thomas, the revisiting of the Winter of Discontent had an even more profound political effect in Britain. He argues it was the 're-presentation' of those events after 1979 that made it 'crucial to the ideological success of Thatcherism' by providing 'the most potent popular image by which social democracy could so effectively [be] condemned as offering "no alternative."'[70]

The Labour Party's failure to provide viable opposition to the Tories throughout the 1980s and early 1990s underlines the strength of Thomas' argument. In 1990, the burden of Labour's history was apparent. As *Guardian* journalist Hugo Young noted,

> Labour may have reformed themselves, but many unions have not. They once again look like vultures, awaiting their prey's arrival. If the voters are prisoners of the past, it is that part of the past, from the winter of discontent backwards, which stands most in need of exorcism.[71]

Young was not simply engaging in journalistic hyperbole. As Labour's director of communication after the party's loss in the 1992 general election noted:

> Immediately after the election I said that the main reason why, when it came to the crunch, people felt that they could not vote Labour, was because they were concerned about Labour's history. They were not just

---

[66] Thomas, 'Bound in by History,' 275.
[67] Connerton, *How Societies Remember*, 48.
[68] Greg Philio, 'Political Advertising, Popular Belief and the 1992 British General Election,' *Media, Culture, & Society* 15, no. 3 (July 1993): 1
[69] Philio, 'Political Advertising,' 1.
[70] Thomas, 'Bound in by History,' 269.
[71] 'Locked in the Prison of a Painful Past,' *Guardian*, May 17, 1990.

concerned about their perception of Labour's links to the trade union movement. [...] Our canvassers discovered [...] that people on the doorstep were remembering 1979.[72]

These impressions illustrate the growing prominence of a specific view of the Winter of Discontent that loomed powerfully enough to affect voting behaviour even in 1992.

Consequently, it was incumbent upon the Labour modernizers to liberate the party from its past. New Labour architect Peter Mandelson declared after Labour's successful re-election in 2001 that the party was 'no longer trapped in the memories of the party's recent past.' More specifically, he explained,

> The public's memories of crisis-ridden Labour governments have been almost entirely banished. Gone is the winter of discontent, replaced by low inflation, low mortgage rates and social security bills under control. Gone is the International Monetary Fund crisis, replaced by record sums available for investment. Gone is opposition of the sale of council houses, replaced by the patient-centred NHS. [...] The dropping of policy and ideological baggage pre-1997 was vital to this.[73]

Mandelson's assertion does not refute the negative myth of the Winter of Discontent, but instead appropriates it as a dismal and regrettable fact, thereby extricating the party from a seemingly militant and inescapable reputation.[74] From 1979 to 1997, and even later on, the shape of this understanding of the Winter of Discontent has been nudged and kneaded to take form and function for both the Conservatives and Labour.

Conclusion

The Winter of Discontent has cast a pall over British collective memory; this is nowhere more apparent than in the dirge-like vocabulary evoked to describe it. Like Robert Taylor's description of events as 'a harsh internecine conflict,' others have followed suit with similarly grim and creative descriptions such as: 'hangover,' 'violent,'[75] 'hues of the blackest

---

[72] David Hill, 'The Labour Party's Strategy,' in *Political Communications: The General Election Campaign of 1992*, ed. Ivor Crewe and Brian Gosschalk (Cambridge: Cambridge University Press, 1995), 38.
[73] Peter Mandelson, *The Blair Revolution Revisited*, rev. ed. (1996; London: Politico's, 2002), xv.
[74] Thomas, 'Bound in by History,' 278.
[75] Beckett, *When the Lights Went Out*, 2.

black,' 'evil ogre,'[76] 'revenge,' 'self-interest,'[77] and even 'hara-kiri.'[78] Like Francisco Goya's *Saturn Devouring his Son*, journalists and academics appear to gorging on every dismal word in their respective thesauruses in order to appropriately describe the Winter of Discontent. Alwyn Turner's history of the 1970s epitomizes this trend:

> Britain was effectively talking itself into having a crisis, as though it somehow felt more comfortable with its back to the wall, imbibing the spirit of the Blitz. Having spent the whole decade making its flesh creep by telling horror stories about how bad things were, steeping itself in a popular culture that frequently verged on the apocalyptic, the nation finally found its nightmares coming true with the winter of discontent in early 1979.[79]

Obviously even the syntax of retrospective accounts is not immune to the pervasively grim myth of 1978–1979.

In this chapter I have demonstrated that the vocabulary and imagery used to depict the Winter of Discontent have been in part shaped by the Conservative Election campaign of 1979. They influenced the outline of the myth of the Winter of Discontent with a narrative of secondary picketing, striking gravediggers, uncollected rubbish, and closed hospitals. Nevertheless, the Winter of Discontent was not solely the result of inspired and cynical creativity. Lorry drivers did go on strike, and rubbish did go uncollected. Therefore, the prevalence of the myth and political bias urges the historian to do more than examine how the manipulations were embedded in this legend. Instead, it focuses our attention on how the Winter of Discontent grew in size and proportion as subsequent election campaigns pointed to it as the dire backdrop to a glorious national rebirth of sorts, but all the while resonating with a harder truth held among the British public.

However, when every evocative word and vivid image has been exhausted, we are left with confronting a much rockier, contradictory, and possibly hopeful historical reality. By readjusting our focus to incorporate local as well as national voices, especially the previously ignored experiences of women, West Indians, and Asians, the simple and compact myth becomes a more complex and textured panorama of experiences. George Lipsitz describes this transition:

> Myth provides legitimation for the world as it is; it reconciles people to the disparity between their desires and their opportunities. [...] History,

---

[76] Tiratsoo, 'You've Never Had It So Bad,' 186.
[77] Foot, *The Vote*, 396.
[78] Morgan, *Callaghan: A Life*, 650.
[79] Turner, *Crisis? What Crisis?*, xiii.

on the other hand, involves a search for hidden truths and a look beyond surface appearances. History explores how things came to be, and it inevitably confronts all the roads not taken and all the blasted hopes of the past.[80]

These untravelled roads and obscured hopes, therefore, will come into view as we begin to analyse the complex set of forces in post-war Britain that culminated in the Winter of Discontent.

---

[80] Lipsitz, *Time Passages*, 217.

2

The Winter of Discontent: Causes and Context

On the eve of January 1, 1970 British journalists waved a 'haggard goodbye' to the 1960s. For those steeped in the energy of blossoming social movements, the decade was one of unprecedented shows of solidarity amongst British youth, and the next decade was the one where they had the chance to 'make the world a better place.'[1] Yet, by the time the 1970s came to a close, little was left of this enthusiasm and hope. On December 7, 1979 punk band the Clash released a startling epitaph for the decade in their song 'London Calling':

> All that phoney Beatlemania has bitten the dust.
> London calling, see we ain't got no swing
> 'Cept for the ring of that truncheon thing.
> The ice age is coming, the sun is zooming in
> Engines stop running and the wheat is growing thin
> A nuclear error, but I have no fear
> 'Cause London is drowning and I – I live by the river.[2]

For songwriters Joe Strummer and Mick Jones, the revelry of the 1960s was reduced to 'the ring of that truncheon thing,' and all that was certain was an apparently disastrous end.

Within the span of ten years, the vision of making the world a better place had turned into a portent of the nation's demise. In order to understand this mood of profound pessimism, it is necessary to ask: What were the undercurrents present within the British economic and political system that had come to a head during the 1970s? Why were political parties less

---

[1] 'And What Happens Now?,' *Guardian*, January 1, 1970; Richard Branson, 'Enter the Peaceful Drop Out,' *Daily Mirror*, December 31, 1969.

[2] The Clash, 'London Calling,' by Joe Strummer & Mick Jones, released December 7, 1979, *London Calling*, CBS.

able and/or willing to deliver on the promises of the post-war settlement? How did political lines, both Left and Right, shift as society changed? In particular, what reconfigurations in class, race, and gender shaped the political terrain in the 1970s? And, finally, how did these shifts set the stage for the strikes of the Winter of Discontent?

The early 1970s represented a 'watershed in the development of Western capitalist economies' as the global economy experienced the most dramatic economic downturn in post-war history.[3] The economic shocks of this decade were all the more unsettling because they followed an era of unprecedented economic prosperity, known as the 'Golden Age.'[4] Prior to 1973, the industrialized countries of the world experienced the longest period of uninterrupted growth at the highest rates ever seen in history after the Second World War.[5] From 1950 to 1973, the real GDP of the top OECD countries rose by an average annual rate of 4.8 per cent.[6] Britain too was experiencing its own form of economic development and affluence as Britons came to experience the most dramatic rise in living standards in British history.[7] From 1951 to 1963, wages rose by 72 per cent.[8] The effects of increased disposable income became visible as modern amenities and consumer goods, like televisions and washing machines, quickly became staples in many British households. For instance, from September 1957 to November 1959, consumption of televisions increased by 32 per cent among British households, and that of washing machines and refrigerators increased by 54 and 58 per cent respectively.[9]

Nevertheless, even before the economic tribulations of the 1970s, Britain was already facing a chronic problem that tarnished the veneer of this 'Golden Age': creeping inflation. Post-war Britain's commitment to ensuring full employment and a strong welfare state posed a particular challenge to

---

[3] Derek Aldcroft, *The European Economy: 1914–1990*, 3rd ed. (London: Routledge, 1989), 195.

[4] Michael Kitson, 'Failure followed by success or success followed by failure? A re-examination of British economic growth since 1949,' in *The Cambridge Economic History of Modern Britain*, ed. Roderick Floud and Paul Johnson (Cambridge: Cambridge University Press, 2004), 48.

[5] Rondo Cameron, *A Concise Economic History of the World* (New York; Oxford: Oxford University Press, 1997), 375.

[6] A.G. Kenwood and A.L. Lougheed, *The Growth of the International Economy, 1820–1990: An Introductory Text*, 3rd ed. (London: Routledge, 1992), 245.

[7] Roger Middleton, *The British Economy since 1945: Engaging with the Debate* (Houndmills: MacMillan Press Ltd., 2000), xv.

[8] David Childs, *Britain since 1945: A Political History*, 3rd ed. (London: Routledge, 1992), 105.

[9] Dominic Sandbrook, *Never Had It So Good: A History of Britain from Suez to the Beatles* (London: Abacus, 2005), 110.

combatting inflation. In order to prevent this trend while continuing to fulfil their commitment to maintaining full employment, incomes policy or wage restraint was seen as a necessary imposition on British workers.[10] From as early as 1948 both Labour and Conservative governments attempted to tackle this problem with such a policy.[11] In 1961, for instance, Harold Macmillan's Conservative government imposed a 'Pay Pause' on all government employees, as historians Malcom Pearce and Geoffrey Stewart observe, 'with the faint hope that the private sector would feel morally bound to come in line.'[12] This temporary measure was followed nine months later by a declaration that rises were to remain within 2 to 2.5 per cent.[13] This 'manifestly discriminatory'[14] pressure on the public sector characterized both Labour and Conservative incomes policies throughout the post-war era. For decades it not only created pronounced pay disparities between private and public sector workers, but it deepened divisions among their trade unions, fractures of which would eventually be central to the upsurge in industrial activity during the Winter of Discontent.[15]

With the problem of inflation still looming, Harold Wilson's Labour government followed the Conservatives' example, and in 1966 imposed a wage freeze in Britain. Consequently, trade unions were placed in the awkward position of fighting for the interests of their membership, which included wage increases, while maintaining their support for the Labour government. British workers resisted the current form of wage restraint *en masse*. One such strike was the 1967 seamen's strike that defied the Labour government's 3 to 3.5 per cent wage ceiling just after doctors, judges, and civil servants were given rises.[16]

These long-term problems of inflation and wage restraint only became more acute in the hostile economic environment of the early 1970s. After the economic boom of 1972–73, one of the worst recessions, characterized by both

[10] John Sheldrake, *Industrial Relations and Politics in Britain 1880–1989* (London: Pinter Publishers, 1991), 63–64.
[11] Leo Panitch, *Social Democracy and Industrial Militancy: The Labour Party, the Trade Unions and Incomes Policy, 1945–74* (London: Cambridge, 1976), 20.
[12] Malcom Pearce and Geoffrey Stewart, *British Political History 1867–1990: Democracy and Decline* (London: Routledge, 1992), 480.
[13] William Brown, 'Industrial Relations and the Economy,' in *The Cambridge Economic History of Modern Britain*, ed. Roderick Floud and Paul Johnson (Cambridge: Cambridge University Press, 2004), 408.
[14] Panitch, *Social Democracy and Industrial Militancy*, 49.
[15] Steve Ludlam, 'Too Much Pluralism: Not Enough Socialism: Interpreting the Unions-Party Link,' in *Interpreting the Labour Party: Approaches to Labour Politics and History*, ed. John Callaghan, Steve Fielding, and Steve Ludlam (Manchester: Manchester University Press, 2003), 158. See also Hay, 'Chronicles of a Death Foretold,' 446–470.
[16] Childs, *Britain since 1945*, 182–183.

high inflation and unemployment, or 'stagflation,' hit the Western world in 1974–75.[17] Underlying this recession were an assortment of interlocking factors. First of all, President Johnson's decision to finance the Vietnam War through budget deficits pushed inflation upwards around the world. Second, from 1971 to 1973 the Bretton Woods system deteriorated, contributing to an increase in the prices of primary commodities such as food, raw materials, and energy.[18] The pressure on energy prices was simply exacerbated by OPEC price rises in 1972–74 and 1978–79. In 1972, oil prices rose by 420 per cent in retaliation for the West's support for Israel in the Yom Kippur War.[19] From 1978 to 1979, the Iranian Revolution and panic buying also contributed to the inflationary climate of the 1970s.[20] It is no surprise, therefore, that world inflation leapt from 5.9 per cent in 1971 to 15 per cent in 1974.[21] In response to the rise in prices, workers around the world began to demand higher wages, which further expanded inflationary pressure.[22] In 1975, industrial production fell by 7 per cent in Europe and by 9 per cent in Japan and the US, while the average unemployment rate almost doubled in the period 1962–73 in most Western capitalist countries.[23]

These economic upheavals erupted while Britain was undergoing profound transformations in industry and manufacturing. The industrial landscape of factories and billowing smoke stacks began to give way to the clutter of dishes and the chimes of cash registers as manufacturing in Britain began to contract as service and public sector employment expanded. Although manufacturing continued to have a significant foothold in the economy with 40 per cent of the British workforce employed in this sector in the mid-1970s,[24] from 1966 to 1979 2.9 million jobs in production were lost, three-quarters of which by men, and while the overall labour force remained constant, male employment declined by 5 per cent.[25]

Many of the jobs that would replace those disappearing were in both the service and public sectors. From 1963 to 1983, industrial employment

---

[17] Childs, *Britain since 1945*, 182–183.

[18] Richard Coopey and Nicholas Woodward, 'The British Economy in the 1970s: An Overview,' *The British Economy in the 1970s: The Troubled Decade* ed. Richard Coopey and Nicholas Woodward (London: University College London Press, 1996), 4.

[19] Coopey and Woodward, 'The British Economy in the 1970s,' 6.

[20] Coopey and Woodward, 'The British Economy in the 1970s,' 8.

[21] Kenwood and Lougheed, *The Growth of the International Economy*, 247.

[22] Aldcroft, *The European Economy*, 206.

[23] Aldcroft, *The European Economy*, 199.

[24] Linda McDowell, Sundari Anitha, and Ruth Pearson, 'Striking Images: Gender, Ethnicity, and Industrial Politics in the 1970s, Reflections On/Of Grunwick,' Manuscript to be published in *Women's History Review*, 32.

[25] James Cronin, *Labour and Society, 1918–1979* (New York: Schocken Books, 1984), 194.

in Britain declined from 49 per cent to 34 per cent, while employment in services rose from 48 per cent in 1963 to 64 per cent in 1983.[26] In 1966, 3.7 million people, or 15.7 per cent of the British workforce, were employed in the public sector. By 1976, the public sector employed 5 million people, 27.3 per cent of the workforce.[27]

Women's movement into employment was also part of this dramatic economic overhaul. Although in 1971, 92 per cent of working-age men were employed compared to 56 per cent of working age women,[28] from 1966 to 1979, women's employment in service industries grew by one-third, while growth among men in the same sector was only 3 per cent. The overall rise in the participation of women in the workforce was also significant. In 1961 the proportion of women over the age of 15 who worked was 37.3 per cent. By 1977, that number was 47.4 per cent.[29]

The picture was much more complex for Asian and West Indian women. Black women continued to participate in manual work at a higher rate than white women. While 63.5 per cent of black women were employed in manual work in 1972, 45 per cent of white women were similarly employed.[30] Also, Asian and West Indian women as a whole participated in full-time work at a higher rate than British women as a whole.[31] These workers became an increasingly significant part of this expanding service and public sector, especially within the NHS. Due to the nationalization of the health service, cheap labour in the form of overseas health staff and nurses began to arrive from the Caribbean, Hong Kong, Malaysia, and Ireland in the 1960s. However, many of these women were directed into acquiring nursing qualifications that were only recognized in Britain, undercutting any opportunity for significant economic advancement.[32] Particularly in the case of women from the West Indies, having to accept these auxiliary nursing degrees not only limited their ability to reach the upper echelons of nursing, but it also turned auxiliary nursing into a 'a *job* for women of the working class, particularly for black and other migrant women.'[33]

[26] Eley, *Forging Democracy*, 386.
[27] Cronin, *Labour and Society*, 195.
[28] McDowell, Anitha, and Pearson, 'Striking Images,' 32.
[29] Cronin, *Labour and Society*, 195.
[30] Ron Ramdin, *The Making of the Black Working Class in Britain* (Aldershot: Wildwood House, 1987), 239.
[31] Ramdin, *The Making of the Black Working Class*, 260.
[32] Ramdin, *The Making of the Black Working Class*, 310–311.
[33] Ramdin, *The Making of the Black Working Class*, 310. For an exploration of the gendered and racialized history of similar work in the United States see: Eileen Boris and Jennifer Klein, *Caring for America: Home Health Care Workers in the Shadow of the Welfare State* (New York: Oxford University Press, 2012).

The influx of women into the workforce, however, did not ameliorate gender inequality in Britain. In 1978 the *Economist* pronounced that 'Women's lib is half dead in Britain.' While women made up about 40 per cent of the British workforce and participated in the labour force at a higher rate than that of West Germany and Italy, by the end of the decade, skilled manual jobs were largely out of their reach. Only one in 12 women, in comparison with one in two men, had a skilled manual job.[34] The low pay that often accompanied unskilled work later played a central role in the disputes of the Winter of Discontent.

These relatively depressed wages appeared at a time when women's paid employment was increasingly crucial to the family income and critical to keeping up with the rising standard of living in the post-war era. First of all, women's wages played a key role in providing for their families' basic needs. As David Vincent argues, 'given the absence of the minimum wage, and the presence of such obstacles as the wage stop, which particularly affected large families of low earners, the wife's labour was in fact the only absolute guarantee of basic subsistence.'[35] Vincent here acknowledges that a woman's wage was often not secondary, but central to a family's survival. Furthermore, as historian Dolly Smith Wilson has noted,

> The spread of affluence changed ideas about acceptable standards of living, affecting the definition of what it meant to 'need' to work. Sociological studies of working women in post-war Britain found that educational expenses became one such priority, paying for school uniforms, and school travel holidays. Therefore, work for women was more than for survival, but neither was it for mere pin money if by 'pins' are meant pleasant little frivolities for personal enjoyment. For most women the aim was a higher standard of living.[36]

Therefore, whether part of large families living at the margins or families with at least incrementally higher wages, women's contribution to the overall household income was important in post-war Britain.

With inflation exerting increasing pressure on households in the 1970s, such conceptions of 'pin money' became all the more obsolete. For Mrs M.P. Blackley, writing in the *Manchester Evening News* in 1974, 'Happy Homebird's' earlier letter, which claimed that 'women who go out to work fritter their wages on bingo and pubs,' especially irked her.

---

[34] 'Women's Work,' *Economist*, December 16, 1978, 120.

[35] David Vincent, *Poor Citizens: The State and the Poor in Twentieth-Century Britain* (London: Longman, 1991), 144–145.

[36] Dolly Smith Wilson, 'A New Look at the Affluent Worker: The Good Working Mother in Post-War Britain,' *Twentieth Century British History* 17, no. 2 (2006): 216–217.

Like me, most of my friends work because they have no choice. I work a full day from 8 30 am to 5 pm, and I work! Our family does not have a colour TV set or a car. I don't play bingo or visit the pub except on the very rare occasion when my husband and I go out for a quiet drink. We haven't even a washing machine. This we are saving up for, and we are buying our own house.[37]

Such assertiveness amongst working women was also reflected in their increasing presence in trade unions. From 1966 to 1979, while the trade union movement as a whole experienced a dramatic rise in membership, female membership increased by 73 per cent while male trade union membership rose by 19.3 per cent in the same period.[38] Overall, Asian and West Indian workers had higher levels of unionization compared to white workers. In 1977, 61 per cent of black male workers were unionized compared to 47 per cent of white male workers.[39] By the end of the decade, women overall would come to make up 29.4 of trade unionists.[40]

Furthermore, the growth in women's trade union membership was an effect, in part, of the trade unions' increased penetration into the expanding public sector. These increases in particular unions reflected a wider trend of public sector unionization. While 1974 saw a continued overall union density of 50 per cent, union density in the public sector reached 83.1 per cent. Key public sector industries that were to become central to the strikes of 1978 and 1979, furthermore, experienced significantly high levels of unionization. In 1974, unionization in the health service was 90.5 per cent, in education 61.9 per cent, and in local government 60.9 per cent.[41]

With a greater numeric presence in the trade union movement, these unions began to flex their industrial muscle. In the strike wave from 1968 to 1972, 'traditional' industries like mining and the motor industry continued to feature prominently; nevertheless, public sector strikes were also increasing in number. For instance, from 1964 to 1968 there were 135 strikes in the public sector, involving 35,000 workers. Soon thereafter, from 1969 to 1973, this number more than doubled, and there were 347 strikes in the public sector, involving 744,000 workers.[42] By the mid-1970s, over half of the Trades

---

[37] Mrs M.P. West Blackley, 'Postbag' (letter to the editor), *Manchester Evening News*, October 16, 1974.

[38] Chris Wrigley, 'Women in the Labour Market and in the Unions,' in *British Trade Unions and Industrial Politics: The High Tide of Trade Unionism, 1964–79*, ed. John McIlroy, Nina Fishman, and Alan Campbell (Aldershot: Ashgate, 1999), 44.

[39] Ramdin, *The Making of the Black Working Class*, 362.

[40] Wrigley, 'Women in the Labour Market and in the Unions,' 44.

[41] Phil B. Beaumont, *Public Sector Industrial Relations* (London: Routledge, 1992), 44.

[42] Cronin, *Labour and Society*, 190.

Union Congress (TUC) membership was in the public sector.[43] Also, those unions with the largest increases in female membership, such as NUPE, the Confederation of Health Service Employees (COHSE), the Transport and General Workers' Union (TGWU), and the General and Municipal Workers' Union (GMWU), had their membership based entirely or partly in the public sector in 1978.[44]

Important political alignments amongst the trade union leadership were also occurring. In 1967, Hugh Scanlon, 'a more militant and strong advocate' of industrial democracy, assumed the leadership of the Amalgamated Union of Engineering Workers (AEUW), while two years later Jack Jones became General Secretary of the TGWU. Jones' support for the devolution of union power from full-time officials to shop stewards worked so well with Scanlon's 'militant' support of industrial democracy that they were called 'the dubious duo.'[45] Their trade unionism had been forged in the industrial climate of the Second World War. The model of the Joint Production Committee was formative for them both, and they sought to incorporate collective bargaining and democratic representation at the workplace through one representative trade union body. Furthermore, they assumed that there would be parity of representation with management over key decisions at the workplace. Their ideas about industrial democracy developed and crystallized through their participation in the Institute of Workers' Control, which brought together Left union officials, shop stewards, and intellectuals.[46]

The wider industrial and political ferment occurring in the late 1960s and early 1970s produced another generation of activists that further invigorated the British labour movement. In 1968, workers and students across Europe began to press for democratic reforms in the workplace, universities, and society at large. With their ties to Left politics, two transformations occurred to fuel the labour movements in the late 1960s. First of all, both Nikita Khrushchev's revelations of Stalinist purges and the Hungarian revolution in 1956 undermined 'Communism's granite orthodoxies' in Europe.[47] To fill this political vacuum, previously un-translated Marxist thinkers, like Antonio Gramsci who wrote on workers' councils, came to refresh the intellectual currents of Marxism in Europe. These 'rediscovered' ideas

---

[43] Steve Ludlam, 'Labourism and the Disintegration of the Postwar Consensus: Disunited Trade Union Responses to Public Expenditure Cuts, 1974–1979' (PhD thesis, University of Sheffield, 1991), 156.

[44] Wrigley, 'Women in the Labour Market and in the Unions,' 66.

[45] Robert Taylor, *The Trade Union Question in British Politics: Government and Unions since 1945* (Oxford: West Blackwell, 1993), 149–150.

[46] Lewis Minkin, *The Contentious Alliance: Trade Unions and the Labour Party* (Edinburgh: Edinburgh University Press, 1991), 173–174.

[47] Eley, *Forging Democracy*, 362.

provided inspiration for an upsurge of militancy and democracy on the Left and in the labour movement.[48] The emphasis was on direct action and grassroots links between workers and local working-class communities. Wildcat strikes in 1968's 'hot autumn' in Milan, Italy, for instance, operated outside the grips of established trade unions and Left parties, leading 'a generation of Italian student theorists and their followers to conclude that [...] workers' autonomy – as tactic and objective – was the path to the future.'[49] Even in the United States, a confident form of rank-and-file activism was apparent. For example, when trying to gauge this new militancy, a New York television talk show host in 1975 asked a panel of workers if it were management or the union that 'had the power to change the situation.' The panel was unanimous in their assessment: 'the rank and file.'[50]

The British Left and the labour movement did not go untouched by this flourishing political culture. First of all, 'Marxism found space between the CPGB and the labour movement's cultural institutions.'[51] Enmeshed in this political ferment, a new generation of Left activists rushed into political parties and into the labour movement. West German political activist Rudi Dutschke described this phenomenon as 'the long march through the existing institutions.' During this time as a new generation of activists went to work in education, the civil services, health care, mainstream Left parties, and, most importantly for this discussion, trade unions and the Labour Party.[52] Eventually, many of these people steeped in this dynamic political environment would have a profound effect on radicalizing the politics of some factions of the Labour Party and key trade unions, especially the politics of the public sector union NUPE.

If the blossoming Left politics of the 1960s infused unions with a new energy, the Women's Movement would fuel trade unions' increased efforts to organize women workers. Feminists began to put pressure on the trade union movement to put more emphasis on the needs and claims of working-class women.[53] For example, in late 1970, activists in the Women's Movement joined forces with working women to organize cleaners in what

---

[48] Tony Judt, *Postwar: A History of Europe since 1945* (London: Random House, 2007), 402–403.

[49] Judt, *Postwar*, 415.

[50] Cowie, *Stayin' Alive*, 8.

[51] Eley, *Forging Democracy*, 362. A more detailed examination appears in Geoff Eley, *A Crooked Line: From Cultural History to the History of Society* (Ann Arbor: University of Michigan Press, 2005).

[52] Eley, *Forging Democracy*, 364.

[53] Sheila Rowbotham, *The Past is Before Us: Feminism in Action since the 1960s* (London: Pandora Press, 1989), 182.

became an extended action known as the Night Cleaners' Campaign.[54] Feminists also struggled with trade unions to put issues such as abortion and domestic violence on the agenda and to take up cultural aspects of women's subordination, such as sexist imagery in the media, in their efforts to organize women.[55] The Women's Movement helped to reframe not only how the trade union movement regarded women's work, but also extended the scope of the issues faced by women workers.

Such energized grassroots politics was also present on the Right. One of the most notable right-wing groups to gain momentum in the 1970s was the National Association for Freedom (NAFF), launched in the 1975.[56] Their Charter of Rights and Liberties included:

> Freedom to withdraw one's labour, other than contrary to public safety.
>
> Freedom to belong or not to belong to a trade union [...]
>
> The right to private ownership.[57]

Like the Socialist Workers' Party, they sold papers on the streets in London. John Gouriet, the director of NAFF in the 1970s, was part of a Right wing that, as journalist Andy Beckett puts it, had a 'sense that the world was tilting dangerously towards Leftism and anarchy.'[58]

After the defeats of Conservative Government in 1974, such right-wing movements began to find a receptive audience among the middle classes of Britain. According to historian Nick Tiratsoo, up to the 1970s, 'the middle class had hardly been visible as a coherent social interest group.' However, as inflation cut into middle-class salaries, and an evolving aspirational and individualistic ethos arose, 'the mood began to change. The middle class felt under threat, and many argued that it needed to reassert itself.'[59] Joe Moran further asserts that the 1976 IMF crisis fostered a feeling of 'middle class anxiety, embattlement and resentment.'[60] Throughout the political spectrum, therefore, a feeling of restlessness found expression in a variety of grassroots movements.

The inability of British mainstream parties to harness such energy also

---

[54] Sheila Rowbotham, 'Cleaners Organizing in Britain From the 1970s: A Personal Account,' in *The Dirty Work of Neo-Liberalism*, ed. Luis Aguiar and Andrew Herod (Oxford: Basil West Blackwell, 2006), 181.

[55] Jenny Beale, *Getting It Together: Women as Trade Unionists* (London: Pluto Press, 1982), 14–15. See also, Sarah Boston, *Women Workers and the Trade Unions*, rev. ed. (1980; London: Lawrence & Wishart, 1987).

[56] Beckett, *When the Lights Went Out*, 377.

[57] Beckett, *When the Lights Went Out*, 379.

[58] Beckett, *When the Lights Went Out*, 381.

[59] Tiratsoo, 'You've Never Had It So Bad,' 187–188.

[60] Joe Moran, '"Stand Up and Be Counted": Hughie Green, the 1970s and Popular

became increasingly apparent in British general elections. Support for the two-party system began to erode as electoral support for minor parties developed. Moreover, the supposed cornerstone of British political loyalty, class, appeared to have become increasingly destabilized as cross-class voting began to increase in 1970.[61] More specifically, manual workers' support for the Labour Party 'dropped sharply,' although Labour's support amongst the non-manual workers remained relatively stable.[62] Nevertheless, British women's support for the Conservative Party tended to outpace that of men's support. In February 1974, for example, men voted for Labour at a rate 14 per cent higher than women. This gender gap continued, but at a slightly decreased rate, in the October 1974 election, with a disparity of 12 per cent.[63]

Despite the emergence of these shifting economic, social, and political currents, the intractable problem of inflation continued to plague Britain. Trade union power came to be seen not only as a key source of inflation, but as a major impediment to Britain's overall economic progression. For the Labour Party in the late 1960s, the debate over how to resolve this problem set a crucial precedent for the struggles throughout the 1970s, and the Winter of Discontent especially.

The Wilson government commissioned the Donovan Report in 1968 to report on the state of industrial relations in the Britain. The unofficial nature of many of the strikes during the 1960s led the authors of the report to argue that 'two systems of industrial relations' existed in Britain. The first was the 'formal' system, which consisted of trade unions and employers bound by industry-wide agreements. 'Formal' agreements contrasted with what the Donovan Report called 'informal' agreements bound by 'custom and practice,' agreed upon by local shop stewards and managers.[64] In 1969, the Labour government provided a quick response to the Donovan Report with Barbara Castle's white paper *In Place of Strife*. The white paper proposed ways to deal with this dual system of industrial relations. Members were to be balloted prior to taking strike action, and the government could impose legal sanctions on unions if such procedures were not followed.[65] The already strained relationship between unions and the Labour government reached breaking point. Ironically, one of the most prominent voices of opposition

---

Memory,' *History Workshop Journal* 70, no. 1 (2010): 176, doi: 10.1093/hwj/dbq025. For further insight into right-wing grassroots political culture, see Sandbrook, *Seasons in the Sun*, 362–385.

[61] Pippa Norris, *Electoral Change in Britain since 1945* (Oxford: Blackwell Publishers, 1997), 3.

[62] Anthony Heath, Roger Jowell, and John Curtice, *How Britain Votes* (Oxford: Pergamon Press, 1985).

[63] Lisanne Radice, *Winning Women's Votes* (London: Fabian Society, October 1985), 5.

[64] Minkin, *The Contentious Alliance*, 113–114.

[65] Alan Sked, *Post-War Britain: A Political History* (Brighton: Harvester Press, 1979), 260.

to *In Place of Strife* was the Chancellor of the Exchequer and later Prime Minister during the Winter of Discontent, James Callaghan. Callaghan disagreed with making unions liable to pay fines for unofficial strikes, and that it would be the government, not the employers, who would bring the strikers to court. Callaghan explained:

> I declared my opposition to the legal sanctions in the White Paper on three grounds, which I repeated *ad nauseam*. The legal sanctions would not pass through Parliament. The proposals would not stop unofficial strikes. The proposals would create tension between government and unions as a time when morale was low, to no effective purpose.[66]

The TUC joined Callaghan's opposition to the proposal. Labour's subsequent capitulation after the TUC's rejection of *In Place of Strife* resulted in the TUC's 'solemn and binding undertaking' that TUC workers would abide by TUC guidelines concerning unofficial strikes.[67] This settlement only temporarily ameliorated a conflict that would plague governments throughout the 1970s. This lack of clear resolution of the relation between the state and trade unions became a central problem during the mid-1970s.

It would be the Tories' opportunity to tackle the issue of wage restraint in 1970. That year the Wilson government was shocked as a 20 per cent Labour lead in the polls[68] turned into a Conservative majority of 30 seats on election day.[69] The new Conservative Prime Minister, Ted Heath, entered Number 10 Downing Street in June of 1970, assuring the British public, 'Our purpose is not to divide but to unite and, where there are differences, to bring reconciliation and create one nation.'[70] Heath's proclamation set the tone for the Conservative government's agenda of 'One Nation Toryism,'[71] which sought a departure from earlier governments by initiating a change in its approach to controlling wages and industrial legislation. The Conservative government believed that incomes policy during the previous Wilson government had failed to stem the tide of wage and price increases; therefore, the government did not issue an across the board wage limit for workers. Instead, they sought to keep wages down through a strategy called

---

[66] James Callaghan, *Time and Chance* (London: Politico's, 1987), 274.
[67] Sked, *Post-War Britain*, 260.
[68] James Cronin, *New Labour's Pasts: The Labour Party and Its Discontents* (Harlow: Pearson Longman, 2004), 117.
[69] Martin Holmes, *The Failure of the Heath Government*, 2nd ed. (1982; London, MacMillan Press, 1997), 8.
[70] Quoted in Holmes, *The Failure of the Heath Government*, 9.
[71] Pearce and Stewart, *British Political History*, 490.

'N minus one' whereby the government attempted to ensure that each pay settlement was 1 per cent lower than the previous pay settlement.[72]

Although Heath's pay policy provided a novel approach, the uneven implementation between the private and public sectors continued. Private sector employers could evade such wage restraint with the justification of retaining their skilled workers with higher wages.[73] Such disjointed wage restraint was apparent in 1970 when striking postmen successfully won a rise of 9 per cent, but the settlement simply made the government take a more 'resolute stand [against] the public sector [rises].' Nevertheless, an equivalent call to private industry to follow their example was ignored as private employers continued to make pay deals in excess of the inflation rate.[74] Heath, like his predecessors in the Wilson government, saw legislating industrial relations as instrumental to effectively tackling inflation. The Conservatives' passage of the 1971 Industrial Relations Act attempted to emulate the United States' Taft–Hartley Act. Integral to Heath's reforms was the 'resolve to pursue industrial relations reform rather than wage controls' through this 'Quiet Revolution.'[75] Heath-style Conservatives reasoned that legislation would keep wage claims at a reasonable level, remove obstacles to productivity deals, and reward individual workers for their performance, thus keeping inflation down without an incomes policy.[76] While enhancing the individual rights of workers to take strike action and ensuring protection from unfair dismissal, the Industrial Relations Act aimed to restrict unions on an institutional level. First of all, a register of unions would be created to supervise unions' rules and further extend its reach by exerting such powers as asserting the binding nature of collective agreements. The Act also established the National Industrial Relations Court. One of the court's many functions was to impose fines on unions taking part in 'unfair industrial relations practices.'[77] Finally, under this new legal structure, employers and trade unions' collective agreements were enforceable under law unless otherwise agreed.[78]

The TUC, encouraged by their defeat of Labour's *In Place of Strife*, issued an immediate response. The TUC 'strongly advised' unions not to register

---

[72] Taylor, *The Trade Union Question*, 188. Also see Holmes, *The Failure of the Heath Government*, 57.

[73] Chris Wrigley, 'Trade Unions, Strikes and the Government,' in *Britain in the 1970s: The Troubled Economy*, ed. R. Coopey and N. Woodward (New York: St. Martin's Press, 1996), 287–288.

[74] Taylor, *The Trade Union Question*, 189.

[75] Cronin, *New Labour's Pasts*, 128.

[76] Taylor, *The Trade Union Question*, 185.

[77] Cronin, *New Labour's Pasts*, 128–129.

[78] Taylor, *The Trade Union Question*, 182.

Causes and Context

with the Trade Unions and Employers' Associations.[79] Although trade unions' individual responses to non-registration were uneven, the case of five dockers accused of 'blacking' the Midland Cold Storage and taken before the National Industrial Relations Court in July 1972 provoked upheaval amongst trade unionists. In response to what the TUC saw as an all-out attack on trade union power, it mobilized a one-day strike, demonstrations outside prisons, and thousands of dockers stopped work. The case eventually reached the House of Lords, whose members ruled in favour of the unions, thus discrediting the Industrial Relations Act.[80]

Heath's 'Quiet Revolution' began to unravel further as inflation reached 9.2 per cent.[81] In July 1971 the situation worsened when the National Union of Mineworkers (NUM) rejected a 7 per cent pay claim for one of 47 per cent (£5 to £9).[82] An industry already in decline, pay that was not catching up with rising prices, long hours, and perilous work conditions made this more than a simple increase in take home pay: it became an all-out confrontation with the government.[83] The miners' strike of January–February 1972, furthermore, resulted in a 21 per cent increase for the miners. Heath believed such a settlement further aggravated inflation, but he was unwilling to fully confront the powerful demonstrations.[84]

The second part of Heath's U-turn commenced with him seeking some form of incomes policy. The government, the TUC, and the Confederation of British Industry (CBI) held talks aimed at creating a voluntary wage policy for industry.[85] The platform of free collective bargaining fell by the wayside by November of 1972 as the government began to impose the first of three stages of wage restraint with 90 days of a wages standstill. Stage II capped wage increases at 4 per cent, plus £1 to £250 per year, while 1973's Stage III would set a limit of £350 per year or 7 per cent.[86] The miners' subsequent resistance to Stage III of the incomes policy proved opportune for the strikers because the dispute coincided with a 70 per cent increase in oil prices by OPEC.[87] The increased demand for coal put them in a powerful bargaining position with the government. To prevent shortages of power and fuel during the winter, the government called a state of emergency

---

[79] Darlington and Lyddon, *Glorious Summer*, 20.
[80] Taylor, *The Trade Union Question*, 201–202.
[81] Sked, *Postwar Britain*, 341.
[82] Darlington and Lyddon, *Glorious Summer*, 36.
[83] Darlington and Lyddon, *Glorious Summer*, 31.
[84] Cronin, *New Labour's Pasts*, 130.
[85] Cronin, *New Labour's Pasts*, 130.
[86] Pearce and Stewart, *British Political History*, 493.
[87] Holmes, *The Failure of the Heath Government*, 107.

in November 1973,[88] implementing a three-day week, along with speed restrictions of 50 miles per hour, and TV ending at 10:30 pm.[89]

The dramatic and almost surreal effects of these strikes could be seen clearly on February 21 of that year when *Blue Peter* presenters Peter Purves and co-presenter John Noakes demonstrated on the programme how to use layers of newspaper to keep the elderly warm when faced with power cuts. After the lesson the presenters concluded, 'And if you do that, the old folks will stay warm as toast.'[90]

The scene at Whitehall was much more frantic. Brendon Sewill, a special advisor to the Chancellor of the Exchequer, admitted in the midst of the blackouts, 'I heard the Treasury Permanent Secretary talking about the possible need to activate regional government centres, as in the case of nuclear war. Because if all the lights went out, there would be no way of governing the country from the centre.'[91]

Faced with the 'most severe crisis since Suez in 1956,'[92] Heath called a general election for February 28.[93] He presented the general election as a referendum on the power of the state over that of the trade unions. 'Who Governs?'[94] became both the Conservative campaign slogan and the overarching political question of 1974. The answer to that question would disappoint the Tories but provide a problematic victory for a Labour Party struggling with its own identity.

Ideological Division in the Labour Party: 1970-74

For the last four years, Labour had been rife with internal conflict and dissension, leaving the party deeply divided and embattled once they took the reins of power. Two divergent camps began to emerge over its purpose.

One group, based primarily in the Parliamentary Labour Party, supported no major shift away from the Wilson government's direction of Labour and held strongly to Parliament's role in change.[95] Furthermore, it was steeped in a socialist Revisionism espoused most prominently by Anthony

---

[88] Cronin, *New Labour's Pasts*, 132.
[89] Pearce and Stewart, 494.
[90] Beckett, *When the Lights Went Out*, 65–66.
[91] Beckett, *When the Lights Went Out*, 65.
[92] Holmes, *The Failure of the Heath Government*, 107.
[93] Holmes, *The Failure of the Heath Government*, 113.
[94] Pearce and Stewart, *British Political History*, 494.
[95] Patrick Bell, *The Labour Party in Opposition: 1970–1974* (London: Routledge, 2004), 115; Hillary Wainwright, *Labour: A Tale of Two Parties* (London: The Hogarth Press, 1987), 14. Both hold divergent perspectives on Labour from 1970 and 1974, but both, basically, agree on the nature of the split within the Labour Party.

Crosland in *The Future of Socialism*. Crosland argued for a socialism based upon the foundations of the post-war welfare state. He asserted that the rise of both the welfare state and public sector checked the power of private business, forcing Labour to adopt a new approach to their politics. This combination of the welfare state and the new restraint placed on the private sector predicated that Labour abandon its call for an assault upon existing economic relations.[96] In particular, the state now exerted sufficient control over the economy that nationalization was unnecessary.[97] Instead, the achievement of full socialism would come about through stable economic growth.[98] Croslandite Revisionism shaped the trajectory of the party from the 1950s, eventually becoming a key intellectual component among many in the leadership of the 1974–79 Labour government.[99]

Stuart Holland's *The Socialist Challenge*, on the other hand, embodied the counterpoint to Croslandite Revisionism. Holland took a critical look at British capitalism and argued that the state exerted far less agency over private capital than the Revisionists asserted. Rather, small and powerful multinational corporations were able to increase prices, despite fluctuations in demand, resulting in rising profits for corporations, but aggravating inflation for national governments.[100] He believed that this trend was only growing worse and predicted that by the 1980s, 100 companies could control up to 66 per cent of net manufacturing input.[101] In addition to the spectre of inflation, these multinationals now had the freedom to increase prices rather than input, affecting Keynesian governments' ability to assure full employment to their citizens.[102] Furthermore, such concentration would allow multinationals to transfer-price goods, so they would not have to pay taxes in the UK.[103] With governments like the British in such a vulnerable position, Holland proposed that the top 20 to 25 companies should be nationalized, bringing a halt to uncompetitive, monopolistic pricing, and creating a more competitive market that would result in lower prices. Moreover,

---

[96] Michael Kenny, *The First New Left: British Intellectuals after Stalin* (London: Lawrence & Wishart, 1995), 126.

[97] C.A.R. Crosland, *The Future of Socialism* (1956; Westport: Greenwood Press, Publishers, 1963), 318.

[98] Kenny, *The First New Left*, 126.

[99] Mark Wickham-Jones, *Economic Strategy and the Labour Party: Politics and Policy-Making, 1970–83* (New York: St. Martin's Press, 1996), 43.

[100] Stuart Holland, *The Socialist Challenge* (London: Quartet Books, 1975), 132–133. See also Wickham-Jones, *Economic Strategy and the Labour Party*, 58.

[101] Patrick Seyd, *The Rise and Fall of the Labour Left* (London: MacMillan Education, 1987), 26.

[102] Wickham-Jones, *Economic Strategy and the Labour Party*, 56.

[103] Wickham-Jones, *Economic Strategy and the Labour Party*, 56.

instead of profits going to shareholders, profits would go to reinvestment.[104] Holland's ideas formed the basis for the AES, one of the key policies that became the centrepiece of ideological struggle during the 1970s.

For those opposed to Holland's ideas, the strategy represented a dangerous level of state interference in the economy at a point when it was most vulnerable. Tony Crosland, more specifically, alleged that Holland overestimated the level of monopolization of firms in the UK and that global competition among such large firms still occurred.[105] Others, like Roy Jenkins, refuted the idea that the AES' intention of creating more equality in society would actually result from nationalization.[106] Overall, many on the Right saw the AES as a dinosaur of a policy that, if implemented, would deter rather than increase economic investment in Britain.[107]

Neither did the Left of the Labour Party wholeheartedly embrace the AES. Some of the traditional Left believed that those supporting the AES were a young generation of academics deftly bypassing Labour's commitment of Clause Four.[108] Some, even its most famous proponent, Tony Benn, did not believe the AES was a 'comprehensive transformation strategy' of the economic system, but that it at least represented the beginning of broader change.[109] Peter Doyle, a Young Socialist member of the NEC who voted for the nationalization of 25 major industries as a part of the Labour Manifesto, reflected that it 'didn't go far enough.' For him, the nationalization should have had a wider sweep, including the insurance industry.[110] Doyle's measured criticism contrasted with those in the Socialist Workers' Party that wholly denounced the AES as 'authoritarian, reformist, impractical, and chauvinistic.'[111]

Socialist feminist criticism of the AES pointed to larger problems not only of industrial strategy, but of the role of women in the labour movement. In 1981 feminist Anna Coote concluded that, 'in spite of its radical pretensions, it is embedded in the same old-fashioned patriarchal values that inform and distort all mainstream political thinking today.'[112] Socialist feminist critics

[104] Holland, *The Socialist Challenge*, 75–76.
[105] Wickham-Jones, *Economic Strategy and the Labour Party*, 86.
[106] Wickham-Jones, *Economic Strategy and the Labour Party*, 89.
[107] Wickham-Jones, *Economic Strategy and the Labour Party*, 89.
[108] Michael Hatfield, *The House that the Left Built: Inside Labour-Policy Making, 1970–75* (London: Victor Gollancz, 1978), 104.
[109] Wickham-Jones, *Economic Strategy and the Labour Party*, 61.
[110] Peter Doyle, interview by author, December 2011.
[111] Bob Rowthorn, 'The Politics of the Alternative Economic Strategy,' *Marxism Today* (January 1981): 5.
[112] Anna Coote, 'The AES: A New Starting-Point,' *New Socialist* 2 (November–December

raised a range of biases implied in the AES. They alleged that the AES prioritized male-dominated manufacturing, ignoring industries like health and education with largely female workforces.[113] Moreover, the emphasis upon production created a dichotomy between making things and serving human need.[114] Furthermore, the AES' failure to take note of the sexual division of labour and the role of the family, by framing the standard worker as the male breadwinner, ignored women's unwaged labour in the home.[115] They pressed for the inclusion of child benefits, parental leave, and extending the social wage. Socialist feminists pointed to a broader social economy that questioned simply increasing productivity and pay.[116]

The emphasis women's liberation placed on process also connected with the shop stewards' combines, which were a type of industrial democracy. One of the key components of industrial democracy included employers notifying employees 90 days before any decision made affecting the enterprise and discussing alternative proposals with workers.[117] A more 'radical conception of planning agreements' involved workers developing alternative proposals for companies.[118] The supporters of this plan looked to the example of the Victor Works of Lucas Aerospace in Liverpool.[119] When the management of Lucas announced redundancies in 1978, the workers organized themselves into the Lucas Aerospace Combine Committee and pressured the Confederation of Shipbuilding and Engineering Union (CSEU) to set up a 14-man committee to provide alternatives to the job cuts.[120] For its supporters industrial democracy would inspire similar 'creativity and enthusiasm'

1981): 4–7, quoted in Seyd, *The Rise and Fall of the Labour Left*, 202.

[113] Anne Phillips, *Hidden Hands: Women and Economic Policies* (London: Pluto Press, 1983), 32.

[114] Rowbotham, *The Past is Before Us*, 174–176. See also: Hillary Wainwright, 'Reporting Back from Conditions Not of Our Choosing,' in *Beyond the Fragments: Feminism and the Making of Socialism*, ed. Sheila Rowbotham, Lynne Segal, and Hilary Wainwright, rev. ed. (1979; Pontypool: Merlin Press, 2013), 30–32.

[115] Rowthorn, 'The Politics of the Alternative Economic Strategy,' 7. See also Phillips, *Hidden Hands*, 28.

[116] John Callaghan, 'Rise and Fall of the Alternative Economic Strategy: From Internationalisation of Capital to Globalisation,' *Contemporary British History* 14, No. 3 (Autumn 2000): 129.

[117] Wickham-Jones, *Economic Strategy and the Labour Party*, 69.

[118] Wickham-Jones, *Economic Strategy and the Labour Party*, 67.

[119] Coventry, Liverpool, Newcastle, N. Tyneside Trades Council, *State Intervention in Industry: A Workers' Inquiry* (Nottingham: Spokesman, 1982), 65.

[120] Coventry, Liverpool, Newcastle, N. Tyneside Trades Council, *State Intervention in Industry*, 136.

among workers and 'be a practical demonstration of the potentialities of democratic socialism.'[121]

The Right of the Labour Party did not feel the same levels of excitement over the prospect of industrial democracy. To many on the Right the AES posed a further impediment to British industry's competitiveness. As Tony Crosland's advisor, David Lipsey stated, 'Crosland was at least as hostile to planning agreements as to public ownership.'[122]

If industrial democracy represented a visionary move towards 'uncharted territory,'[123] the Labour Party still had to contend with the trodden path of wage restraint. Holland's ideas would also prove influential in this debate. He argued that rising prices, not wages were the primary cause of Britain's economic decline, thereby obviating a statutory incomes policy. However, the Revisionists, who believed that rising wages were the culprit, still held sway in the party.[124]

It would be up to the Labour–TUC Liaison committee newly formed in 1972 to hammer out a concrete policy in the midst of these debates. What came out of a series of meetings with this group was the Social Contract. In the document *Economic Policy and the Cost of Living*, Labour and trade unions came to agree that the future Labour government would enact price controls in exchange for the trade unions' agreement to abide by a voluntary form of wage restraint.[125]

Within the framework of the Social Contract, once in government, Labour would pass a series of pro-worker policies in exchange for workers' voluntary adherence to wage restraint.[126] One, the government promised 'a fundamental and irreversible shift in the balance of wealth and power in favour of working people and their families' through redistributive taxation and increased social expenditure.[127] Two, the government was to extend public ownership to failing industries such as shipbuilding, and the state would acquire an interest, but not nationalize more profitable industries.[128] Three, the government was held to specific legislative promises such as repealing Heath's Industrial Relations Act and introduced legislation to expand both union and individual workers' rights.[129]

---

[121] Rowthorn, 'The Politics of the Alternative Economic Strategy,' 7.
[122] Wickham-Jones, *Economic Strategy and the Labour Party*, 91.
[123] Wickham-Jones, *Economic Strategy and the Labour Party*, 69.
[124] Wickham-Jones, *Economic Strategy and the Labour Party*, 58.
[125] Wickham-Jones, *Economic Strategy and the Labour Party*, 130.
[126] Wickham-Jones, *Economic Strategy and the Labour Party*, 71
[127] The Labour Party Manifesto, February 1974, *Let Us Work Together – Labour's Way Out of the Crisis* (London: The Labour Party, 1974), 15.
[128] Panitch, *Social Democracy and Industrial Militancy*, 229.
[129] David Marsh, *The New Politics of British Trade Unionism: Union Power and the Thatcher*

This agreement became solidified into a distinct policy promise when the Labour Party Conference convened in 1974. At the conference James Callaghan and three colleagues proposed for the inclusion into the Manifesto of the following clause.

> As it is proved that the Government is ready to act – against high prices, rents, and other impositions falling most heavily on the low paid and on pensioners – so we believe that the trade unions voluntarily (Which is the only way it can be done for any period of a free society) will cooperate to make the whole policy successful.[130]

Despite policy papers and the Party Manifesto, the Social Contract did nothing to settle the debate on wage policy in the Labour Party. In fact, it proved a sieve through which varying interpretations of wage restraint emerged, reflecting the deepening divisions in the party. For Harold Wilson and others in the Parliamentary leadership, the Social Contract was 'a way of life based on economic and social justice, aimed at replacing conflict and confrontation with cooperation and conciliation.'[131] Others in the Parliamentary leadership believed that it was an 'unrealistic manifesto.'[132] Some left-wing supporters, on the other hand, contended that the Social Contract was a 'contract for a socialist industrial programme,' rather than a return to the wage restraint of *In Place of Strife*.[133] However, trade unions believed the Social Contract to be a return to free collective bargaining and reflation.[134] These divisions were not absolute, but fissures existed among these different wings of the labour movement. For instance, some on the Left condemned the TUC for collaborating with the Labour government in what was seen as a form of 'crony capitalism' because such a pact would stifle grassroots trade union militancy.[135]

Therefore, when Labour finally came to power, they were tied to election promises to which many in the party were opposed. Furthermore, even those commitments that garnered a good degree of broad support within the party were also unstable as the factions' respective understandings or definitions of those policy promises were dramatically divergent. Poised at the helms of government, these fractures in the Social Contract would prove especially destabilizing once in power.

Legacy (London: MacMillan, 1992), 41.
[130] Cited in Hatfield, *The House that the Left Built*, 227–228.
[131] Wickham-Jones, *Economic Strategy and the Labour Party*, 94.
[132] William Rodgers, 'Government under Stress: Britain's Winter of Discontent,' *The Political Quarterly* 55, no. 2 (April 1984): 171.
[133] Wickham-Jones, *Economic Strategy and the Labour Party*, 94.
[134] Wickham-Jones, *Economic Strategy and the Labour Party*, 130.
[135] Taylor, 'The Rise and Fall of the Social Contract,' 70–71.

Labour in Power: 1974

When Labour won in February 1974, the deeply divided party faced a compounding problem: a slim margin of victory. Labour's win in February 1974 with 37.1 per cent of the popular vote was actually less than the Conservatives' 37.8 per cent. Even after another election in October of that same year, Labour's lead was only 39.2 per cent to the Conservatives' 35.8, along with a slim majority of three seats in Parliament.[136] The inconclusive results in the 1974 elections also reflected what some political scientists recognized as a larger trend emerging in the 1970s. British voters no longer demonstrated stalwart loyalty to either the Conservative or Labour Party. While from 1951 to 1955, only one in 25 voters refused to vote Labour or Conservative, by October 1974, one in four people were voting for parties outside the two major parties.[137] Moreover, Labour's slim majority was complicated by gains by the Liberal Party. For the Liberal Party, the 1974 general election was a 'significant breakthrough at the national level'[138] with 25 per cent of voters supporting the Liberals in the February and October elections.[139]

The precarious lead Labour held in government mirrored the similarly delicate balance it had to strike between the Left and Right in its own party as it assumed power. The new Prime Minister would now have to temper the zeal of the Left, and implement the changes of the Labour Manifesto, while balancing a Right wing tied to consensus politics and critical of the feasibility of following through with Manifesto promises under current international economic conditions. Initially, a veneer of unity and stability emerged, while conflicts were manageable enough to prevent the emergence of a full-blown crisis.

First and foremost, Labour repealed the Industrial Relations Act and passed such pro-union legislation as the Health and Safety at Work Act. In addition to legislation, the Labour budget came to fulfil many other promises of the Social Contract. In the Chancellor of Exchequer's two budgets of March and July 1974, Denis Healey increased subsidies on basic foodstuffs by £500 million, froze public and private sector rents, and increased taxes on the wealthy.[140] Women, in particular, benefited from the passage of key laws such as the Employment Protection Act and the Sex Discrimination

---

[136] Cronin, *New Labour's Pasts*, 52.

[137] Ivor Crewe, Bo Sarlvik, and James Alt, 'Partisan Dealignment in Britain 1964–1974,' *British Journal of Political Science* 7, no. 2 (Apr. 1977): 130.

[138] Norris, *Electoral Change in Britain*, 40.

[139] Butler and Kavanagh, *The British General Election of 1979*, 142.

[140] Taylor, *The Trade Union Question*, 230.

Act.[141] The Domestic Violence and Matrimonial Proceedings Act of 1976 also made it easier for women to obtain legal protection from abusive husbands. The effects were soon notable. In 1972 300 women had applied for such protection, but in 1976, 3,000 did so.[142] Able once again to engage in free collective bargaining, the TUC chose to uphold its side of the Social Contract by setting guidelines for wage negotiations that would act as a form of 'self-restraint' so that wage rises would not further aggravate inflation.[143]

From 1975 the Labour government's shift away from other policy commitments became apparent. The nationalization of major British industries came to be one of the first Labour Manifesto promises to come under fire. Like many of the Manifesto promises, the conflict over this policy reflected deeply-rooted rifts within the Labour Party itself. The Labour Left initially proposed the nationalization of industry in all major sections of the economy. The Cabinet majority, however, supported nationalization only when companies could not attain such goals as improved export performance or regional balance. Central to their idea of nationalization was co-operation with the private sector. Secretary of Industry Tony Benn's white paper put forward a less radical proposition. The February 1975 Industry Bill would have required businesses to share information with trade unions and proposed to fund the National Enterprise Board with £700 million in order to reorganize major industries.[144] The commitment among those in the Labour leadership was already antagonistic to calls for nationalization. In particular, Harold Wilson was seen to have strategically adopted a 'radical gloss' during the 1973 Labour Conference by vaguely supporting nationalization when his key priority was to 'dump the proposal to nationalize the 25 companies and avoid being tied to precise commitments.'[145] Now in office, the Cabinet and the Prime Minister asserted that they were not willing to antagonize the business community at a time when economic growth was so crucial. Wilson's subsequent removal of Benn as Secretary of State of Industry not only signalled a readjustment of Labour's industrial strategy, but it would become part of a broader U-turn within the Labour government as key elements of the Social Contract were challenged.[146]

The Labour government had inherited an economy already riddled with weaknesses, such as rising retail prices, a rising balance of payments deficit of over £1 billion in 1973, and a public sector borrowing requirement (PSBR)

---

[141] Rowbotham, *A Century of Women*, 405. See also Sandbrook, *Seasons in the Sun*, 43.
[142] Tiratsoo, 'You've Never Had It So Bad,' 175.
[143] Taylor, *The Trade Union Question*, 233.
[144] Cronin, *New Labour's Pasts*, 164.
[145] Wickham-Jones, *Economic Strategy and the Labour Party*, 93.
[146] Shaw, *The Labour Party*, 124.

of over £4 billion that same year.[147] Public expenditure, therefore, came under increasing scrutiny from the Treasury and from the Chancellor of the Exchequer, Denis Healey. Even before entering office, as early as 1973, Healey warned his colleagues about 'expecting too much. We might have to cut public expenditure.'[148] Later, on March 14, 1974, spurred on by exploding rates of inflation, he warned that Cabinet that the economic situation was 'probably the worst we had ever faced in peacetime.' Healey dispatched a memo to the Cabinet stating that it should not increase any part of public expenditure, except for subsidies and pensions uprating.[149] In particular, he urged,

> the Cabinet to agree that net additions to public expenditure should be limited to those affecting personal incomes and expenditure [...] and that in the view of these additional expenditures and the risk of subsidies being needed for the nationalised industries, any other net additions to public expenditure programmes in 1974–1975 should be avoided.[150]

When Healey followed up this warning for a proposed £1 billion in public expenditure cuts in 1975, his bid was successful.[151] The cuts directly affected workers in the public sector and came to further fuel public sector workers' dissatisfaction with their pay, conditions, and the Labour government. As Chief Whip, Bob Mellish warned Healey, 'This means the virtual destruction of the Manifesto and the impossibility of continuing the Social Contract. You are going to see the most major revolt in your history.'[152] Mellish recognized that the cuts would be seen as a betrayal of the promises of the 1974 Manifesto within the labour movement. The Social Contract would come under additional strain as the pound began to plummet, pushing the government to even harsher methods to control inflation and undermine the Social Contract.[153]

---

[147] Healey, *The Time of My Life*, 392.
[148] Wickham-Jones, *Economic Strategy and the Labour Party*, 88.
[149] Barbara Castle, *The Castle Diaries, 1974–76* (London: Weidenfeld and Nicolson, 1980), 42.
[150] 'Conclusions of a Meeting of the Cabinet,' 14 March 1974,' Cabinet Office Papers, CAB/128/54/3, CC (74), National Archives at Kew.
[151] Cronin, *New Labour's Pasts*, 168–169.
[152] Quoted in Cronin, *New Labour's Pasts*, 169.
[153] For a critique of this myth of the IMF's influence on Labour's public expenditure cuts see Steve Ludlam, 'The Gnomes of Washington: Four Myths of the 1976 IMF Crisis,' *Political Studies* XL (1992): 713–727.

The Sterling Crisis and the IMF Loan of 1976

As the Labour government turned the corner into 1976, it began to quickly lose its ability to manage the multitude of crises affecting Britain. OPEC 1 and 2 rocked the British economy, triggering the explosion of inflation from rates of 16 per cent in 1974 to an all-time high of 24 per cent in 1975.[154] Harold Wilson's May 1976 resignation appeared to be an ominous act signalling more instability for the Labour government ahead. When centre-Right James Callaghan won the leadership election as Prime Minister, it proved to be an important turning point in which the Labour government began to retreat even further away from its initial obligations of the Social Contract.[155]

As Callaghan took the helm of the Labour government, sterling was already under pressure. The government's attempts to stabilize the pound reveal global changes in exchange rates, divisions among Labour's Cabinet, the Treasury, and the Bank of England, placing additional strain on the already fragile Social Contract with British trade unions.

In 1969 the US Federal Reserve was in talks with the Bank of England and the Treasury about global exchange rates.[156] Influenced by the growing prominence of Milton Friedman's advocacy of floating exchange rates in order to free up capital flows among nations,[157] exchange rates began to float in 1972, and in the words of Edmund Dell, the former Paymaster General and later Secretary of State for Trade in the Labour government,

> A major realignment of exchange rates had been agreed [...] Before long, exchange rates were floating. Governments expected that floating would ensure balance in their current accounts and thereby restore some measure of national autonomy to an increasingly interdependent world.[158]

However, for Chancellor of Exchequer Denis Healey, this change proved difficult for national governments. 'In such a regime the value of a currency depended on the demand for it in the financial markets, which were not subject to control of any government.'[159]

This did indeed occur, and on March 4, 1976, the Bank of England

---

[154] Cronin, *New Labour's Pasts*, 168.
[155] Cronin, *New Labour's Pasts*, 174–175.
[156] Forrest Capie, *The Bank of England: 1950s to 1979* (Cambridge: Cambridge University Press, 2010), 417.
[157] Capie, *The Bank of England*, 417.
[158] Edmund Dell, *A Hard Pounding: Politics and Economic Crisis, 1974–1976* (Oxford: Oxford University Press, 1991), 4.
[159] Healey, *The Time of My Life*, 433.

reduced its holdings of sterling from £1,800 to £800 million.[160] When the Bank lowered interest rates the next day, it appeared as if it were trying to 'push down the pound,'[161] causing the pound to 'suffer its largest ever fall in a single day.'[162] Even more troubling was that the value of the pound continued to fall throughout 1976. This prolonged slide indicated that financial markets had lost confidence in government policy. Instead of facing a declining current account deficit, the government now had to resolve how to 'raise foreign exchange to replace growing withdrawals of capital.' This is the point when the government began to look for help from other banks and, eventually, the IMF.[163]

In negotiations with the IMF, the Treasury had to provide key financial forecasts of the British economy, in particular, the PSBR. The Treasury had forecast the PSBR to be £10.5 billion for 1977/8, a number that was central to negotiations with the IMF.[164] However, the PSBR turned out to be £5.6 billion.[165] The overshoot of this forecast created suspicions in the Labour Party that 'the Callaghan government had been the victim of a subtle campaign in 1976 by right wing Treasury officials to make it accept cuts in public spending.'[166]

This accusation reveals a long-standing power struggle between the government's Policy Unit and the Treasury. Edmund Dell, the then Paymaster General, defended his actions and those of the Treasury:

> Economics is not a matter of science, only of judgment. The judgment now had to include, as an essential ingredient, the opinion of the market. [...] The market clearly had not, been persuaded for long, [sic] by the measures of July 1975, nor by the public expenditure cuts of January 1976 and July 1976. This was the fourth attempt to get things right and it had to succeed. [...] In short, the argument was for overkill. If it proved to be overkill, we could always add back.[167]

However, the £4.9 billion in 'overkill' would require the government to enact massive public expenditure cuts to receive the IMF loan.

---

[160] Sangster to McMahon/Richardson, 'Events of the afternoon of Thursday 4 March 1976,' 5 March 1976, C43/779, quoted in Capie, *The Bank of England*, 743.

[161] Healey, *The Time of My Life*, 426.

[162] Capie, *The Bank of England*, 744. For a review of the debate over the intentional nature of the March 4, 1974 selling of sterling and subsequent lowering of rates see Kathleen Burk and Alec Cairncross, *'Goodbye, Great Britain': The 1976 IMF Crisis* (New Haven & London: 1992).

[163] Burk and Cairncross, *'Goodbye, Great Britain,'* 29.

[164] Joel Barnett, *Inside the Treasury* (London: André Deutsch, 1982), 102.

[165] Beckett, *When the Lights Went Out*, 355.

[166] Beckett, *When the Lights Went Out*, 355.

[167] Dell, *A Hard Pounding*, 284–285.

If the Labour government was fractured along the lines of Left and Right, the visceral opposition to such dramatic reductions in public expenditure cuts initially united these various factions. Once the IMF proposed the cuts, Prime Minister Callaghan knew that he would need to get the Cabinet to approve it, yet groups of opposition were forming within the Cabinet. For Callaghan, it was a priority to 'carry' the Cabinet with him, or more cynically, neutralize the left- and right-wing opposition to the proposal. Callaghan detailed his plan by asserting 'The best way to guide the Cabinet towards a united conclusion in the face of their deeply held opposing views was not to suppress Ministers' unhappiness or attempt to bludgeon them but to bring everything out in the open.'[168] Therefore, Callaghan invited those with alternative plans, namely Tony Crosland, Peter Shore, and Tony Benn, to present their alternatives on December 1, 1976.

Of particular importance was Tony Benn's presentation. As the IMF loan was seen as an historic 'watershed' in many ways,[169] it was especially pivotal in divesting the Labour Left of the momentum it gained from 1970 to 1974, but also ideologically disorienting the Revisionists. Although Benn had already been demoted from Secretary of Industry to Secretary of Energy, he still believed that elements of the AES could be an alternative to IMF-imposed austerity. However, the Policy Unit had not only armed the Prime Minister with questions to undermine Benn's presentation of the AES,[170] but the opposition throughout the Cabinet was tipped off and had questions ready, too. Furthermore, it was noted that 'without the Treasury behind him, Benn was pulverised. Even non-economic ministers, primed with briefs from No 10, joined in to expose the weakness of his assessment for import controls, direction of investment and a siege economy.'[171] Benn came to realize that 'the whole Cabinet was devoted to the extermination and ultimate destruction of my paper.'[172] According to plan, only a minority of the Cabinet, which included Michael Foot, Albert Booth, Stan Orme, Peter Shore, and John Silkin, supported Benn's plan.[173]

Revisionists like Tony Crosland also began to feel the political sands shift beneath their feet. Public spending was inextricably intertwined into the Revisionist view of socialism, but under the pressure of IMF cuts, this vision

---

[168] Callaghan, *Time and Chance*, 434.

[169] Burk and Cairncross, '*Goodbye, Great Britain*,' xi.

[170] Bernard Donoughue, *The Heat of the Kitchen: An Autobiography*, rev. ed. (2003; London: Politico's, 2004), 286–287.

[171] Stephen Fay and Hugo Young, 'The Day the Pound Nearly Died,' *Sunday Times*, May 14, 21, and 28, 1978 quoted in Burk and Cairncross, '*Goodbye, Great Britain*,' 97.

[172] Phillip Whitehead, *The Writing on the Wall: Britain in the Seventies* (London: Michael Joseph, 1985), 195.

[173] Donoughue, *The Heat of the Kitchen*, 287.

began to unravel. Crosland's proposal in early December 1976 was to use import deposits as an alternative to public spending cuts.[174] He eventually, and begrudgingly, accepted the cuts on 'pragmatic' grounds.[175] Callaghan had successfully encircled Cabinet opposition on the Left and 'killed off any rebellion from the Right,' and by December 6 the Labour government agreed to the sale of £500 million worth of British Petroleum shares, £1 billion in cuts for 1977/8, and £1.5 billion in cuts for 1978/9.[176]

The loan simply accelerated an already occurring erosion of the Labour Manifesto. Months before the final settlement was agreed, the shift in Labour's trajectory became apparent. Jim Callaghan articulated this change at the Labour Party Conference on September 28, 1976 when he announced that:

> Britain has for too long lived on borrowed time, borrowed money, borrowed ideas. For too long, perhaps ever since the war, we postponed facing up to fundamental choices and fundamental changes in our society and in our economy […] the cosy world we were told would go on forever, where full employment would be guaranteed by a stroke of the Chancellor's pen, cutting taxes, deficit spending, that cosy world is gone […] to think that you could just spend your way out of a recession and increase unemployment by cutting taxes and boosting Government spending, I tell you in all candour that that option no longer exists and insofar as it ever did exist, it worked by injecting inflation into the economy.[177]

The assumption of the IMF loan and the subsequent adoption of austerity measures has been the source of historical debate. While some believe that the Labour government was forced to temporarily temper their genuine zeal for reform in the face of economic crisis,[178] others believe that Callaghan and Healey were already convinced that public expenditure cuts and monetarism were legitimate economic trajectories even before entering office.[179] Some contend that the disillusion of key components of the Social Contract was occurring before 1976 and that it was a calculated ploy on the part of the Labour government to adopt the IMF loan as a form of political cover to deflect the wrath of the trade unions.[180]

---

[174] Burk and Cairncross, *'Goodbye, Great Britain,'* 98.
[175] Anthony Arblaster, 'Anthony Crosland: Labour's Last "Revisionist"?', *Political Quarterly* 48 (1977): 416–428 quoted in Wickham-Jones, 101.
[176] Burk and Cairncross, *'Goodbye, Great Britain,'* 101. See also Barnett, *Inside the Treasury*, 109.
[177] Quoted in Callaghan, *Time and Chance*, 425–426.
[178] Cronin, *New Labour's Pasts*, 186–187.
[179] Sandbrook, *Seasons in the Sun*, 502–503 and 690–691.
[180] Ludlam, 'Labourism and the Disintegration,' 91.

The public expenditure cuts further deepened the profound rifts within the trade union movement because they affected their respective memberships unevenly. While the largest unions, such as the TGWU and the GMWU, did have members in the public sector, unions like NUPE based entirely in the public sector were especially hard hit by the cuts. By the end of the 1970s, half of NUPE membership was in local government; one-third was in the NHS, and the rest in universities and the water industry.[181] Fuelled by an already established campaign against low pay within their own ranks and an activist leadership, NUPE became a key player in the establishment of the National Steering Committee against the Cuts (NSCAC), holding a demonstration of 60 to 80,000 people in November of 1976.[182] Although these unions were publicly critical of the cuts, they attempted to maintain support for the Social Contract within their own ranks. In May 1977, a composite motion to return to collective bargaining was put forward at the NUPE national conference. However, it was Alan Fisher, the bogeyman of the Winter of Discontent, who put forward an argument to criticize the Social Contract, but not withdraw from the agreement entirely. Fisher was victorious, and the composite motion to reject the Social Contract was defeated 6,562 to 3,520.[183]

The reductions in public expenditure also divided the trade union along left-wing public sector versus right-wing private sector lines. Frank Chapple, General Secretary of the Electrical, Electronic, Telecommunications, and Plumbing Union (EEPTU) expressed this cleavage succinctly. 'Nothing is more galling to those who contribute to the country's wealth through their productivity and skills, than to have their rewards determined by a group whose productivity is nil.'[184]

The combination of falling real wages and growing economic inequality was putting additional pressure on British workers overall. In December 1978 the *Economist* reported how a more equal distribution of wealth under the Heath government had stalled under Labour. Between 1971 and 1974 the richest 1 per cent of the British populace's wealth declined from 31 per cent to 23 per cent of total wealth. In 1975 and 1976, this 1 per cent's wealth increased to 25 per cent of total wealth.[185] Also, between 1975 and 1980, real wages fell by 13 per cent, a reduction not felt by British workers since 1931–32.[186]

---

[181] Ludlam, 'Labourism and the Disintegration,' 669.
[182] Ludlam, 'Labourism and the Disintegration,' 372.
[183] Stephen Williams and R.H. Fryer, *Leadership & Democracy: The History of the National Union of Public Employees, Vol. 2, 1928–1993* (London: Lawrence & Wishart, 2011), 281.
[184] Ludlam, 'Labourism and the Disintegration,' 111.
[185] 'The Rich Grow Richer Under Labour,' *Economist*, December 23, 1978, 90.
[186] Hay, 'Chronicles of a Death Foretold,' 450–451.

The Labour government then undermined yet another central tenet of the Social Contract: Labour's commitment to free collective bargaining. Held in the vice of loyalty to members' desire for free collective bargaining and passionate desire not to return to a Conservative government, trade union leaders came to support the government's new call for incomes policy. General Secretary of the TGWU Jack Jones was instrumental in the devising of a form of wage restraint. He successfully influenced the TUC General Council to approve a voluntary 6 a week wage increase policy, exempting those workers making more than £8,500 a year in 1975.[187] The plan was to be in effect for only a year with the possibility of being renegotiated and extended, but a return to 'free collective bargaining' was to take place in 1978.[188] However, the Labour government doubted the TUC's ability to hold the line on pay restraint, and thus drew up sanctions to enforce wage restraint if the TUC failed to do so.[189] Although this policy was relatively successful at reducing inflation, it was yet another step in undermining the Social Contract. The retreat from nationalization, cuts in public expenditure, and the continuing push for wage restraint were unravelling the core of the Social Contract. Unions and their members were now expected to deliver with less and less incentive from the government to comply. Such crucial political changes within the Labour government were not isolated, as we shall see. Significant shifts were occurring across the political landscape.

Tory Resurgence and Planning

The election of Margaret Thatcher as the Conservative Party leader in 1975 not only established an alteration in party strategy, it signalled the consolidation of a critique of the post-war consensus. As a member of Heath's Cabinet, Thatcher saw first-hand what she had come to regard as the causes of Conservative defeat. She wrote:

> we owed our later successes to our inside knowledge and to our understanding of earlier failures. The Heath Government showed, in particular, that the socialist policies pursued by Tory politicians are if anything even more disastrous than socialist policies pursued by Labour politicians.[190]

Thatcher and a cohort of right-wing Conservatives departed from both major parties' dedication to key elements of the post-war consensus such

---

[187] Taylor, *The Trade Union Question*, 237.
[188] Cronin, *New Labour's Pasts*, 172.
[189] Taylor, *The Trade Union Question*, 237.
[190] Margaret Thatcher, *The Path to Power* (London: HarperCollins, 1995), 196.

as commitment to the welfare state and the planned economy. Economist Friedrich Hayek emerged as one of their leading influences. In *The Road to Serfdom*, he argued that the rise of Nazism in Germany was rooted in nineteenth-century German social planning. Hayek further asserted that groups such as trade unions exploited this state intervention at the expense of other groups in society.[191] Another influence on Thatcher was Colm Brogan, conservative author and journalist. He criticized the Left historically because in his view they did not come from the working class, but from 'a burgeoning bureaucracy determined to exploit every opportunity to increase its numbers and enlarge its power.'[192] According to Thatcher the implications of social democracy not only weakened democracy, but exerted a profoundly negative effect on the British economy. The burgeoning demand for public expenditure that was characteristic of social democratic societies resulted in high rates of inflation without positively affecting production or unemployment.[193]

Despite many Conservatives' continued allegiance to post-war corporatism, soon after Thatcher's assumption of the party leadership, she moved to align party policy towards overtly restricting trade union power in Britain. In the summer of 1977, Thatcher advisor John Hoskyns co-authored a policy paper with Norman Strauss called 'The Stepping Stones.' The paper was distributed to key members of the Shadow Cabinet. So important was it that the authors emphasized to their readers, 'I know that time is short, but I hope you will find the time to read the paper at least twice and mark every point which is not clear.'[194] They first outlined that winning the next election was merely 'the first stepping stone in a longer term process'[195] of bringing about national recovery.[196] In Hoskyns' opinion, the 'major obstacle' to this national revitalization was 'the negative role of the trades unions.'[197] Instead of working together with unions as both Conservative and Labour governments had done in the past, the paper pointed out that it was exactly this relationship that should be broken. The rest of the paper carefully detailed a communications strategy that would co-ordinate Tory policy and media with the end of 'creating a climate of opinion which will

---

[191] Thatcher, *The Path to Power*, 51.
[192] Thatcher, *The Path to Power*, 51–52.
[193] Thatcher, *The Downing Street Years*, 7–8.
[194] 'Stepping Stones' Report (Final Text)' 14 November, 1977, Archive (Thatcher MSS), Source: THCR 2/6/1248, Margaret Thatcher Foundation, http://www.margaretthatcher.org/document/111771.
[195] 'Stepping Stones,' 8.
[196] 'Stepping Stones,' S-1.
[197] 'Stepping Stones,' S-1.

first reject socialism and [...] make it impossible for the trades union role to remain unchanged.'[198]

Thatcher was quick to act on the paper's suggestions, and in January 1978 she formed the 'Stepping Stones Steering Group' made up of shadow ministers like Keith Joseph and Nigel Lawson, and other political 'outsiders' charged with drawing up new policy initiatives and disseminating literature and speeches to make trade union reform central to Tory policy.[199] Not only did the paper and policy group mark a shift in the party, but it would later allow the Conservatives to effectively capitalize upon the conflicts between the Labour Party and the trade unions of late 1978 and 1979.

Labour in Power

While the Tories had a new leader and were invigorated by new policies, the Labour government was also able to register a few indications of optimism in 1977. After years of spiralling, inflation had decreased from 24.2 per cent in 1975 to 8.3 per cent in 1978. While the percentage of GDP represented by public expenditure declined from 46.4 per cent in 1975 to 42.9 per cent in 1979, social expenditure did increase by 2 per cent.[200] The expectation of revenues from North Sea oil also made the economic forecast brighter for Labour. However, their hold on power was fragile. After the defection of two Labour MPs to the Scottish Labour Party in 1976 and Labour losses in the January 1977 by-election, Labour held a majority of only one seat. Consequently, in March 1977, the Labour government formed an alliance with the Liberal Party. The 'Lib-Lab Pact,' as it became known, gave the Liberals the power to veto legislation before it reached the House of Commons, and Labour was to help the Liberals on issues of housing and local authorities. In addition to providing Labour a badly needed majority, the Liberals were to support Labour on Europe and devolution.[201]

A mood of cautious optimism tempered the outlook for the next general election. That year, Callaghan's lead policy advisor, Bernard Donoughue, submitted an analysis of the potential election dates. Donoughue reflected,

> Just before Christmas 1977, I had sent Jim [Callaghan] a long paper analysing potential election dates, which concluded that October and especially November 1978 promised best, because there would then be a brief opportunity when the economy would be good, and many people

---

[198] 'Stepping Stones,' 15.
[199] Thatcher, *The Path to Power*, 422–423.
[200] Cronin, *Labour and Society*, 186.
[201] Pearce and Stewart, *British Political History*, 499.

would also then receive significant increases in welfare benefits. After that the forecasts grew murky, with growing pressures from our pay policy.[202]

The government's success at attaining a degree of economic and political stability did nothing to ameliorate its difficulty in avoiding industrial unrest however. Two key strikes in particular would presage the changing dynamics of industrial conflict that would characterize those of the Winter of Discontent.

The 1977 Fire Brigades' strike, first of all, illustrated the challenges the government would face in holding a firm line on wage restraint when those calling for rises were providing essential services. In defiance of the government's 10 per cent incomes policy that year, the Fire Brigades went on strike for a 30 per cent rise, along with a reduction of working hours to 42 hours a week.[203] The Fire Brigades faced the quandary of withholding their labour at the risk of endangering lives. Bernard Cahill, a leading firefighter in Finchley, explained this dilemma:

> Firemen's consciences have been the root cause of our having no strikes within the fire service to date. The same abstract phenomenon that has kept us poorly paid for years, working part time to supplement our wages, has enabled us to listen to people telling us we were special but must continue to live on the breadline until we conquer inflation.[204]

During the Fire Brigades' strike, the TUC stood by the government and refused to support the workers. Eventually, Callaghan called a state of emergency and had the Army replace the fire brigades.[205] Although the government was successful in heading off this claim, the strike still became an important precursor to the government's stance on public sector strikes during the Winter of Discontent. In the midst of the strike, Cabinet discussions noted that if the government settled for in excess of the pay policy, 'it had to be remembered that there were many major groups waiting to see if the Government would breach its own guidelines. If that happened there would be very great difficulty in containing the breach.'[206] If the Social Contract bound the Labour government and the trade union movement together in theory, the Fire Brigades' strike reveals that in practice the

---

[202] Donoughue, *The Heat of the Kitchen*, 298.

[203] Tony Benn, *Conflicts of Interest: Diaries 1977–80*, ed. Ruth Winstone (London: Arrow Books, 1990), 226. See also: 'Conclusions of a Meeting of the Cabinet,' 10 November 1977, The Cabinet Papers, CAB/128/62/13, National Archives at Kew, UK.

[204] 'Fire Service Strike: A Personal View,' *Labour Monthly*, Jan/Feb. 1978, 38.

[205] 'Conclusions of a Meeting of the Cabinet,' 17 November 1977, The Cabinet Papers, CAB 128/62/14, National Archives at Kew, UK.

[206] 'Conclusions of a Meeting of the Cabinet,' 24 November 1977, The Cabinet Papers, CAB 128/62/15, National Archives at Kew, UK.

government was willing to intervene on the grounds that unions were defying incomes policy. However, it also reveals that the TUC was not flippant in its support for the government's pay policy. As Cabinet minutes reveal in December of 1977, Denis Healey stated,

> There was also evidence of growing positive trade union support for the policy. The 12-month rule was holding absolutely and trade union leaders were showing more than just a grudging acquiescence in the 10 per cent guideline. This was noticeable in the decision of the Trades Union Congress (TUC) General Council the previous day not to undertake a campaign in support of the firemen.[207]

In terms of escalating militancy and polarizing opinion, the Grunwick strike was also critical. In August 1976 Jayaben Desai, accompanied by her son and three other young Asian men, walked out of Grunwick Processing Laboratories Ltd. in protest against low pay rates and the harsh conditions in the laboratory.[208] The walkout sparked a larger-scale strike among the workforce, the majority of whom were South Asian women concerned about issues of dignity in the workplace, mistreatment by the predominantly white male management and owners, and workplace solidarity.[209] Media images of petite South Asian women striking became iconic, while the ethnic and gender diversity of the strikers,[210] including many Afro-Caribbean and some male strikers, were muted in the uproar.[211] As the strike gained momentum and national attention, it revealed many characteristics recognizable in the Winter of Discontent. As Linda McDowell, Sundari Anitha, and Ruth Pearson have noted in their research, 'The strike [...] contained the seeds of future unrest as a feminised service sector workforce succeeded the old white male industrial proletariat who were once the stalwarts of both the workplace and the picket line.'[212]

However, the strike eventually generated marches of 1,400 to 8,000 from April to November 1977. Violence began to break out and the visibility of white male trade unionists supporting became all the more conspicuous.[213] More than its significance as an industrial dispute that highlighted the issues

---

[207] 'Conclusions of a Meeting of the Cabinet,' December 22, 1977, The Cabinet Papers, CAB/128/62/19, National Archives at Kew, UK.

[208] McDowell, Anitha, and Pearson, 'Striking Images.' See also: Jack Dromey and Graham Taylor, *Grunwick: The Workers' Story* (London: Lawrence and Wishart, 1978); Joe Rogaly, *Grunwick* (Harmondsworth: Penguin, 1977).

[209] McDowell, Anitha, and Pearson, 'Striking Images.'

[210] McDowell, Anitha, and Pearson, 'Striking Images.'

[211] McDowell, Anitha, and Pearson, 'Striking Images.'

[212] McDowell, Anitha, and Pearson, 'Striking Images.'

[213] McDowell, Anitha, and Pearson, 'Striking Images.'

of race, gender, and class, the media portrayal of the violence associated with the strike directly fuelled calls for the restrictions on trade unions that would become so urgent during the Winter of Discontent. Margaret Thatcher judged that such hostile media coverage would help to legitimate the Conservatives' nascent 'Stepping Stones' plans for trade union reform. In a 1977 letter to John Gouriet, she reflected,

> We feel that the scenes of wild violence portrayed on television plus the wild charges and allegations being thrown in certain quarters, are enough in themselves to put most of the public on the side of the right and are doing more than hours of argument.[214]

The Conservatives were beginning to learn the power of media images to further their anti-trade union agenda, a lesson that would prove crucial to their election campaign after the Winter of Discontent.

The Conservatives' opportunity arose soon when the relationship between the Labour government and the trade unions soured as the decade came to a close. Callaghan's announcement in the spring of 1978 of a 5 per cent pay limit crystallized opposition to the Social Contract. According to Callaghan the inflation rate forecast for late 1978 was 7 or 8 per cent, which he saw as too high in comparison with the rates of other industrialized countries. He publicly put forward the 5 per cent norm on January 1, 1978 when asked about inflation on his New Year's Broadcast. He later admitted that 'the 5 per cent idea hardened and popped out when the interviewer tempted me to outline my hopes for the coming year.'[215] According to Bill Rodgers, 'concealed' Treasury growth reports of 10 to 11 per cent were not made known to Callaghan, so the Prime Minister's wage limit was based on the more restricted forecasts for growth.[216]

On the day he announced the 5 per cent limit at TUC headquarters, former Cabinet member Barbara Castle 'was horrified' and as the announcement continued, the National and Local Government Officers' Association (NALGO) General Secretary Geoffrey Drain leaned over to Castle and said, 'Barbara, we cannot deliver.'[217] According to Roy Hattersley some TUC leaders, despite their opposition to the policy, thought they would 'blind it through.' He explains, 'The unions' high command believed that rank-and-file resistance would collapse in the face of an assault by a determined government. They were wrong.'[218]

---

[214] Thatcher, *The Path to Power*, 399.
[215] Callaghan, *Time and Chance*, 519.
[216] Rodgers, 'Government under Stress,' 172
[217] Barbara Castle, *Fighting All the Way* (London: MacMillan, 1993), 507.
[218] Roy Hattersley, *Who Goes Home: Scenes from a Political Life* (London: Abacus, 1995), 107.

The 5 per cent announcement also shocked many close to the Prime Minister. Chancellor of the Exchequer Denis Healey observed:

> Jim [Callaghan] had become obsessed by inflation; he would have preferred a zero norm, and actually proposed a three per cent at one meeting. He told me privately that he was so disenchanted with the behaviour of the unions that he was contemplating legislation to control them.[219]

Callaghan remained confident that the unions would concede to another year of incomes policy if they desired to keep Labour in office.[220] In May of 1978 he attempted to gauge his ability to maintain the 5 per cent wage ceiling when he invited a group of senior journalists and editorial executives from the *Daily Mirror* for lunch in Downing Street. When Callaghan asked the group if the fourth stage of the Social Contract would be successful, the majority asserted that it would be difficult, but that it was feasible. Journalist Geoffrey Goodman disagreed and told Callaghan that it would be impossible for national trade union leaders to quell their members' opposition to pay policy. Callaghan replied, 'Alright, if that is the case, then I will go over the heads of the trade union leadership and appeal directly to their members – and the voters. We have to hold the line on pay or the government will fall.'[221] Others continued to warn Callaghan of the difficulty in implementing the 5 per cent wage limit. In a letter from Roger Carroll on August 31, 1978 to the Prime Minister and his principal advisors, Carroll warned that the 5 per cent limit would be unacceptable without providing workers something in return:

> The central problem of securing acceptance of the five per cent limit: this year our target is running <u>below</u> prices whereas last year, prices were moving below the ten per cent pay target. In the previous year, as I recall, the Chancellor was able to sweeten the pill, even though inflation was high, by net reductions in tax. We have probably neither of these advantages open to us this time, at least at the moment. So might we consider as an alternative, an alteration in the structure – not the total – of direct taxation, to make the five per cent more palatable?[222]

Despite the ominous signs spelled out to the Prime Minister with regards to incomes policy, Callaghan made another choice that resulted in the wage limit being even more unpalatable to unions. At a secret dinner party held days before the TUC Conference in September 1978, Callaghan invited

---

[219] Healey, *The Time of My Life*, 398.
[220] Callaghan, *Time and Chance*, 526.
[221] Goodman, *From Bevan to Blair*, 221–223.
[222] Letter From Roger Carroll to Prime Minister James Callaghan, David Lipsey, and Tom McNally, 31 August, 1978, James Callaghan Papers, Minutes to the Prime Minister from David Lipsey, 1978, Box 139, Bodleian Library, Oxford, UK.

Moss Evans, General Secretary of the TUC Len Murray, David Basnett (GMWU), Alfred Allen (USDAW), Geoffrey Drain (NALGO), and Hugh Scanlon (AUEW) to discuss his election plans. When Callaghan asked whether or not he should hold an autumn election, the entire group, with the exception of Hugh Scanlon, exhorted Callaghan to hold an autumn election because there was no way they could ensure industrial peace for the coming winter.[223] Days later, the decision was apparent when Callaghan cryptically announced in song that 'I have promised nobody that I shall be at the altar in October. Nobody at all.'[224] There would be no November election, and for the unions, there would be no strong justification to hold true to an incomes policy. Workers had little to hold them back from striking in the winter to come. Callaghan's actions throughout 1978, from the imposition of the wage limit to the cancellation of the autumn election, illustrate his decision to have a showdown with trade unions over economic policy.

The most significant trends that came to a head and ignited the strikes of the Winter of Discontent emerged from the fractures in the post-war British state and economy that became full-blown divisions by 1978 and 1979. First of all, the post-war commitment to the welfare state and full employment had national governments look to wage restraint as the key to keeping inflation in check. With a tradition of wage restraint falling disproportionately on public sector workers, compounded by sky rocketing levels of inflation in the 1970s, wage restraint made public sector workers less and less receptive to appeals from the government, especially when private sector workers were successfully breaking wage limits. Second, a combination of new political ideas and the increased presence of women, black, and Asian workers in trade unions were in the process of reshaping the parameters of the labour movement and calling into question assumptions to which trade union and the Labour Party adhered. Differing interpretations of the role of trade unions and political parties, combined with a lack of deference to established leaders, were further accentuated by generational political ruptures in the British labour movement in the late 1970s. Third, profound divisions among the Labour Left, Right, and trade unions created a gulf between the theory, interpretation, and implementation of the Social Contract, which made the agreement inherently unstable. Fourth, leaders in the Labour government, especially Prime Minister Callaghan, were increasingly willing to 'go over the heads of trade union leaders' and challenge the unions' justification to reinstate free collective bargaining in Britain. Finally, within the national political parties, both Conservative and Labour, an increasing scepticism

---

[223] Goodman, *From Bevan to Blair*, 226–227. See also: Sandbrook, *Seasons in the Sun*, 702–703.

[224] Quoted in Sandbrook, *Seasons in the Sun*, 703.

towards the post-war consensus was spreading. All these currents refashioned British society and politics in radically different ways that departed from the mould cast soon after the Second World War. The mounting tension and currents built up during the 1970s would erupt in the strikes of the Winter of Discontent.

3

The Floodgates Open: The Strike at Ford

A little more than two weeks after James Callaghan announced to the TUC Conference in Brighton that there would be no autumn election, the mounting pressure building up against the 5 per cent wage limit came to a head among workers at Ford Motor Company. On September 22 the first workers at the Halewood plant outside of Liverpool walked out on strike, triggering not only industrial action at other plants in the UK, but also creating an important precedent for other trade unionists. As the eight-week strike wore on and the negotiated rates were increasingly in excess of government policy, the *Economist*'s headline, 'After Ford, the Deluge?'[1] became prescient. The dispute at Ford did indeed open the floodgates. Other workers, from lorry drivers to NHS domestic cleaners, were encouraged by Ford workers' eventual successful claim, which struck at the heart of the government's policy.

While the Winter of Discontent has played a central role in debates surrounding the nature of Britain's economic decline, it is somewhat ironic that the first waves of strikes actually began within the American-owned, Ford Motor Company. Ford workers' central claim in September 1978 was a wage rise in excess of the government's 5 per cent pay policy; however, the national strike was rooted in both the company's history of industrial relations and Ford workers' evolving approaches to militancy and politics. While Ford CEOs and managers established new strategies to spur productivity amongst its workforce during the 1960s and 1970s, Ford workers were in the midst of developing their own workplace culture. On the shop floor, new forms of political and industrial militancy began to emerge. These changes were rooted in the evolving face of the workforce at Ford.

In this chapter, I will chart developments within Ford, laying specific

---

[1] 'After Ford, the Deluge?,' *The Economist*, November 4, 1978, 10.

emphasis on the shifts occurring amongst the rank and file. I will focus on the social, political, and cultural experiences of four Ford workers to demonstrate the impact these forces had on their actions during the strike of 1978. What will become apparent is that Ford workers were motivated by a complex set of forces rather than simply rash 'bloody mindedness' or crass greed. Instead, I will argue that the constellation of political identities that emerged in the Ford strike not only inspired their actions that winter, but also reflected broader social and political changes in Britain in the late 1960s on into the 1970s.

Ford Culture and Militancy

> *'Halewood. If one of them sneezed, they would come out on strike! Ford was renowned for it, wasn't it?'* – NUPE shop steward and wife of Halewood worker, Celia Newman[2]

Since its inception in the United States, the Ford Motor Company was infamous for its hostility towards any form of trade union organizing. Resistance to the unionization of their plants was rooted in the 'Ford industrial creed,' which affirmed that management exclusively knew what was in the best interests of the company and its workers.[3] Contradiction was inherent in this creed, for trade unions not only posed a threat to this paternalistic relationship, but their very existence was perceived as undermining workers' freedom. As Henry Ford noted, 'Labour union organizations are the worst things that ever struck the earth because they take away a man's independence.'[4] Ford UK would not prove any different as it inherited this philosophy of industrial relations and applied it to a British workforce. It was not until 1941, 30 years after it began to assemble cars in Britain, that Ford reluctantly acquiesced to union recognition.[5] From 1944 to the 1960s, Ford UK approached its relationship to its workforce within the classic 'Fordist paradigm,' characterized by tight supervision, uniform work standards, and exclusive negotiations with national trade union officials.[6] This arrangement suited the two major unions in the

---

[2] Mike and Lorraine Donovan and Celia Newman, interview by author, October 2006.
[3] Henry Friedman and Sander Meredeen, *The Dynamics of Industrial Conflict: Lessons from Ford* (London: Crom Helm, 1980), 21.
[4] Huw Beynon, *Working for Ford*, 2nd ed. (Harmondsworth: Penguin, 1984), 43.
[5] Beynon, *Working for Ford*, 55–56.
[6] Thomas Fetzer, 'Walking Out of the National Workplace: Industrial Disputes and Trade Union Politics at Ford in Britain and Germany in the 1970s,' in *Ford: The European History, 1903–2003*. ed. Steven Tolliday, Yannick Lung, and Hubert Bonin (Paris: P.L.A.G.E., 2003), 394.

motor industry, the TGWU and the AUEW. The unions themselves also had highly centralized organizational structures. During the 1950s, for instance, General Secretary Arthur Deakin's 'iron-handed austerity' of the TGWU was beneficial to both Ford and the national leadership of unions.[7] Ford management and national unions had secured a relationship whereby they could continue bypassing shop floor negotiations, without any threat from rank-and-file members.

Nevertheless, shop floor militancy soon began to erode this relationship. Throughout the 1950s and the early 1960s, the number of unofficial strikes at Ford grew to such a point that the Donovan Commission had deemed that a form of 'dual unionism' had developed, a system by which workers were bypassing trade unions and directly challenging management.[8] It would be the distinctive workplace culture that emerged at Ford in the 1960s and 1970s that further strengthened this wave of labour unrest and propelled Ford workers to the forefront of the industrial disputes during the Winter of Discontent.

Across Ford factories in Britain, but especially the two largest plants, Halewood in Liverpool and Dagenham in London, in the late 1960s Ford saw an influx of a new generation of young workers, primarily in their early twenties.[9] These young workers brought with them a variety of regional and political traditions to the shop floor. Ford managers at Halewood, for example, recruited workers locally from the Merseyside area. These workers brought with them traditions of trade unionism and politicization shaped in places like the Liverpool docks.[10] John Bohanna was part of this new generation of young men from Merseyside who were beginning their careers at Halewood. Still in his twenties, Bohanna began working in the framing part of the plant in 1969 and eventually became a shop steward, a choice that was influenced by his father's trade union activism. Bohanna's father was an immigrant from Ireland who worked as a labourer in the water department and later became the shop steward in his section. He also became politically active in the Labour Party, immersing his son in the labour movement from an early age:

> And then the elections came, and I can remember local elections, national elections and my father asking us to go out with pieces of wood with a little poster on top with 'Vote Labour!' With one slogan or another,

---

[7] Beynon, *Working for Ford*, 248.
[8] Fetzer, 'Walking Out of the National Workplace,' 394.
[9] 'The Ford Strike: Where does it take us? An Interview with Dan Connor,' *Marxism Today*, February 1979, 36. See also: Beynon, *Working for Ford*, 192–193.
[10] Beynon, *Working For Ford*, 192–193.

looking like idiots. Not marching, but going around the streets, shouting at people, and we were only kids.[11]

The composition of the various Ford plants' workforces differed. At Dagenham, unlike Liverpool, Ford was no longer able to recruit workers locally. Workers were drawn from 25 to 30 miles away from Dagenham and beyond.[12] West Indian and Asian workers were prominent, making up 60 per cent of the workforce at Dagenham.[13] They also played a major role in Ford factories outside of London. At the Leamington factory in the West Midlands, the West Indian or Asian workers comprised 80 per cent of the workforce, and at the Langley factory outside London, they made up 75 per cent of the workforce.[14] Dagenham engine plant worker Johnny Slowly began working there in 1969 while still in his early twenties. Originally from Jamaica, Slowly describes how in the late 1960s there was not much work available, but at the time Ford was hiring 'hundreds' of workers. For a young man, the atmosphere was dynamic and exciting because the workforce was very 'multicultural' with many people from places like Ghana and Jamaica.[15]

Roger Dillon, who began working at Ford after this initial influx of workers during the late 1960s, describes why Ford became a magnet for so many West Indian and Asian workers. Dillon, the son of West Indian immigrants, was raised in a rural mining community in Wales. Unwilling to 'go down to the coal mines,' at the age of 20, Dillon left for London, like many young men of his era, to find work. Dillon explains that during that time it was especially difficult for West Indians and Asians to secure employment, but Ford was one of the few places where work could be found. Dillon states that part of the reason for this was because white working-class men from the area, or what Dillon termed 'Essex men,' saw work at Ford 'right at the bottom because that's where the dregs work – the blacks, the Asians.'[16]

This new generation of employees began to forge a new political dynamic at Ford. In the 1950s, the majority of workers supported the Labour Party, and those with more Left politics joined the Communist Party. In the late

---

[11] John Bohanna, interview by author, June 2006.
[12] 'The Ford Strike: Where does it take us?,' 34.
[13] 'We are the Majority at Fords,' *Race Today*, November 1976, 223.
[14] John Matthews, *Ford Strike: The Workers' Story* (London: Panther, 1972), 39.
[15] Johnny Slowly, interview by author, September 2007. Jefferson Cowie observes an interesting parallel in the United States with a 1972 strike at a General Motors (GM) plant in Lordstown, Ohio. *Newsweek* described the young and multi-cultural workforce as 'an industrial Woodstock,' as they sported 'shoulder-length hair, beards, Afros and mod clothing along the line.' *Stayin' Alive*, 7–8.
[16] Roger Dillon, interview by author, October 2007.

1960s, a wider spectrum of Left groups like the International Socialists and the International Marxist Group emerged.[17] Also, a number of West Indian and Asian shop workers brought into Ford the politics of the emerging Black Power movement and the Indian Workers' Association.[18] In the foundry at Dagenham, Rod Finlayson noted the excitement of working with a similarly diverse workforce made up of Turkish immigrants, West Indians, and Asians. However, it was working with Irish Catholics that proved the most engaging aspect of his work life. Finlayson came from a Protestant Scottish family 'quite bigoted' against Catholics, so working at Ford allowed him to break away from those traditions. Rebellion marked Finlayson's life for his immediate family was not politically active:

> I was pretty unhappy when I came to London, and I got mixed up in the Young Communist League and 'Ban the Bomb.' And I went on the 'Ban the Bomb' marches, and I thought they were brilliant. [...] There were these people, very full of life. [...] There were some very weird people, but there were also some very friendly, honest people that struck me as not hypocritical. I suppose one of the things that I hated was hypocrisy.[19]

The experiences of these men provide a snapshot of some of the shifting currents of workplace culture at Ford in the 1960s and 1970s.

The tedious, intense, and sometimes dangerous nature of the work at Ford also fostered distinctive forms of solidarity that would further shape industrial militancy at this time. Huw Beynon's *Working for Ford* provides a detailed portrait of the atmosphere at Halewood during the early 1970s. In an interview with Beynon, one Halewood worker notes that work at the plant was so mind numbing that '[...] a robot could do it. The line here is for morons.'[20] The 'monotonous and repetitive' work at Ford inspired Finlayson to become a shop steward at Dagenham. He explained, 'You've got to do what you want to do in life, so I gradually found the job very boring, and I needed something to keep me alive.'[21] Rank-and-file activism afforded some Ford workers, like Finlayson, the opportunity to derive some meaning and purpose from a seemingly meaningless and rote job.

The ties among workers eventually developed into a form of what

---

[17] Friedman and Meredeen, *The Dynamics of Industrial Conflict*, 332.
[18] Rod Finlayson, interview by author, June 2007.
[19] Finlayson, interview.
[20] Beynon, *Working for Ford*, 124.
[21] Finlayson, interview. Jefferson Cowie states a similar current could be found at the Wixom Ford plant in the United States. One employee there explained, 'There's only three ways out of here. You either conform and become deader each day, or you rebel, or you quit.' *Stayin' Alive*, 7.

Beynon described as 'factory class consciousness.'[22] Despite pressure from management to constantly speed up production, Slowly found the atmosphere with his fellow workers 'really enjoyable,' especially on breaks when he and his co-workers would play dominos or just 'exchange ideas.' For Slowly, then, it would be the connections he made with his co-workers, not any political ideology, that inspired him to 'put his fellow workers first' and resist what he perceived as unjust actions by management.[23] Despite such camaraderie, racial divisions continued to be stark. For example, Dillon, who had been raised in a predominantly white community in Wales, was shocked when he realized that it was not customary for West Indians and whites to sit together, something he had become accustomed to back in Wales. Instead, whites, West Indians, and Asians all sat at their respective tables during their tea break.[24] Although workplace solidarity was present at Ford, these connections were also contingent on larger divisions of race and ethnicity.

These shop floor ties became further strengthened in the face of the company's often-hostile treatment of their workforce. Bohanna describes how at Halewood men would be laid off in the middle of shifts at four or five in the morning. Since there was no public transportation that early in the morning, men would attempt to stay in the canteen until they could find a way home, but Ford would send security to force the men out.[25] Finlayson argues that the unofficial strikes were the result of everyday power struggles:

> You've got to understand the intensity of the work and the pace of the work. If the management expects you not to have a tea break one day because they've got no tea, that would pose a problem, so you would have a strike over a cup of tea, but it's actually a strike over being treated as a proper human being and not a cup of tea.[26]

Behind the numbers and statistics that made unofficial strikes problematic to Ford management and government officials were instances where underlying shop floor conflicts of power and authority erupted. More specifically, as Finlayson illustrates, workers used one of the few tools at their disposal, strikes, to assert their right to respect as 'proper' human beings. Whether they are described as a form of 'factory class consciousness' or simply loyalty and friendship, these ties of mutual support and obligation provided a solid basis for shop floor activism at Ford.

Finlayson's account of striking over tea might also reaffirm stereotypes that 'a union official [...] would spot a minute failing, say a stale roll on

[22] Beynon, *Working for Ford*, 129.
[23] Slowly, interview.
[24] Dillon, interview.
[25] Bohanna, interview, June 2006.
[26] Finlayson, interview.

sale in the canteen, and tell the membership to stop work.'[27] However, the other side of that coin would be the prevalent managerial culture in Britain at the time. As Nick Tiratsoo illustrates, few British executives in the 1970s held academic or professional degrees; therefore, labour relations were framed between the options of being a 'bastard' or a 'hard bastard.'[28] More egregious examples of this managerial prerogative could be seen in 1970 when one man criticized how his bosses had 'individual towels and fancy soap' while workers were resigned to 'rough towels' and 'cheese cake soap.' In another case it was observed that managers and workers entered by different gates and ate in segregated canteens.[29]

Therefore, a new industrial and political dynamism was at play at Ford in the 1960s and the 1970s, which soon found expression at the national level.

Shop Floor Militancy Goes National

'Those tarts taught us a lesson. We ought to go down there and shout a fucking big 'thank you.' – Halewood worker on the 1968 Dagenham Equal Pay Strike[30]

The first group of workers to take advantage of this developing shop floor presence and take it to a national level was a relatively small group of female sewing machinists working at Ford Dagenham.[31] In 1967, Ford introduced a new wage structure in which sewing machinists were classed as 'unskilled' workers, although, unlike any of their male colleagues, they were hired based on their ability to pass three tests. Consequently, in the summer of 1968, 187 sewing machinists struck to be graded as skilled workers. The strike soon garnered national attention, and Barbara Castle, Secretary of State for Employment and Productivity, personally intervened. Castle obtained a settlement where the women would receive 92 per cent, instead of 85 per cent of an unskilled male worker's rate, although the women were still classed as 'unskilled.'[32] The strike not only led to the Labour government introducing equal pay legislation, it influenced Ford shop stewards and conveners to press grading claims with 'much greater determination' than before.[33] Moreover,

---

[27] Tiratsoo, 'You've Never Had It So Bad,' 181.
[28] Tiratsoo, 'You've Never Had It So Bad,' 181.
[29] Sandbrook, *Seasons in the Sun*, 266.
[30] Quoted in Beynon, *Working for Ford*, 176.
[31] 'The Ford Strike: Where does it take us?,' 34.
[32] Friedman, *The Dynamics of Industrial Conflict*, 44–46; Wrigley, 'Women in the Labour Market and in the Unions,' 55.
[33] Friedman, *The Dynamics of Industrial Conflict*, 255.

it caused 'a turning of the tide in the industrial power relationships at Ford' after defeats in 1957 and 1962.[34]

The strike also raised the issue of gender at Ford. The women were a tiny minority in an overwhelmingly male workforce, yet their strike had a major impact in the media and startled men at Ford. The 1968 Sewing Machinists' Strike for equal pay strongly resonates with Ava Baron's assertion that 'Gender is created not simply outside production but also within it. It is not a set of ideas developed separately from the economic structure but a part of it, built into the organization and social relations at work.'[35] The Ford women exploded the stereotype of women as passive and unable to resist. By bringing to light gender inequality, they became the touchstone for a wider spirit of militancy. Hence, gender was inherent in the history of industrial conflict at Ford.

This 'turning of the tide' was apparent in the workers' response to Ford's yearly wage offer in 1969. That year Ford's offer was tied to a clause that indicated that if workers engaged in 'unconstitutional action,' or unofficial strikes, they would forfeit their entitlement for six months and their right to claims off the 'Income Security Plan.' Halewood workers rejected the offer, sparking a national strike against such 'penalty clauses.'[36] The government was forced to intercede, coming to a settlement for increases in salary pay, with some compromises made in regards to unofficial, shop floor action, yet many of the original penalty clauses remained in place.[37] Nevertheless, yet another national rank-and-file confrontation with management added to the growing momentum of their movement.

After the 1969 strike, workers pushed through important changes on the National Joint Negotiating Committee (NJNC). Since the late 1950s, the NJNC, a group of company and trade union officials, had been charged with the responsibility of negotiating wages and conditions for Ford workers.[38] After the 1969 strike, workers forced the resignation of trade union officials on the NJNC who had originally accepted Ford's offer. They then advocated having a group of conveners placed on the NJNC, and Ford eventually conceded.[39] This act was followed by an overall attempt by management to 'adopt a more accommodating and integrating approach towards shop

---

[34] Friedman, *The Dynamics of Industrial Conflict*, 255. See also: Sheila Cohen, 'Equal Pay – or what? Economics, Politics, and the 1968 Ford Sewing Machinists' Strike,' *Labor History* 53, no. 1 (February 2012): 51–68.

[35] Baron, 'Gender and Labor History,' 37.

[36] Beynon, *Working for Ford*, 253.

[37] Beynon, *Working for Ford*, 285.

[38] Friedman, *The Dynamics of Industrial Conflict*, 61.

[39] Big Flame, 'Shop Stewards at Ford,' *Radical America* 8, no. 5 (September–October 1974): 121.

stewards.'[40] For example, union representatives were now allowed to take part in decisions concerning job allotments and timings.[41] Changes in union leadership also altered this relationship with rank-and-file Ford workers. In the late 1960s, Jack Jones became the General Secretary of the TGWU, and Hugh Scanlon became the General Secretary of the AUEW. Forged in a tradition of anti-fascism that sprang from Jones' service in the Popular Front in Spain and Scanlon's early membership in the Communist Party, both brought a new political tradition to these two unions dominating the British car industry. As the 'terrible twins of the Left,' Jones and Scanlon moved away from their unions' centralized systems of negotiation to one that sought to embrace what they called 'shop floor democracy.' While there was no intention of cutting all ties the former system, which included its ties to the Labour Party, they did bring to the TGWU and the AUEW a formal recognition of the legitimacy of this rank-and-file movement at Ford.[42]

Nevertheless, changes at Ford and among the trade union leadership did not stem this rising tide of labour unrest. When Ford introduced a pay offer in 1971, they were now confronted with a workforce that had gained confidence from previous challenges to management. The offer also came as miners were successfully opposing Heath's Industrial Relations Act, adding to the overall industrial militancy of British workers. The response to Ford's offer of a £2 rise was immediate. 'One minute the shop was working, the next minute it was empty. I've never seen such a walkout,' related one shop steward.[43] Followed soon by workers at Dagenham, Langley, and Southampton, the TGWU and the AUEW made the strike official. Ford workers' central claim was for parity with other workers in the motor industry. They also demanded equal pay and an abolition of the remaining penalty clauses from the 1969 strike.[44] Jones and Scanlon's commitment to shop floor democracy soon faded. The two made a secret deal with Ford and imposed a secret ballot to accept the settlement and end the strike without consulting the NJNC.[45] Despite the bitterness many felt towards Jones and Scanlon, the momentum of the successful strikes from the late 1960s to the early 1970s infused Ford workers with 'enormous confidence' that fed into the strikes of 1978.[46]

Riding on the tide of these successes, the ever-expanding spectrum of

---

[40] Fetzer, 'Walking Out of the National Workplace,' 395.
[41] Beynon, *Working for Ford*, 350.
[42] Minkin, *The Contentious Alliance*, 162–163.
[43] Matthews, *Ford Strike*, 91.
[44] Matthews, *Ford Strike*, 86.
[45] Friedman and Meredeen, *The Dynamics of Industrial Conflict*, 272.
[46] John Bohanna, interview by author, October 2006.

Left groups became more energized and active. While the political culture at Ford continued to be dominated by a loyalty to the Labour Party, those attracted to Left groupings were becoming more heavily involved. Bohanna, a shop steward at the Halewood plant by that time, notes that his politics were 'Labour Party-based' during the mid-1970s, but, at the same time, he was beginning to become influenced by a political group called 'Big Flame.' Disillusioned with what he perceived as Labour's unwillingness to truly represent working-class people, Big Flame's politics began to appeal to him. As a spin off from the Lotta Continua group in Italy, Big Flame advocated an organic growth of revolution from workers, instead of by a formal party construct. What also attracted Bohanna to Big Flame was the group's regular newsletters, which reported on what was happening on the shop floor. Additionally, the newsletters attacked the company, unions, and right-wing shop stewards with a 'fearlessness' that Bohanna admired. Soon thereafter, he often contributed to the newspaper, inspiring him to begin his own paper during the strike of 1978.[47]

At Dagenham, the Communist Party continued to wield influence on the shop floor. Although the Party had only 40 members at Dagenham, two leading shop stewards in the mid-1970s and during the Winter of Discontent, Sid Harroway and Danny Connor, were members.[48] Nevertheless, the Communist Party was but one part of a spectrum of political groups that made up the dynamic and multifaceted political culture at Dagenham. Finlayson, who eventually became a shop steward, observed:

> The other side to Dagenham at the time was on the political Left. And it was extraordinary! It was like a big university of left-wing ideas. There would be an 'Autonomy Group,' an Italian Autonomy group. There were anarchists. There were pro-Serbia Communists, Chinese Communists. There was more than one kind of pro-Albanian Communists. There was every kind of Trotskyite movement you could think of. There were all sorts of things. There was a Black Power movement. Indian workers – there were groups that were part of the Indian Workers' Association. There were a lot of political people. There were also fascists. The fascists came in later as part of three different kinds of factions. You'd call them the ATA, the National Front. There were different Nazi factions ... Dagenham was a magnet. If you wanted to work and earn money and also fight for your rights, it was a good place to go.[49]

---

[47] Bohanna, interview, October 2006.

[48] John McIlroy, 'Notes on the Communist Party and Industrial Politics,' in *British Trade Unions and Industrial Politics: Trade Unions and Industrial Politics*, ed. John McIlroy, Nina Fishman, and Alan Campbell (Aldershot: Ashgate, 1999), 239–240.

[49] Finlayson, interview.

Politicized Ford workers, including Finlayson, came together in April 1978, five months before the strikes of the Winter of Discontent, to form an independent shop stewards' movement called 'The Ford Combine.'[50] That same year, Ford had invited 21 conveners into the NJNC in an attempt to further integrate shop floor leadership into national negotiations.[51] The Ford Combine was created as an alternative to the seemingly 'moderate' and 'institutionalized' shop stewards' movement that had been seen as both co-opted by the NJNC and dominated by the Communist Party.[52] The Ford Combine attracted a broader range of Left groups like Big Flame, the Socialist Workers Party, and the International Marxist Group.[53]

Nevertheless, the widening spectrum of left-wing political culture coexisted alongside a stalwart trade unionism that was loyal to the Labour Party. Dillon's father, for instance, had instilled trade unionism into his son at an early age. He described how when he was a young boy, he would go to his father's workplace in Cardiff, and although his father was a supervisor, the first thing he did was introduce Dillon to the shop steward. Such experiences left a profound impression on him, and throughout his life Dillon saw his politics as that of a generally 'Labour-minded' based on a strong allegiance to trade unionism and the Labour Party.[54]

The Social Contract was especially divisive and proved to further widen the gulf between shop floor activists and the national trade union leadership. General Secretary of the TGWU Jack Jones was one of the principal architects and advocates of the Social Contract from its inception in 1974. For three years Jones successfully convinced not only his own union, but also the trade union movement as a whole to uphold the government's incomes policy. However, by the time he retired in 1978, his union had grown restless and rejected the government's pay policy. Jones, like many leaders at the time, was placed in an inopportune position. He noted that

> Without a socialist background – without my record as a consistent fighter for working people – I don't think I could have got through what we did in 1974 [the Social Contract]. We strove very hard to keep our understandings with the Government in my time. I broke my neck on it.[55]

---

[50] *Big Flame*, April 1979, 11.

[51] Darlington and Lyddon, *Glorious Summer*, 140.

[52] Darlington and Lyddon, *Glorious Summer*, 145–146. The dominance of the Communist Party over the NJNC shop stewards movement is noted in *Socialist Challenge*, January 11, 1979, 11. Finlayson, interview.

[53] *Big Flame*, April 1979, 11.

[54] Dillon, interview.

[55] Jack Jones, quoted in Fountain, 'A Long Hot Winter,' *Guardian (Weekend)*, September 25, 1993.

Jones' successor Moss Evans was 'typical' of a new generation of full-time union officials that emerged in the 1950s and 1960s 'from a long experience of shop floor "unofficial" unionism behind them.'[56] Furthermore, he was the chairman of the trade union side of the NJNC in 1971, so he had first-hand experience with rank-and-file disenchantment with Jones and Scanlon and the secret settlement they had made with the company at the expense of the union membership.[57] His background and his rejection of the incomes policy made him immediately unpopular with the Labour government. While James Callaghan and Denis Healey saw Evans as out of touch with the reality of inflation and the looming threat of a Tory government,[58] others in the Labour government simply saw Evans as a weak figure in comparison to Jones or 'at best a third rater.'[59]

Scepticism of the Social Contract served to strengthen the opposition rife among the Left political culture at Ford. International Socialists observed that many workers agreed to three years of incomes policy because they saw it as a 'short-term investment' in exchange for increasing social expenditure and pro-union legislation. As the hopes that the government would relent on incomes policy dissipated, Left groups like the International Socialists saw the Social Contract as a way of driving a further wedge between trade union officials and workers. The agreement between unions and the Labour government had not only become a 'back-door way to more power' for trade union officials, but it was characterized as 'the worst class-collaboration workers have seen in the history of trade unions in this country.'[60] The Revolutionary Communist League argued that the Social Contract was a cynical way of the British ruling elite to exploit Labour's link with unions in order to pacify British workers. This group asserted that the Labour government had seen that Heath was unable to impose wage limits on British workers in the early 1970s, so Labour chose to use voluntary limits because '*only* a Labour Government could get away with it.'[61] After three years of wage restraint, such arguments began to resonate more and more with the rank and file at Ford.

---

[56] Beynon, *Working for Ford*, 270.
[57] Friedman and Meredeen, *The Dynamics of Industrial Conflict*, 272.
[58] See Callaghan, *Time and Chance*, 521; Healey, *The Time of My Life*, 398.
[59] Donoughue, *The Heat of the Kitchen*, 309.
[60] Independent Socialists, *The Case against the Social Contract* (From the personal collection of John Bohanna, 1978).
[61] Revolutionary Communist League of Britain, *The Lessons of the 1978 Strike, Ford* (From the personal collection of John Bohanna, 1978).

Ford Strike 1978

'Being involved in five minutes of an action is worth fifty years of reading. Being involved in an action is like a burst!' – John Bohanna, Halewood[62]

Not simply politics, but an awareness of Ford's increasing prosperity in 1978 also fuelled this mounting discontent. In 1977, Ford dominated the market share of the automobile industry in Britain for the first time since 1920.[63] Additionally, from 1976–77, Ford's profits doubled from £121.6 million to £246.1 million. Even more indicative of Ford's success in the late 1970s was Ford Chairman and Managing Director Sir Terence Beckett's 80 per cent salary rise in 1978.[64] Ford workers were aware of rising profits that year, and they were poised to reject any 5 per cent offer. A week prior to Ford's offer, the feeling among Halewood workers 'was very high and even the moderates were resigned to the fact that there would be action to the Company's first reply to the claim if it centred on 5 per cent only.' On the shop floor at Halewood, people had already made homemade posters declaring '£20 ON THE NOTES OR ON WITH OUR COATS!'[65] Ford management was also aware of imminent conflict. As Paul Roots, the Director of Industrial Relations at Ford in 1978, later admitted, 'Ford is an extremely sophisticated company, and they don't fall into strikes; they have strikes because usually they know they are going to have them and have decided that is worth having one over a particular issue.'[66] Ford management's knowledge of the disquiet on the shop floor, combined with what was seen as a limiting wage policy, meant strike action was imminent.

Compounding the situation, according to Ron Todd, chairman of negotiations for the TGWU, was rank-and-file dissatisfaction with the restrictions of the Social Contract. He revealed later, in 1987, that such pressure was present in 1977 when skilled workers were pushing for a wage rise, and

---

[62] Bohanna, interview.

[63] Steven Tolliday, 'The Rise of Ford in Britain: From Sales Agency to Market Leader, 1904–1980,' in *Ford: The European History, 1903–2003. Vol. 2*, ed. Hubert Bonin, Yannick Lung, and Steven Tolliday (Paris: P.L.A.G.E., 2003), 48.

[64] Friedman and Meredeen, *The Dynamics of Industrial Conflict*, 270. In a 1987 symposium on the Winter of Discontent, Paul Foot, the Director of Industrial Relations at Ford in 1978, noted 'Ford had declared a profit which was healthier than it had been for many many years, something like £600 million.' Robert Taylor and Anthony Seldon, '"The Winter of Discontent" Symposium,' *Contemporary Record* 1, no. 3 (1987): 40.

[65] John Bohanna, *Report on the Ford Motor Company Halewood Strike over Wages and Conditions, Commencing Thursday, September 21, 1978* (Unpublished personal account, Mimeo, Liverpool, 1979), 1.

[66] Taylor and Seldon, '"The Winter of Discontent" Symposium,' 37–38.

employers were willing to capitulate. In the midst of negotiations with the government, Todd described how 'negotiating chambers were literally invaded by sometimes 50, 60, sometimes a couple of hundred electricians and toolmakers [... insisting] that I leave the negotiating table and address a mass picket outside.' However, according to Todd the TGWU arranged to keep the rises within the strictures of the Social Contract.[67]

On September 21, 1978, Ford announced its wage rise of 5 per cent. Immediately after the announcement, 100 workers walked out of the body plant at Halewood.[68] That evening, Halewood workers on the night shift arrived, but refused to work and left hours later.[69] By September 23, 16,000 other Ford workers at Belfast and Daventry followed Halewood.[70] The unrest at the Dagenham plant was apparent when the vote to strike was called. A reporter described the dynamism of the scene when the shop steward asked workers, 'Right all those in favour?'

> The cavernous canteen was suddenly thick with a forest of arms, white, brown and ebony. The platform party was momentarily obscured by the lush growth of ayes, and a buzz of approval washed across the room.
>
> 'Right, hands down. Nobody keep their hands up', Mr Gill ordered. 'Any against?' There were all of a dozen; all eyes turned on them and they were roundly booed by the majority.[71]

Todd expected at least a brief period of negotiations before any strike was called, 'But this time it was different. Ten thousand men walked out, just like that. I finished up that day with all the workers out. After so many years of incomes policy, it was like a pressure cooker.'[72]

On the heels of Ford workers' actions, the TGWU and the AUEW made the strike official. When the Ford workers' claim was released, the influence of the Ford Combine group was apparent. Combine member Finlayson calculated that the 'moderate' representatives on the NJNC had a history of putting wage claims in to Ford that were in terms of percentages and 'substantial rises.' The Ford Combine found that a definite figure in terms of pounds would prevent any leeway that could result from negotiating a percentage rise, and it would also be in terms that Ford workers would understand.[73] Therefore, at the heart of the claim was a £20 increase on

---

[67] Taylor and Seldon, '"The Winter of Discontent" Symposium,' 40.
[68] *The Lessons of the 1978 Strike*, 5–6.
[69] *The Lessons of the 1978 Strike*, 5–6.
[70] 'Union Backs Stand as 16,000 Walk Out: Ford Workers Mount Battle on 5 pc With All-Out Strike,' *The Guardian*, September 23, 1978.
[71] 'It Took 16 Minutes to Bring Ford Plant To A Standstill,' *The Times*, September 26, 1978.
[72] Fountain, 'A Long Hot Winter.'
[73] Finlayson, interview.

basic rates and a reduction to a 35-hour week.[74] The Ford Combine group easily made this into a slogan: '£20 on pay! 1 hour off the day!'[75] Underlying the wage claim were demands for greater union influence at Ford. Influenced by debates surrounding industrial democracy, the TGWU called for unions to be part of decision-making at Ford, where 'full, free and frank disclosure' of the company's long-term plans was provided to unions.[76] Also, the long-standing struggle over 'penalty clauses' re-emerged, and the union called for lay-off pay for all lay-offs 'regardless of whether the dispute is external to the company or not.'[77] The claim sought to address the specific wage offer of 1978, but it also addressed issues that had been developing throughout the 1960s and 1970s.

Organizing a massive strike in such a large company involved co-ordination and creativity, especially at the Dagenham plant, which employed 2,000 workers and was so large that it was known as the 'Dagenham Square Mile.'[78] In the 1950s, the co-ordination of a strike was facilitated by the local character of the workforce, so union contact with workers could easily be made at local pubs and workingmen's clubs. However, with the more geographically dispersed workforce of the late 1970s, unions, conveners, and shop stewards issued weekly bulletins that were readily available to Ford workers when they went to pick up their strike pay or tax rebates.[79]

Picketing was also challenging at Dagenham because the plant had 25 entrances. Co-operation from delivery drivers, train drivers, and seamen who blacked Ford shipments was crucial, but it was the 24-hour pickets that would be central to this strike. Soon after the strike, pickets covered all 25 entrances.[80]

The mostly 'boring' and tedious nature of picketing, especially as one of Britain's most severe winters in history began to set in, tested the resolve of those at the gates. The 24-hour pickets at Halewood, for instance, had little to entertain themselves, especially in the evening.[81] One night, Bohanna noted,

> Saturday, no news, picket again through the night. The PTA lads caught a rabbit, skinned it, cooked it, and attempted to eat it. The four lads from

---

[74] Transport and General Workers' Union, *Ford Wage Claim, 1978* (from private collection of John Bohanna).
[75] Finlayson, interview.
[76] *Ford Wage Claim, 1978.*
[77] *Ford Wage Claim, 1978.*
[78] Finlayson, interview. See also Friedman and Meredeen, *The Dynamics of Industrial Conflict*, 126.
[79] 'The Ford Strike: Where does it take us?' 37.
[80] 'The Ford Strike: Where does it take us?' 36.
[81] Bohanna, *Report on the Ford Motor Company*, 10.

the MS&B were offered some but we declined, stewards on the picket left a little early, about 5 a.m., for a bit of sleep before the meeting in the morning being held in the Shaftsbury Hotel.[82]

The co-ordination and maintenance of the picket lines also provided relief from the monotony of the being on strike. Finlayson describes how he was a duty steward in charge of a picket line on the entrance to the foundry at Dagenham:

> What our picket line used to do was it used to take the coke and take it to all the other picket lines. And then the coke, it burns inside the iron oil drums; it gives you a lovely heat. And at the far end, there was a picket line where cars were kept next to what is known as a bonded warehouse, which is a high security warehouse where whiskey is kept. And the workers in the bonded warehouse would throw broken pallets over the security fence. So we'd deliver the coke that was part of the job of the picket line, break down the broken pallets and drive back, so that people would have wood and coke to keep warm and to keep certain people entertained.[83]

For Finlayson, the experience of picketing extended to the extremes of both excitement and boredom, but in the end, there was 'a liberating side to it [because] you felt that you were really doing something.'[84]

Not everybody participated in the pickets. When Dagenham workers voted to strike, the practicalities of survival were the primary concern. As a *Times* reporter described it, once Dagenham strikers voted in favour of industrial action,

> Outside, half of them made an Olympic dash for the car park and the bus stops, while others hung loosely around the gates, as if thinking it unwise to return to busy wives at 8:30 in the morning.
>
> 'What do we do now?' one asked of another.
>
> 'Down to the social security, innit?' was the reply born of experience.
>
> 'Right,' said the first. 'Are they open yet?'
>
> 'Not yet, stupid,' the seasoned one said. 'You get paid this week.'[85]

Striking workers were entitled to Supplementary Benefit, which helped with rent and rates. Dagenham workers, however, ran into stumbling blocks when union leaders agreed with the Department of Health and Social Security to have all claims go by post to an office in London, instead of being dealt with

---

[82] Bohanna, *Report on the Ford Motor Company*, 6.
[83] Finlayson, interview.
[84] Finlayson, interview.
[85] 'It Took 16 Minutes to Bring Ford Plant To A Standstill,' *The Times*, September 26, 1978.

personally at the office in Dagenham. As a result, many claims were late and any refusals or underpayments had to be dealt with by post, further delaying the claims.[86] Strike pay that was also meant to sustain workers could easily disappear. Bohanna's house was broken into during the strike. Although his wife Joan interrupted the thieves in the act, they had managed to steal the few pounds they had in strike pay, leaving the Bohannas with no money for the rest of the week.[87]

Strikers had to develop multifarious ways of surviving. Newly employed Dagenham worker Dillon noted that it was common knowledge among Ford workers that once the sirens at Ford went off, signalling a shutdown of the plant, Ford workers rushed out not simply because of a desire to strike, but also for reasons of practicality. Since strikes were common at Ford throughout the 1970s, when the 1978 strike started, Dillon noted that some Ford workers wanted to be the first to land part-time jobs to sustain themselves and their families throughout the strike. In Dillon's case, as soon as the strike was called, he headed straight to the employment agency, where he found a job working in the carpet department at Harvey Nichols until the end of the strike.[88] Slowly was another such worker. Although he was present at all necessary union votes during the strike, he was absent from the pickets because he had taken up odd jobs to support his family until the strike ended.[89]

The Ford Combine's influence continued throughout the duration of the industrial action in the form of their newsletter *Fraud News*, which was given out at the gates and inside the plant. For instance, in November 1978, the Ford Combine campaigned to have workers reject productivity deals that might come with a settlement to the strike. Writers in *Fraud News* explained how productivity deals would result in more accidents in the plant and that there would be penalties for absences and tardiness.[90] Ford Combine's activities were not always so serious. During the strike, a group from Ford Combine wrote the song 'One in the Eye for Sunny Jim' and had it pressed into a record and distributed to workers:

Come on all you women and men
Henry Ford's in trouble again
He's got himself in a terrible jam
With the strikes at Halewood and Dagenham
We put down our tools and out the gate

---

[86] *The Lessons of the 1978 Strike*, 12.
[87] Bohanna, *Report on the Ford Motor Company*, 14–15.
[88] Dillon, interview.
[89] Slowly, interview.
[90] *Fraud News*, November 1, 1978. Reprinted in Beynon, *Working for Ford*, 379.

For twenty pounds on the basic rate!
[...] It's one in the eye for Sunny Jim
Whoopee!!! We're gonna win!![91]

Those who were active, especially those in Ford Combine, were also charged with the task of garnering support from other workers. In the last week of October, Bohanna and one other shop steward at Halewood addressed the National Union of Students at a university in Liverpool, an audience in Manchester, and then a group of miners at Sutton Manor Colliery.[92] These efforts, at times, proved effective in fostering support both in Britain and abroad for the strikes at Ford. For example, one day close to 100 nurses showed up to guard a picket line at Dagenham;[93] another day, the International Metal Workers' Federation pledged financial assistance to the unions.[94] These shows of solidarity were coupled with acts from workers in other countries, which made the strike all the more effective. In support for the strike in Britain, workers at the Bosch plant in Germany refused to produce instrument panels and other electrical components for Ford, and Ford workers in Cologne blacked all work done in Britain.[95]

Public and Government Response

The first challenge to the Labour government's incomes policy garnered significant media attention. On the first day of the strike, the *Financial Times* declared, 'ALL OUT STRIKE CALLED BY FORD.'[96] The right-wing *Daily Mail* saw the dispute as a direct challenge to the Social Contract and the Labour government as it claimed an 'ALL OUT WAR ON JIM'S 5%.'[97] This emphasis on conflict between government and trade union power played into a long-standing theme in the British media; trade unions were seen to wield more power than the government. In 1977, the *Sun* read, 'Move over Jim [Callaghan]! It's Jack Jones and his men who are really in charge.'[98] By early October, public opinion appeared to be on the Labour government's side. On October 19, the more left-leaning *Guardian* reported

---

[91] OHC and the Gappers, 'The Ford Strike Song,' recorded October 9, 1978, Ford UK Workers (vinyl from the private collection of John Bohanna).
[92] Bohanna, *Report on the Ford Motor Company*, 14–15.
[93] Finlayson, interview.
[94] Friedman and Meredeen, *The Dynamics of Industrial Conflict*, 273.
[95] Friedman and Meredeen, *The Dynamics of Industrial Conflict*, 273.
[96] *Financial Times*, September 23, 1978; *Daily Mirror*, September 23, 1978.
[97] *Daily Mail*, September 23, 1978.
[98] *Sun*, July 25, 1977.

on a poll published by the *Daily Mail* indicating that 66 per cent of Britons believed that the 5 per cent limit was 'reasonable.'[99]

Stories of Ford workers' wives campaigning against the strikes also hit the national headlines. In Southampton, a group of these women called for a secret ballot on whether the men should stay out on strike. Susan Charlton, one of the members of the group, organized a petition of 3,000 signatures to support their effort.[100] One of the women attending the meetings had both a husband and a son working at Ford and asserted that 'They are both on strike, and they don't want to be, like the rest of the silent majority.'[101] In response, Ford workers' wives and girlfriends formed the 'Ford Women's Action Group,' which held counter demonstrations to the 'get back to work' protests.[102] They disrupted Charlton's meeting, waving banners and chanting that the strike had to continue until the claim was won.[103]

The women's actions underline, once again, the gendered nature of work at Ford. The masculinized work and strikes at Ford were complemented by the feminized activism of their wives. The women found a conduit through the use of 'domestic' and 'traditionally' female roles as wives and mothers to advocate for or against the strikes. The agency women exerted during the Winter of Discontent revealed the lack of clear boundaries between the public and private sphere, even for those individuals who sought to defend such boundaries in their opposition to the strike.

Moss Evans of the TGWU became the particular focus of ire for those in the British public disgruntled with the industrial action taking place at Ford. During the strike, Evans received letters that ranged from being critical of the strike to personally threatening. In one letter signed 'Trade unionist,' the author criticized Evans' 'deplorable' opposition to the 5 per cent limit. He writes:

> Who do you think you are? Do you imagine that you and the Union Bosses are going to dictate on the economic policy to be adopted by the Government of the day? If so, you had better think again. Big bullying men, like yourself, have tried this before, and have been toppled into oblivion.[104]

---

[99] 'One Line for the Rich and the Poor,' *Guardian*, October 19, 1978.
[100] 'Ford Wives Break Strike,' *Daily Mirror*, October 19, 1978.
[101] 'Ford Workers Afraid, Say Their Wives,' *Daily Telegraph*, October 23, 1978.
[102] *Big Flame*, April 1979, 11.
[103] *Lessons from the Ford Strike*, 5–6. See also Friedman and Meredeen, *The Dynamics of Industrial Conflict*, 274.
[104] Letter to Moss Evans from 'Trade Unionist,' 5 October 1978, Moss Evans and Ron Todd Papers, MSS 126/TG/384/1/1, Modern Records Centre, University of Warwick, Coventry, UK.

This charged environment was further exacerbated by political shifts amongst the parties. Ford workers gained allies in the Labour Party. In the midst of the Ford strike, the Labour Party Conference passed a motion rejecting wage restraint. In early October Ron Todd described how he spoke to James Callaghan about the strike at the Labour Party Conference, defending Ford workers' right to collective bargaining. He added, 'We had about a quarter of an hour. He [Callaghan] put his hand on my shoulder and said, 'Well Ron, I've enjoyed talking to you. Come and see me when I'm a backbencher.'[105] Political alignments appeared to be turned on their head as unions defied the Labour Party, and the Conservatives appeared to champion their cause. The Labour government's resistance provided the perfect opportunity to voice their support for free collective bargaining. Soon after Ford workers walked out of their plants, Margaret Thatcher vowed that a 'Conservative Government would leave trade unions free to work with management.'[106] The British media seized on these conflicts with headlines like 'Let Them Vote Tory.' Soon after the defeat of the wage policy at the Labour Party Conference, the *Economist* noted wryly, 'If the trade unions really believe that market forces should be paramount in setting wage levels, they would be better off permanently washing their hands of the Labour Party.'[107]

The Labour government was served another blow on November 11, when a statement on pay, prices, and inflation failed in the TUC General Council in a tight vote of 14 to 14.[108] TGWU General Secretary Moss Evans played a key role in the failure of this ballot. Although Evans had helped draft the statement, he had gone on holiday when the TUC General Council was called to session. Evans left two union delegates in his place, but they had no instructions on how to vote. One voted in favour of the statement, and the other voted against it.[109] Reflecting on the vote almost 10 years later, Evans revealed that he had been willing to cancel his holiday, but Len Murray advised him to go. At the same symposium in 1987, Murray admitted that he 'wasn't sorry' for the outcome of what eventually was seen as a crucial vote 'because a vote of 15:13 in favour would have been useless as a basis to operate on.'[110]

The government immediately realized that the failed vote would further encourage other groups of workers to press for wage claims higher than the

---

[105] Fountain, 'A Long Hot Winter.'
[106] 'Ford Chairman Attacks Union's Broken Pledge,' *Guardian*, September 28, 1978.
[107] 'By Whose Authority?' *Economist*, October 7, 1978.
[108] *Financial Times*, November 11, 1978. See also: Callaghan, *Time and Chance*, 533; Kenneth O. Morgan, *A Life of Michael Foot* (London: HarperCollins, 2007), 362–363.
[109] Healey, *Time of My Life*, 462.
[110] Taylor and Seldon, '"The Winter of Discontent" Symposium,' 37.

5 per cent limit. Cabinet ministers privately mulled over how the vote was a 'kick in the teeth for the corporate state,'[111] while in public the Labour government acknowledged 'disappointment' over the vote, but still hoped that 'it would not make any difference to pay settlements.'[112]

From the onset of the strike, not only Ford workers, but also the Ford motor company itself expressed a reluctance to adhere to any form of government-imposed wage limits. Days after the talks began, Ford Chairman and Managing Director Sir Terence Beckett deleted from a speech a passage declaring government intervention a '[...] species of tetanus where one set of muscles goes rigid, pulling against another and the patient becomes paralyzed.'[113] Inherent hostility towards incomes policy was coupled with the practical effects the strikes were having on production. Ford was losing £10 million per day during the strike.[114] The effects were to soon be felt across Ford factories in continental Europe. During the strike, 10,900 Ford workers in Europe were either laid off or on short-time working since they lacked parts usually supplied from Britain.[115] Ford eventually relented and asked unions to resume talks.

As it became evident that Labour's 5 per cent limit would be broken, union negotiators attempted to deflect any charges that the unions were making a political stand against Labour. In early November, at a meeting to vote on Ford's most recent offer of 16 per cent, TGWU chairman of negotiations, Ron Todd told Ford workers, 'The media have portrayed this as a confrontation with the Government. There is no way we would have used you in a political fight.'[116] Despite this conciliatory tone, the Labour government saw the Ford workers' settlement for a 17 per cent rise on November 22 as '[...] the heaviest blow, which did so much to determine the course of events in the winter of 1978.'[117]

---

[111] Benn, *Conflicts of Interest*, 391.
[112] BBC Interview with Denis Healey, 14 November, 1978, VT ANBA318D 9.00CIN LISC 418393, BBC Motion Gallery.
[113] Quoted from *Guardian*, September 27, 1978.
[114] Freidman, *The Dynamics of Industrial Conflict*, 271. Paul Roots, the Director of Industrial Relations for Ford in 1978, estimated that about £21 million was lost. Taylor and Seldon '"The Winter of Discontent" Symposium,' 39. Dominic Sandbrook, however, indicates that by the beginning of November £300 million was lost. Sandbrook, *Seasons in the Sun*, 719.
[115] 'Countdown to International Ford Lay Off,' *Guardian*, November 7, 1978.
[116] 'Dagenham quietly says, No,' *Times*, November 4, 1978.
[117] Callaghan, *Time and Chance*, 534.

The Settlement

The Labour government's defeat at Ford became the 'bellwether of the flock,' and in order to stave off further bleeding from their pay policy, the government proposed imposing sanctions on Ford.[118] The sanctions would have stopped all government purchases from Ford; however, the vote was defeated in the House of Commons with a vote of 285 to 283.[119] Compared to the Labour government, Ford emerged from the strikes virtually unscathed; £97.5 million were lost in after-tax earnings, but foreign earnings rose by 9.2 per cent in 1978, amounting to 48 per cent of Ford's total profit that year.[120]

The victory for Ford workers initially came in late November. When union negotiators voted to accept the offer, rank-and-file membership throughout the plants in Britain voted to accept the settlement.[121] Ford workers won a 17 per cent rise in wages, but their success was not absolute because penalty clauses were reintroduced as part of the settlement. In exchange for the rise, there would be 'no increase in labour costs during the twelve months of the Agreement and no strike action to put pressure on the negotiations for the 1979 agreement.'[122] A group of Halewood conveners opposed the settlement based on the reintroduction of the penalty clauses. When the NJNC had voted in favour of the settlement, Bohanna was enraged that they would do so based on an agreement that would penalize unofficial action:

> We didn't come out on an NJNC recommendation, why the hell should we return on one, but on saying that, I know all is lost. It was like walking out in a street of palm leaves and returning with a cross on your back. Never have I seen the stewards so depressed and disillusioned.[123]

More immediately, the success of the strike in November had profound implications for workers across Britain. Ford workers had shown themselves able to both defeat a multinational company *and* the national government on wage policy. Ford's nine-week strike has been described as the first of an on-coming 'self-destructive bonanza'[124] for higher and higher wage claims. There is no denying that wages played a central role in these struggles; however, the claims for increased wages carried with them a wider assertion

---

[118] Callaghan, *Time and Chance*, 534.
[119] Callaghan, *Time and Chance*, 536.
[120] Friedman and Meredeen, *The Dynamics of Industrial Conflict*, 278.
[121] Friedman and Meredeen, *The Dynamics of Industrial Conflict*, 274–275.
[122] Ford Motor Company, 'Ford Employee Information,' 20 November, 1978 (From the personal collection of John Bohanna).
[123] Bohanna, *Report on the Ford Motor Company*, 24.
[124] Samuel Beer, *Britain against Itself: The Political Contradictions of Collectivism* (London: Faber & Faber, 1982), 56.

of Ford workers' independent power within their union and within the Labour Party. Moreover, the emergence of rank-and-file and shop steward pressure nationally was an important element in the strike. The engagement of wives and girlfriends along with attempts to reach out to other workers were innovatory aspects. West Indian and Asian workers also were taking an active part, and this would have an impact on the unions in the early 1980s. A new generation of working-class activists was beginning to bring new attitudes, views, and interests to union politics. They were claiming back time to live their own lives from employers. Constrained in the factory and without creative outlets in their jobs, they resisted in songs, humour, and ideas. This infectious confidence would become increasingly apparent as it spread to lorry drivers, already restless as the cold winter began to envelop Britain.

4

'The Second Stalingrad': The Road Haulage Strikes

As the reality of the Ford workers' successful breach of the incomes policy set in among those in the Labour government, so too did one of Britain's coldest winters on record. In January of 1979, the average temperature was -.04°C, making the winter of 1978–79 one of 50 coldest since records began.[1] Blizzards that greeted New Year's revellers inspired the *Guardian* to proclaim 'The Big Freeze Tightens Its Grip,'[2] while the *Financial Times* grimly reported the deaths of 23 people throughout the UK, France, and West Germany as a result of the 'Arctic weather conditions.'[3] The harsh weather intensified pressure on the Labour government as strikes among lorry drivers came to fruition. In early January, hauliers took industrial action, rejecting the employers' offer of a 15 per cent increase for one of 20 per cent.[4] Since road haulage was now the 'predominant mode of inland transportation,' strikes in this industry had the potential to completely paralyse the nation.[5]

The potency of such industrial action was only matched by the dramatic images that spilled out from the media. Picketing drivers stopping lorries became vividly imprinted in the public imagination as headlines like the *Economist*'s cover screamed 'Britain under Siege.'[6] Some of the most macabre scenes, such as piles of dead piglets and chickens, not only heightened the sense that the British public was personally victimized, but the scenes

---

[1] 'Britain's Coldest Winters on Record,' *The Daily Telegraph*, Picture Gallery, accessed June 27, 2013, http://www.telegraph.co.uk/news/picturegalleries/uknews/8209333/Britains-coldest-winters-on-record-in-pictures.html.

[2] 'Big Freeze Tightens Its Grip,' *Guardian*, January 2, 1979.

[3] 'More Snow On The Way,' *Financial Times*, January 3, 1979.

[4] Sandbrook, *Seasons in the Sun*, 727.

[5] Paul Smith, *Unionization & Union Leadership: The Road Haulage Industry* (London: Continuum, 2001), 65.

[6] *Economist*, January 20, 1979.

would become enmeshed in its ultimate mythologization. Unlike the Ford strike, which was in many ways confined to the industrial estates of Halewood and Dagenham, the lorry drivers' strike could potentially affect everyone in Britain, making the strike appear more personal. Roy Hattersley, Secretary of State for Prices and Consumer Protection in the Callaghan government, observed that the road haulage strike 'was spreading the bad news throughout the country. Every town and village felt like they were affected by the Winter of Discontent.'[7] This was also a pivotal moment when Margaret Thatcher and the Conservative Party began to effectively tap into the widespread panic and frustration these images helped to foster. Her general calls for restrictions on practices like secondary picketing would lay the foundation for concrete legislation that she and the Conservatives would implement once in government.

The strikes in road haulage, therefore, are central to understanding not only the series of events that took place from 1978–79, but also comprehending the broader emotional and political reverberation of the Winter of Discontent decades later. Hence, in this chapter I seek to understand the root of these strikes not only by briefly outlining the social, political, and industrial forces that incited these actions, but by zeroing in on the lives of two key participants in this strike: William (Bill) Rodgers and Fred Beach. Although both Labour men, Rodgers' political development and eventual rise to Secretary of Transport in the Labour government during the Winter of Discontent will be juxtaposed against the trajectory of TGWU shop steward Fred Beach, who was pivotal to the organization of strikes in Hull. The media attention on these strikes, in particular the claims of food shortages, which became prevalent in the myth will also be interrogated. I further examine what has previously been seen as a backdrop, the extreme weather, and bring it forward as a protagonist in the mythologization of the Winter of Discontent. As David Arnold notes, severe forms of weather like drought, and I would argue the extremely harsh winter of 1978–79, can serve as a 'memory aid' in society, acting 'as a pole around which all other experiences and impressions are organized and collected' and providing 'a link between the world of personal memory and the broader domain of collective consciousness.'[8]

I will argue, therefore, that long-term changes in the road haulage industry and the structure of industrial relations are essential to understanding the causes and the nature of the strike in 1979. I will also assert that while an

---

[7] Roy Hattersley, interview in *Secret History: Winter of Discontent* (Brook Lapping Productions for Channel Four, 1998).

[8] David Arnold, *Famine: Social Crisis and Historical Change* (Oxford: Basil West Blackwell, 1988), 12.

amalgam of half-truths and media chicanery did characterize this strike, efforts to construct and/or manipulate media messages arose from multiple constituents, from employers to journalists to trade unionists. Moreover, I will demonstrate that the lorry drivers' potential threat to vital supplies sharpened the sense of victimization and frustration already felt among the British public in the 1970s, and it was Margaret Thatcher's deft expression of such unease that began to propel both her electoral and policy prospects forward. Finally, I will argue that it was the chilling weather that facilitated the particular resilience of memories of the Winter of Discontent.

The Road Haulage Industry

Changes in technology, the British fuel economy, and politics all shaped the road haulage industry in post-war Britain. After 'a limited programme of denationalization' in 1951, road haulage began to eclipse rail as the key form of inland transportation in Britain.[9] Unionization took a distinctive form, too. Unlike dockers or London busmen, a sense of militancy and unity did not take root within the road haulage industry immediately after the Second World War.[10] When Jack Jones assumed the leadership of the TGWU in 1956, his imposition of district-wide organization that unified workers in disparate depots and companies fostered a sense of solidarity among these workers.[11]

As a result, wage militancy among lorry drivers also developed from 1968 to 1978. After the imposition of the Wilson government's pay freeze, different groups of hauliers throughout the country breached the government's wage limits and won rises. Their organizational power grew as labour shortages and the closed shop began to proliferate throughout the industry and culminated in subsequent victories throughout the 1970s.[12] The four-week strike of 6,000 drivers in Scotland in 1974, for example, eventually spread and won hauliers a £40 rise, and demonstrated this growing militancy and organizational confidence in defiance of incomes policy.[13]

The changes in the industry were set within the dynamism of post-war British politics. William Rodgers' own political development reflected these shifting currents within the Labour Party. Born in Wavertree in

---

[9] Smith, *Unionization and Union Leadership*, 65–66.
[10] Smith, *Unionization and Union Leadership*, 47.
[11] Smith, *Unionization and Union Leadership*, 65.
[12] Smith, *Unionization and Union Leadership*, 77.
[13] Smith, *Unionization and Union Leadership*, 79.

1928,[14] he never ended up identifying as 'Scouse.'[15] Although his regional identity was not so powerful, his class identity and education became formative in his political evolution. He began to identify as a member of the *petite bourgeoisie* because, as he explained, 'I decided that my family, provincial, suburban and just a cut above the skilled working class, fitted neatly in that category.'[16] A conviction for social justice could be seen as a young man when he trespassed on land in Knowsley. Upon being ejected by the bailiff, Rodgers cried in protestation that 'This is the people's.'[17] His father worked with people from across the political spectrum and was not committed to a political view, a factor Rodgers cited as influential in his own evolution as a moderate.[18]

When he studied at Oxford, he joined the Labour Club and came to run the Fabian Society once he completed his university studies. In the process of becoming further entrenched in Labour politics and ultimately getting elected to Parliament, his Revisionist politics found expression. His ideology was, in part, shaped by Evan Durbin's assertion that capitalism was not doomed to collapse. Rodgers was attracted to Durbin's idea of restraining the most egregious excesses of capitalism. Even more influential were the writings and personality of Tony Crosland. Rodgers poignantly expounded upon the profound effect *The Future of Socialism* had on him and a generation of Revisionists like himself. He reflected, 'By the late 1950s, this book [*The Future of Socialism*] had become the bible of Revisionists, who rejected both "consolidation," if it meant inertia, and "socialist advance," if it meant utopianism.'[19]

As he began to scale the ministerial ladder in the Wilson and Callaghan governments, Rodgers' right-leaning Labour politics became all the more resolute. His speech titled 'Socialism without Abundance,' for instance, contrasted starkly with the rising left-wing opinion in the party during the 1970s. In 1977 he explained that people wanted 'more money to spend' and were not so convinced of the benefits of nationalization. He was also critical of government housing policy. 'I was in favour of giving men and women more control over their lives, and referred to the brutalising consequences

---

[14] Bill Rodgers, *Fourth among Equals* (London: Politico's, 2000), 2.
[15] Rodgers, *Fourth among Equals*, 9.
[16] Rodgers, *Fourth among Equals*, 5.
[17] Rodgers, *Fourth among Equals*, 17–18.
[18] William Rodgers, transcribed interview by Mike Greenwood, *The History of Parliament* website, http://www.historyofparliamentonline.org/volume/oral-history/member/rodgers-william-1928.
[19] Rodgers, *Fourth among Equals*, 49.

of tower blocks and massive council estates without public transport or community facilities.'[20]

By contrast, TGWU shop steward Fred Beach's labour activism primarily found expression through the trade union movement. Beach's commitment was spurred on by his involvement in the 1967–68 unofficial strike by truckers, and he identified himself as a Labour man from the 'broad left.' The political apathy among lorry drivers in his branch set Beach apart from his cohort. He explained, 'The political nuance of the average lorry driver is zero. They were working too hard. Too tired. You'd go to meetings and mention something political, and nobody would know what you were talking about.'[21]

The gradual progression of these men's trajectories in the labour movement would eventually be caught up in the immediacy and urgency of events that began in 1978. By the end of the decade, militancy also began to develop among hauliers, which boded ill for the continued viability of the Social Contract. Key changes, for instance, were occurring in the industry during the 1970s that intensified criticism of Labour's incomes policy. The new European Economic Community regulations, for instance, set out mandatory eight-hour driving days, a reduction from the previous standard of 10 hours. This change provoked worry among drivers over a decrease in real and national overtime hours. With wages making up such a significant component of their costs, employers, in organizations such as the Road Haulage Association (RHA), also became more strident in their attempts to cap wages in the 1970s. Finally, with the introduction of the tachograph, drivers grew nervous about such new efforts to monitor their performance.[22]

These broader currents in the industry exacerbated the stress particularly on hire and reward hauliers. By the late 1970s, disparities between the 'hire and reward,' haulage services provided by contract, versus 'own account,' where transport of goods is part of a company's own distribution systems, began to grow throughout the decade. By March 1978 those lorry drivers in car transport earned £130 to £150 per week, while those in oil transportation earned an average of £110, but the highest paid hire and reward drivers earned £56 a week.[23] By 1978 work conditions and pay had coalesced into a general feeling of dissatisfaction among truckers. As Beach describes:

> To lorry drivers, low pay and long hours was just a way of life. Drivers were ten-a-penny. Ex-army men with heavy-goods licenses. Easy sacking,

[20] Rodgers, *Fourth among Equals*, 169.
[21] Beckett (includes interview with Fred Beach), in *When the Lights Went Out*, 486–487.
[22] Paul Smith, 'The "Winter of Discontent": The Hire and Reward Haulage Dispute, 1979,' *Historical Studies in Industrial Relations* 7 (Spring 1999): 32.
[23] Smith, *Unionization & Union Leadership*, 143.

easy hiring. Weak regulatory authorities. Sixty, seventy, eighty hours a week was normal. The lorry driver was a mobile tramp, a nonentity. The lorry driver didn't have any respect; their employers didn't have respect for them. If you don't like it, lump it. A heater in your cab? Never heard of it. Good training for a cold picket line.[24]

In a letter to the *Northern Echo*, one man echoed Beach's description of the lorry drivers' work conditions. He wrote, 'I've been driving for thirty-four years, with two holidays (seven days) in this country, a ten year-old-car (off the road), and nothing left for the sales.'[25]

As an organized workforce, however, hauliers did hold some key advantages. First of all, by comparison with other workers in the TGWU, tanker drivers and those in road haulage were 'far better paid' than many other British workers.[26] Second, road haulage was expanding in the 1970s, so there was an 'almost permanent shortage of drivers,' giving 'drivers bargaining leverage.'[27] Also, despite previously being relegated to specific districts and cities, by 1978 the TGWU RTC (Road Transport Commercial) became an effective organizational force. Smith argues that it was this unification of TGWU branches that 'was an indispensable factor' in 'provoking' the road haulage disputes during the Winter of Discontent.'[28]

By 1978, a prevailing mood of restlessness, confidence, and unity among hauliers was tangible. As Beach explained, 'If you went into a café, everyone was saying, "This effing job." We'd had three years of pay restraint, and people had got fed up.'[29] The January 1978 strike of 2,000 hauliers in South Wales, who successfully secured a pay claim in excess of government policy, for instance, was emblematic of this feeling.[30] This sentiment began to percolate up to the national level when the TGWU RTC group hire and reward conference met in August 1978 and voted for a claim of £64 a week and a 35-hour work week.[31] This claim contrasted with the RHA's offer in support for the Labour government's 5 per cent policy, no meal allowance, and no decrease in work hours.[32]

Although the RHA hoped to garner support from the government by putting forward this offer, Smith argues that this was a fatal mistake because

[24] Beckett (includes interview with Fred Beach), in *When the Lights Went Out*, 485–486.
[25] Newton Aycliffe, 'In Defence of Lorry Drivers: Hear All Sides,' Letter to the Editor, *Northern Echo* (Darlington), January 22, 1979.
[26] Sandbrook, *Seasons in the Sun*, 720.
[27] Smith, *Unionization & Union Leadership*, 145.
[28] Smith, *Unionization & Union Leadership*, 142.
[29] Beckett (includes interview with Fred Beach), in *When the Lights Went Out*, 33.
[30] Smith, *Unionization & Union Leadership*, 82.
[31] Smith, 'The 'Winter of Discontent,' 33.
[32] Smith, *Unionization & Union Leadership*, 146.

neither the government nor the RHA 'showed any comprehension of the potential scale of the impending conflict.'[33] In particular, the government pinned its hope on the fact that they still had control over price increases as a way to keep employers within pay guidelines. The government's vow to enforce pay policy by refusing to agree to price increases eventually influenced the RHA to increase its offer to £60 a week for 40 hours.[34] Bill Rodgers explains:

> When in November I discussed the latest round of negotiations with the Chairman of the RHA, I was told they hoped to keep within the guidelines, and I reported accordingly to Number 10. But as 1979 opened, the RHA jumped to thirteen per cent in a clumsy attempt to get a quick settlement.[35]

Despite the increased offer, an unofficial conference of drivers on December 16 called for industrial action and, as Smith asserts, 'The conference crystallized what hitherto had been only a fragmented mood of discontent into the beginning of a national movement. The initiative began to slip from the TGWU's authoritative bodies and officials.'[36] When oil tankers imposed an overtime ban in early 1978, the government was becoming increasingly aware that 'The enthusiasm for this dispute comes from shop stewards. [...] It is not clear what degree of discipline can be exercised over the shop stewards by the TGWU national officers.'[37] Beach underlined the importance of the mood and organization at the grassroots level. 'By the end of 1978, there was a vast and efficient communication between shop stewards. [...] We were disciplined. We knew people everywhere. Lorry drivers do. The mood was very, very strong, and it was universal. I think it was unstoppable.'[38]

The government had already prepared for such threats to vital goods when oil tankers threatened to strike in late 1978. On December 23, 1978 the *Economist* reported that the threat among oil tanker drivers forced the government to consider bringing in troops to 'move essential supplies' and had the government print 'millions of ration coupons.'[39] The media reports were well founded, and in the autumn of 1978 the Civil Contingencies Unit (CCU), a group of ministers, civil servants, and members of the military,

---

[33] Smith, 'The 'Winter of Discontent,' 35.
[34] Smith, *Unionization & Union Leadership*, 146.
[35] Rodgers, *Fourth among Equals*, 181.
[36] Smith, *Unionization & Union Leadership*, 147.
[37] Letter from M.G. Jeremiah to Principal Private Secretary, 30 September, 1978, Prime Minister's Office: Correspondence and Papers, 1974–1979, PREM 16/1707, National Archives, Kew, UK.
[38] Beckett (includes interview with Fred Beach), *When the Lights Went Out*, 486–487.
[39] '15 % is Now the Going Pay Rise,' *Economist*, December 23, 1978.

was activated to manage the flow of essential supplies when threatened by industrial action.[40] A strike among petrol tanker drivers would prove especially crippling in the midst of winter, so the CCU developed 'Operation Drumstick,' a plan to call for troops that would be put on 72-hour standby to take over for oil tanker drivers.[41] On December 21 contingency plans were formulated to put 160 instructors on notice to report to central training after Christmas, and 9,000 troops were expected to be placed on notice that they would be available for duties on January 2.[42]

The CCU was preparing for a variety of strikes in 1978, but by December 21, priority was given to preparing troops for a lorry drivers' strike.[43] Rodgers notes the severity of the threat when he explains, 'If the tanker drivers dispute was a warning to the Government, the road haulage strike was the battle fully joined.'[44]

Strike

Such certainty became manifest when the first lorry drivers came out on strike and began to effectively shut down the flow of goods in key localities throughout Britain. On January 2 Rodgers notified the Chancellor, the Prime Minister, and the Cabinet that a stoppage in road haulage 'was imminent.' He warned that 'The long-term effects of a strike could obviously be very serious, but it would be wrong to put any pressure on the Road Haulage Association to improve an offer so far beyond the guidelines.'[45] From Scotland to Liverpool to Birmingham to Oxford, the unofficial movement took the initiative to propel the action forward on January 3.[46] The spread of industrial action provoked intense responses due to the particular vulnerability of medicine and food to the onslaughts of such a series of actions.

One of the first cities to feel the effects of these unofficial strikes was Hull, where Beach was a shop steward of the local TGWU branch. Since only two major roads flowed in and out of the city, with the strike's effective

---

[40] Beckett, *When the Lights Went Out*, 481.
[41] Ken Stowe, 'Oil Tanker Drivers' Pay Negotiation,' 12 December, 1978, Prime Minister's Office: Correspondence and Papers, 1974–1979, PREM 16/1707, National Archives, Kew, UK.
[42] Ken Stowe letter to Prime Minister, 15, December 1978, Prime Minister's Office: Correspondence and Papers, 1974–1979, PREM16/1707, National Archives UK at Kew, UK. See also: Benn, *Conflicts of Interest*, 413–428.
[43] 'Army Trains to Break Strikes,' *Guardian*, December 21, 1978.
[44] Rodgers, 'Government under Stress,' 175.
[45] Rodgers, *Fourth among Equals*, 180.
[46] Rodgers, *Fourth among Equals*, 181. See also: Roy Hattersley letter to Secretary of State, 14, December 1978, Prime Minister's Office: Correspondence and Papers, 1974–1979, PREM16/1707, National Archives UK at Kew, UK.

organization, lorry drivers eventually blockaded the city. As Beach reflected, 'We were amazed that this city was locked tight. Nothing coming in; nothing going out.'[47] Their hold was magnified by the clout the TGWU's Dispensation Committee began to assume. This committee, a group of shop stewards led by Beach, determined what items could leave or enter the city by lorry. The committee would meet from 8 am to 4:30 pm at the union's local headquarters, and employers would line up, sometimes all day, to have the group of stewards determine if the movement of their supplies was essential.[48] The Dispensation Committee considered hospital supplies, food, and animal feed crucial and permitted them to leave or enter the city.[49]

With employers now asking strikers for permission to move goods, a transformation in power relations began to occur:

> It always started amicably. They [employers] were coming to beg. I use the word without any pleasure because it gives me no satisfaction to recall some of our arrogance or impudence of that day or that time. I don't think we were consciously arrogant or impudent. It just went along with the job. When you have that power, and you had the authority to impose on people these restrictions, and I suppose as time went on, and we saw our success and how it was biting and how it was hurting, I think we got some satisfaction from it.[50]

Newspapers soon declared Hull 'Siege City' and a 'Second Stalingrad.' Union activists often embraced such publicity because it was a sign of the effectiveness of the strike and brought trade unionists' claims to a broader audience. 'We had the feeling that we were being successful. Every night, you'd read the headlines, "Siege City." Well, that's what we aimed for. If it was a measure of our success, then we were being very, very successful,' reflected Beach.[51] Ironically, the bad press often made strikes appear more effective than they really were, to the unions' benefit.[52] The *Economist* glibly crystalized this trend: 'The "siege city" image has been fostered by some trade unionists (good for strikers' morale), by a few local industrialists (good union-bashing ammo) and by journalists (good copy).'[53] The idea that

---

[47] Fred Beach, interview by Paul Smith, November 21, 1996.
[48] Beckett (includes interview with Fred Beach), in *When the Lights Went Out*, 489–490.
[49] Fred Beach, interview by Paul Smith.
[50] Fred Beach, interview by Paul Smith.
[51] Fred Beach, interview by Paul Smith.
[52] Hay, 'Narrating Crisis,' 253–277; Hay, 'The Winter of Discontent Thirty Years On,' 545–552; Hay, 'Chronicles of a Death Foretold,' 446–470. For a debate addressing Hay's thesis see: Lawrence Black and Hugh Pemberton, 'The Winter of Discontent in British Politics,' *The Political Quarterly* 80, no. 4 (October–December 2009): 553–561.
[53] 'Warrington's Soft Siege,' *Economist*, January 27, 1979.

the Winter of Discontent was purely a 'constructed crisis,' therefore, has to be nuanced for trade unionists contributed to the production of a media narrative.[54]

The strikers' reach had its limitations, however. In 1979 the RHA represented less than half of all private haulage firms, leaving trucks among owner-operated fleets, non-unionized hauliers, and the non-striking National Freight Corporation still moving.[55] Union activists overcame these challenges with secondary picketing and flying pickets. Secondary picketing, where strikers would picket industries not directly involved in the dispute, arose almost immediately with lorry drivers, as well as TGWU dockers, refusing to cross picket lines throughout Britain.[56] Even after oil tanker drivers accepted a 15 per cent wage rise, some refused to cross pickets in solidarity with striking road haulage drivers.[57]

Solidarity, particularly between oil tanker and lorry drivers, proved especially helpful to the flying pickets in Hull. Beach described how the Dispensation Committee would organize a fleet of cars and drive out to local refineries. Sympathetic oil tanker drivers would throw out a piece of paper with their destination scribbled on it, and the flying picket would then meet the tanker with a picket line, which would not be crossed. The tanker would then have to turn around without completing its delivery. Beach stated that 'The depot managers were furious – the tankers would come back full. On their way back the drivers would wave to our pickets, sometimes give a thumbs up.'[58] For Beach, the flying pickets were like a game of 'cowboys and Indians,' where pickets were 'enjoying themselves, flying after lorries.'[59]

This excitement among local trade union leaders contrasted starkly with the sense of crisis that resonated throughout the country. 'Lorry Men Threaten Food Supplies, New Strike Could Halt Britain'[60] and 'Britain Faces Food and Oil Shortages as Strikes Bite'[61] declared the *Daily Mail* and the *Guardian*. Such serious threats provoked very real responses among the British public. On January 6 the *Financial Times* reported that food company

---

[54] NUPE Regional Secretary, Rodney Bickerstaffe comments on trade union use of the media: 'What we did do – there is no doubt about this – we made the best in PR terms in regards to what action was going on. And I think nowadays they call it "spin."' Rodney Bickerstaffe, interview by author, May 2006.

[55] 'British Workers. More, Much, Much, More,' *Economist*, January 6, 1979.

[56] 'Pickets are Main Problem,' *Daily Telegraph*, January 8, 1979.

[57] 'Ports Crippled by Picketing, Tanker Men Accept Deal: Lorry and Tran Drivers Threaten Official Action,' *Daily Telegraph*, January 9, 1979.

[58] Beckett (includes interview with Fred Beach), in *When the Lights Went Out*, 489.

[59] Fred Beach, interview by Paul Smith.

[60] *Daily Mail*, January 3, 1979.

[61] *Guardian*, January 6, 1979.

Bejam 'blamed the media for the wave of housewives which swept through the stores yesterday, stripping bare shelves of all frozen vegetables.'[62] This was not an isolated incident; it was reflected in the increasing sense of fear and frustration that was becoming pervasive.[63] In a letter to Moss Evans, the General Secretary of the TGWU, one member of the public parodied the union members' participation in the strike:

> Dear Comrade Moss,
>
> The lads and I hope that you will make the transport strike official, and also that you will render every possible support to the tanker drivers in their heroic struggle.
>
> With their efforts and the full support of the Union, they hope and trust that what they are doing will bring the country to its knees, and thereby hasten the day of the Glorious Revolution. [...] My branch are already openly saying 'Moss for King', good luck to you in your efforts, and we are all fully behind you.
>
> Sergei Czarnowska[64]

This sardonic attack provides one perspective, while Nicola Watson from Stockport gives a picture of the specific conditions antagonizing people:

> Sir. – So Mr John Pardoe (Letters, January 15) thinks we should sweat it out through the various strikes that now face us by withdrawing our demand for the labour which the strikers are withholding. If I were writing from a warm office in the House of Commons I would doubtless voice the same sentiments, but I live in Greater Manchester.
>
> Let me tell you what things are like here. Last weekend I could buy neither smokeless fuel nor paraffin and the old lady next door will be unable to get a replacement gas cylinder when her present one runs out. All the local shops were out of [...] decent electric heaters. This last week we have had rush hour buses only and even if I owned a car, petrol was virtually unobtainable.[65]

Watson's emphasis on the weather and the inability to acquire 'decent electric heaters' underscores the role the cold weather conditions played in framing the view of the strikes. She was not alone in perceiving the strikes refracted through the lens of harsh weather. Headlines such as the *Guardian*'s 'Freeze Piles on Agony for Labour,' and descriptions of how

---

[62] 'Shoppers Urged to Stop Food Panic Buying,' *Financial Times*, January 6, 1979.

[63] Sandbrook, *Seasons in the Sun*, 727–728.

[64] Sergei Czarnowska to Moss Evans, 6 January, 1979, Moss Evans and Ron Todd Papers, MSS/26/TG/384/1/1, Modern Records Centre, University of Warwick, Coventry, UK.

[65] Nicola Watson, letter to the editor, *Guardian*, January 18, 1979.

'Arctic weather conditions over much of the country added to the industrial misery of Britain yesterday,' echoed the way the effects were easily collapsed into deprivation as a result of the extreme weather.[66]

Labour Prime Minister James Callaghan's attendance at the Strategic Arms Limitation Talks (SALT II) in the Caribbean only exacerbated the feeling that Britain was engulfed in problems that the government was seemingly unwilling to solve. Callaghan's political adviser at the time, Tom McNally, recounted that while at the summit and the three days' holiday the Prime Minister later took in Barbados, the Press Corps, especially the *Daily Mail*, was 'briefed to get a picture of the Prime Minister in a bathing suit,'[67] a trap into which Callaghan easily strolled.[68] The *Daily Mail* got their pictures and asked, 'Can nothing be done to stop greedy and ruthless unions from inflicting incalculable discomfort on their fellow workers, and even endangering life?'[69] The resentment built up to a climax as the reader continued through the issue as the holiday photos contrasted with 'Britain under siege [...] But 4,000 miles Away, Callaghan Enjoys the Sun, Dear Jim, Glad to See You're Having a Good Time, Thought You'd Like to Know How We've Been Getting on Over Here.'[70]

Upon his return to Britain on January 10, Callaghan's advisors debated whether or not the Prime Minister should immediately hold a press conference or return to Downing Street first. They finally decided to have Callaghan speak immediately as he arrived at Heathrow Airport. McNally recounted that he encouraged Callaghan to speak to the press at the airport to show that:

> 'Jim's Back! 'Jim's in Charge!' And that would give us leadership and ownership of the problem. I walked into that press conference believing that was exactly what he [Callaghan] was going to do. Instead, of which, he turned all whimsical and started talking about his swimming in Barbados. And I just thought, 'This isn't it.'[71]

The situation went further awry when a member of the press asked Callaghan what he thought of the 'mounting chaos' that the strikes were supposedly causing in Britain. Callaghan responded defensively, 'Please don't run down your own country by talking about mounting chaos.

---

[66] 'City predicts rise in minimum lending rate: Freeze piles on agony for Labour,' *Guardian*, January 24, 1979.
[67] (Lord) Tom McNally, interview in *Secret History: Winter of Discontent* (Brook Lapping Productions for Channel Four, 1998).
[68] *Daily Mail*, January 8, 1979.
[69] *Daily Mail*, January 8, 1979.
[70] *Daily Mail*, January 8, 1979.
[71] McNally, interview in *Secret History*.

If you look at it from outside, you can see that you are taking a rather parochial view. I do not feel that there is a mounting chaos.'[72] McNally immediately knew that Callaghan had just made a serious mistake. 'I'm standing behind him during that interview, and I knew he was getting it wrong. It was one of those terrible things where you feel like you would like to yank your man off and start again.'[73] The press immediately pounced upon the apparent disconnect; the iconic 'Crisis? What Crisis?' headlined in the *Sun*.[74]

Callaghan's speechwriter, Roger Carroll explains the resonance of this fabricated quote. 'He never actually used the words, 'Crisis? What Crisis?' But what Jim said was not that far away from 'Crisis? What Crisis?' He asked for it, I'm afraid, and he got it.'[75] This phrase continues to be 'used to accuse British politicians of complacency.'[76] Like many other central components of the mythology, construction is present, but at the heart lays a reality to be moulded.

The uproar in the immediate aftermath of this press conference pales in comparison to the scale its impact has had on popular memory. When commenting on Callaghan's misstep 20 years later, for example, a BBC documentary showed footage of the Prime Minister walking around the tropical island in a Hawaiian shirt as the narrator forebodingly described how the conference scene starkly contrasted with the experience as the British public 'shivered in the snow and a new wave of strikes.'[77] As David Arnold has observed, 'The occurrence of other events of personal or public significance have often been recalled in oral tradition by locating them in relation to a particular famine.'[78] However, in this case, the contrast of weather helps to organize the memory of this event. The pervasive reference to the cold weather intensified the resonance of the memory. As Andy Beckett comments, 'The weather added to the sense of panic.'[79] Images of the bronzed Prime Minister seemingly dumbfounded by claims of national strife was, therefore, refracted through the memory of a chilling cold, making the feeling of Callaghan's apparent disconnect with Britain's problems all the more acute.

[72] 'Thatcher's call for a state of emergency over haulers rejected: Cool Callaghan plays down cries of chaos,' *Guardian*, January 11, 1979.
[73] McNally, interview in *Secret History*.
[74] *Sun*, January 19, 1979.
[75] Roger Carroll, interview in *Secret History: Winter of Discontent* (Brook Lapping Productions for Channel Four, 1998).
[76] Beckett, *When the Lights Went Out*, 484.
[77] *Secret History: Winter of Discontent* (Brook Lapping Productions for Channel Four, 1998).
[78] Arnold, *Famine: Social Crisis and Historical Change*, 12.
[79] Beckett, *When the Lights Went Out*, 466.

This was the moment for Margaret Thatcher's 'Stepping Stones' agenda to find a receptive audience. Only five days after the beginning of the road haulage strike, Thatcher responded with a call for a state of emergency and a list of proposed laws that would curb trade union power. Such restrictions included taxing strikers' social security benefits, allowing the state to pay for postal strike ballots, a 'review of the right to strike in those industries "where unions have the power to hold the nation to ransom," and a review of unions' present legal immunities.'[80] Thatcher's repeated call for a state of emergency after Callaghan's return from the SALT II talks became all the more pointed. Also, the contrast of the sun-tanned Prime Minister 'turn[ing] whimsical and [...] talking about swimming in Barbados'[81] with the calm and sensible presence of the Leader of the Opposition, in a very British sitting room, was very apparent in the Conservative Party Broadcast on January 17. In a media message which some have argued 'won her the election,'[82] Thatcher directly addressed the camera with poise and composure, appearing to transcend political rivalries and show genuine concern for the state of the country:

> Yes, technically, this is a Party Political Broadcast on behalf of the Conservative Party. But tonight I don't propose to use the time to make party political points. I do not think you would want me to do so.
>
> The crisis that our country faces is too serious for that. And it is our country, the whole nation, that faces this crisis, not just one party or even one government. This is no time to put party before country. I start from there.

Legislation outlawing secondary picketing was the first on her list of the reforms she believed would bring Britain out of this state of 'siege.' She was careful not to look as if she were attacking unions, but seemed concerned about the overall welfare of the nation when she closed the broadcast with:

> If the present crisis has taught us anything it has surely taught us that we have to think of others as well as ourselves; that no-one, however strong his case, is entitled to pursue it by hurting others.
>
> There are wreckers among us who don't believe this. But the vast majority of us, and that includes the vast majority of trade unionists, do believe it, whether we call ourselves Labour, Conservative, Liberal – or simply British.
>
> It is to that majority that I am talking this evening. We have to learn

---

[80] 'Cabinet Ready to Use Troops, Ports Shut to Lorries: Mrs Thatcher promises to curb unions,' *Daily Telegraph*, January 8, 1979.

[81] McNally, interview in *Secret History*.

[82] Bell, 'The Conservatives' Advertising Campaign,' 22.

again to be one nation, or one day we shall be no nation. If we have learnt that lesson from these first dark days of 1979, then we have learnt something of value.[83]

Thatcher began to do what the Labour government was seemingly unable to do: take ownership of the problem. Years later Callaghan admitted, 'Mrs Thatcher exploited this attempted usurpation of authority with gusto, and the leaders of the TGWU could not have been surprised at the growing dislike they engendered.'[84]

While Thatcher exuded an air of leadership, the government was attempting to devise concrete tactics to solve the problem. Bill Rodgers activated the Regional Emergency Transport Sub-Committees and had them make contact with local TGWU officials to assure that essential supplies were flowing.[85] On January 12 Rodgers worked with TGWU leaders on a list of priority supplies called the 'Charter for Pickets' and had it sent to regional secretaries. The document warned that 'To prevent intervention of emergency powers and calling in of troops [...] We would recommend to strike committees that to ensure that troops are not used they accept these priorities.'[86] Although his language was quite strident, Rodgers soon became aware that TGWU headquarters 'had only *recommended* priorities for essential supplies, and local strike committees had been given the list "for action at their discretion".'[87] Even in the Cabinet, it was apparent that the TGWU leadership 'had now lost control of its local branches.'[88] At the local level, the Charter for Pickets appeared to have been ignored. When asked about the Charter, Beach replied, 'If headquarters did send one to us, nobody took any notice.'[89]

The inability to exert any pressure on the local strike committees increased the push among members of the Labour Cabinet to call for a state of emergency. On January 13 the responsibility of dealing with the effects of the dispute fell on the CCU. However, any plans to pull in troops could only be pursued once a state of emergency was called, like that which had been declared in Northern Ireland. In Cabinet discussions on January 15, ministers pointed out that, unlike in Northern Ireland, where strikes

---

[83] 'Winter of Discontent Party Broadcast' YouTube video, 8:36, from a Conservative Party Broadcast on January 17, 1979, posted by 'thatcheritescot,' February 4, 2012, https://www.youtube.com/watch?v=Txsslou33HQ.
[84] Callaghan, *Time and Chance*, 537.
[85] 'Conclusions of a Meeting of the Cabinet,' 15 January, 1979, The Cabinet Papers, CAB/128/65/2, National Archives at Kew, UK.
[86] Quoted in Beckett, *When the Lights Went Out*, 492.
[87] Rodgers, *Fourth among Equals*, 182.
[88] 'Conclusions of a Meeting of the Cabinet,' 15 January, 1979.
[89] Beckett (Includes interview with Fred Beach) in *When the Lights Went Out*, 493.

had affected petrol supplies, in Britain, 'the TGWU had undertaken to co-operate over maintenance of deliveries for essential services, a better flow of petrol and oil had been maintained in Great Britain without a state of emergency than would have been possible with one.'[90]

Three days later the debate over calling a state of emergency continued to rage. While the need to intervene was certain, at least to make the Labour government look like it was in control of the situation, it was noted that although the 'supply situation was deteriorating slightly,' 'it was still better than the level of supply which could be maintained with the use of troops alone.'[91] The logistics made the efficacy of the state of emergency questionable:

> The Army only had about 2,000 trucks available, and could requisition a further 8,000, but it would take about 4 days before these could be fully deployed, because of the need to train drivers. For comparison, there were about 530,000 vehicles in the road haulage industry in normal times. It would be very difficult for the Army to maintain more than a tiny fraction of this very complicated distribution network.[92]

Rodgers was among those opposed to the declaration of the state of emergency as he was 'doubtful about the advantages of a state of emergency. Troops could only be used on a limited scale quite legitimately without one.'[93]

More importantly, that same day it was decided that an order would not be introduced to restrict profits of the road haulage industry, leaving the RHA room to increase their offer to unions.[94] This move incensed Rodgers to the point that not only did he plan to resign,[95] but he directly addressed the Prime Minister in a letter after the meeting. He wrote, 'I am gravely concerned with the view you expressed in Cabinet that we should tip the wink to the RHA to settle as soon as possible and presumably on any terms.' He explained his criticism by emphasizing that the British public was not suffering great shortages, but more importantly, the move would be giving into the TGWU and the pickets. For Rodgers, this move was 'not a matter of pay policy but of trade union power and of law and order.' He ended the letter dramatically by declaring:

---

[90] 'Conclusions of a Meeting of the Cabinet,' 15 January, 1979
[91] 'Conclusions of a Meeting of the Cabinet,' 18 January, 1979, The Cabinet Papers, CAB/128/65/3, National Archives at Kew, UK.
[92] 'Conclusions of a Meeting of the Cabinet,' January 18, 1979.
[93] Rodgers, *Fourth among Equals*, 183.
[94] 'Conclusions of a Meeting of the Cabinet,' January 18, 1979.
[95] Rodgers, *Fourth among Equals*, 185.

> I assume that the Government must stand and fight somewhere and at some time. But in this case the Government is not even in the front line. To suggest to others that they should now give in would be defeatism of a most reprehensible kind. I could not be party to it.[96]

Rodgers' anger at what appeared to be capitulation to the trade unions provides a presentiment of his later political shift away from the Labour Party early in the next decade.

In discussions surrounding the state of emergency, the Labour government privately considered implementing some of the same constraints that Thatcher did so publicly. The Cabinet discussed that while trade unions' influence in the past had been positive, the recent strikes revealed how things had 'swung too far in favour of the unions.' The use of secondary picketing, in particular, was seen as a 'serious threat to law and order.' Although not explicitly stating that the practice should be outlawed, the legal contours were explored, implying a consideration of legislation. Furthermore, the Cabinet noted that 'Britain probably had the most generous social security provisions for strikes of any country, and had abandoned any attempt to restrict the right to strike in key services.'[97]

Threats to food and medical supplies were still of concern, however. Rodgers explains that overall food supplies continued to move throughout the country.[98] Claims of deprivation in the north-western city of Warrington, for example, were deemed 'phoney.' As the *Economist* explained, 'Food shortages (mainly tea, sugar, margarines and fats) [...] are no worse than in several other industrial areas of militant north-west England.'[99] Douglas Smith, from the Employment Department of the Cabinet Office, dismissed the assertion that there were vast food shortages during this strike. He adamantly declared at a symposium almost a decade later that 'The only shortage of food I recollect in the whole of the affair was that Kellogg's Cornflakes were difficult to obtain in some supermarkets!'[100] Comments during the Winter of Discontent by the Minister for Agriculture, Fisheries, and Food, John Silkin, appear to vindicate Smith's assertion. On January 18 Silkin explained that there were adequate supplies with some limitations.

---

[96] Letter from William Rodgers to Prime Minister, James Callaghan, 18 January, 1979, Prime Minister's Office: Correspondence and Papers, 1974–1979, PREM 16/2128, National Archives at Kew, UK.
[97] 'Conclusions of a Meeting of the Cabinet,' January 15, 1979.
[98] Taylor and Seldon, '"The Winter of Discontent" Symposium,' 42.
[99] 'Warrington's Soft Siege,' *Economist*, January 27, 1979, 83.
[100] Taylor and Seldon, '"The Winter of Discontent" Symposium,' 42. Kellogg's UK Ltd was picketed, so the supply of this cereal could have been affected. Letter from William Rodgers to Alex Kitson, 17 January, 1979, Prime Minister's Office: Correspondence and Papers, 1974–1979, PREM/16/2128, National Archives at Kew, UK.

'You may not get the brand of cereal you like, but there are still plenty of others.'[101] These public declarations were not merely ways to placate the public, but reflected governmental assessments of the situation. Overall, most basic goods were seen to be 'still in good supply,' but shortages of salt, sugar, and edible oils and fats were reported from all regions of the nation.[102] There were problems getting hydride and acetic acid for the manufacture of penicillin in Yorkshire and Humberside.[103] The most 'critical break in the chain,' however, was the dearth of raw materials for animal feed.[104] In the East Midlands, there were reports of drivers being threatened for delivering Pedigree Pet Foods.[105]

In February, the *Economist* contrasted the dire warnings of food manufacturers and the reality once the strikes began to wind down. One of the first was the January 16 claim by the Food Manufacturers' Federation that food was running out quickly, but, as the *Economist* remarked, 'supermarket shelves stayed well stocked (except for a few items) and Mr Hornby's lay-offs turned out to be as illusory as the CBIs.' In another account the chairman of United Biscuits asserted that food 'will soon be near a halt' due to the strikes, but such shortages, according to the *Economist*, did not materialize.[106]

The complexity of the situation, however, did not put members of the public at ease. As Rodgers observed, 'The loss of jobs turned out to be much less than expected, and there were few serious shortages of food. But from the first days of the strike, the sense of mounting chaos was acute.'[107] John Silkin publicly reiterated Rodgers' claim when he declared in late January that there were no food shortages and only panic buying would create such a crisis.[108] Cabinet discussions underlined the importance of this 'psychological effect,' especially given that 'the impression was that the distribution of foodstuffs was now entirely in the control of the Transport and General

---

[101] 'Join Hunt for Food,' *News of the World*, January 18, 1979.
[102] Daily Situation Report by MAFF/Situation as at 13.00 HRS on 17 January/Report by Ministry of Agriculture, Fisheries and Food, 17 January, 1979, Prime Minister's Office: Correspondence and Papers, 1974–1979, PREM16/2128, National Archives at Kew, UK.
[103] Letter from William Rodgers to Alec Kitson, 17 January, 1979, Prime Minister's Office: Correspondence and Papers, 1974–1979, PREM 16/2128. National Archives at Kew. See also: Taylor and Seldon, '"The Winter of Discontent" Symposium,' 42.
[104] Note of a Meeting at the Cabinet Office on Thursday, January 18 at 11:15/Road Haulage Dispute: National Liaison Group, 18 January, 1979, Prime Minister's Office: Correspondence and Papers, 1974–1979, PREM 16/2128, National Archives at Kew, UK.
[105] Letter from William Rodgers to Alec Kitson, 17 January, 1979, Prime Minister's Office: Correspondence and Papers, 1974–1979 PREM 16/2128. National Archives at Kew, UK.
[106] 'Blame the Bosses, Too,' *Economist*, February 3, 1979.
[107] Rodgers, *Fourth among Equals*, 181.
[108] 'Silkin: No Food Crisis,' *Daily Mirror*, January 23, 1979.

Workers' Union.'[109] Headlines such as 'Join Hunt for Food' from the *News of the World* definitely contributed to this sense of deprivation and panic.[110]

While the public's reactions to the strike were varied, they were all intense. In a letter titled 'We've Had Enough of Flying Pickets' in the *Manchester Evening News*, A.B. Volk expresses frustration:

> We are, I suggest, fed-up with the bully-boys, flying pickets and general intimidation of the silent public. Recognizing that the unions did so much good in the past, I now fear that they may do equally as much harm in the future, in the opposite direction. There is no easy answer, in a democracy, we are all responsible: both for the government and the way people respond. Perhaps it is the time for people to stand-up and be counted.[111]

In London a letter to the editor of the *Guardian* complained about the abuse among secondary pickets:

> Sooner or later society will have to grasp the nettle and support the full enforcement of laws which ban secondary picketing – entirely, and make holding the nation to ransom less of a paying proposition.
>
> The alternative is increasing disruption, accelerating inflation, and a distorted pay structure in which even highly paid workers in over manned occupations can force through big pay increases if they are in a position to cause enough damage to the community.[112]

'Trade Unionist of Cheetham' braced against the tide of negative opinion and pointed out that 'trade unionists have had as much as they can stomach of falling real wages and services,' and it was the 'intransigence of the employers and the government,' not that of striking workers, that was causing the current upheavals.[113]

The 'Lorry Driver's Wife' from Cheshire also acerbically chided such critics:

> I am sick and tired of the constant moans and groans about 'The long suffering citizens being held to ransom. I hope all you citizens will now learn to appreciate the hard-working lorry driver when you shop. Think of yourselves as lucky you moaners. At least the majority of you are getting wages. But not the lorry driver – he has to live on a few pounds of strike

---

[109] 'Conclusions of a Meeting of the Cabinet,' January 18, 1979.
[110] 'Join Hunt for Food,' *News of the World*, January 18, 1979.
[111] A.B. Volk, Postbag (letter to the editor) *Manchester Evening News*, January 19, 1979.
[112] J.A. Nelson, Merton Park, London, letter to the editor, *Guardian*, January 18, 1979.
[113] 'Trade Unionist,' 'Postbag' (letter to the editor), *Manchester Evening News*, January 18, 1979.

pay, which he has paid in over the years. Think about it, who emptied those supermarket shelves? Not us. Now who's greedy?[114]

In Darlington a lorry driver also defended the industrial action among these drivers:

> If we are so work shy, why are all Common Market countries crying out for British workers, not forgetting the Middle East? The political levy is a voluntary payment. We do have Tories, Liberals and Communists in the trade unions. The choice isn't available for the CBI or the RHA.
>
> Ask some RHA members how many drivers are forced to work illegal hours or take a walk. I have not been on strike. I drive for a private firm, and no picket tried to stop me.[115]

Still, these opinions were muted in the back columns of British newspapers. Frustration began to take the form of people taking matters in their own hands. This do-it-yourself attitude emerged in one letter from Fallowfield:

> Trade unions have declared war on society. Some of us believe that work must be for the well-being of society. We are all now being bullied. Pickets don't bother me, woe betide any who try to stop me from earning a living. If the government can't look after us, it is up to us to look after ourselves.[116]

This frustration exploded into violence when 300 women from a Cadbury Schweppes chocolate factory at Bourneville, Birmingham, scattered a picket of 15 lorry drivers. 'Wielding handbags and umbrellas,' the women descended upon the picket line with a 'formidable display of female fury.'[117] Wendy Harris, one of the women from the factory, explained, 'Word spread around the factory that flying pickets were stopping lorries. We were disgusted. We decided to do something about it.'[118] Manchester and Liverpool also saw such demonstrations, as well as counter-demonstrations in support of the strikers.[119]

Such conflicts also erupted in Hull and became a struggle over media messaging. When the correct mixture of feed was failing to reach farmers

---

[114] Lorry Driver's Wife, 'Postbag' (letter to the editor), *Manchester Evening News*, January 23, 1979.

[115] Newton Aycliffe, 'In Defence of Lorry Drivers: Hear All Sides,' letter to the editor, *Northern Echo* (Darlington), January 22, 1979.

[116] W. Ashcroft, Postbag (letter to the editor), *Manchester Evening News*, January 19, 1979.

[117] 'Charge of Angry Factory Women Scatters Picketing Lorry Drivers,' *Daily Telegraph*, January 18, 1979.

[118] 'Shops under Siege – Fury of the Wives,' *Daily Mail*, January 18, 1979.

[119] 'Ban the Pickets: Demo by 500 Wives!' *Manchester Evening News*, January 20, 1979; 'Pier Head Surprise for Strike-Force Mums,' *Liverpool Echo*, January 22, 1979.

in and around Hull, word spread that the farmers were going to stage a dramatic action. Beach recollected:

> The committee was told that there was going to be an incident. We didn't know what, but from Yorkshire, television cameras were appearing [... and the national newspapers] were on the corners. At the given signal, the cameras began to whirl, and the newsmen congregated [...] and a Land Rover drove into the street here. And the cameras are running, and the typical farmer with his cap on, and then he started his speech, so obviously rehearsed. Looking at the cameras [...] and he dropped the door down, and there were beautiful little piglets. 11. All dead. [...] That was us. We were the murderers. [...] What happened in fact was that the mother had laid on them all. And none of them had died from starvation.[120]

Don Avery of the Northern Chicken Growers UK Ltd explains why they took part in the action:

> The only way to bring this to the sympathy of the public and the Transport and General Workers' Union was to say, 'Hey, look! This is what is going to happen to animals'. Unless you publicize your action, you will not get the reaction you are looking for.[121]

While it was a straightforward publicity stunt, farmers did have a legitimate worry. The blockade in Hull put such pressure on the supply of animal feed that the National Liaison Group recommended immediate action 'if a critical situation, particularly on feeding stuffs, was to be avoided.'[122]

Other forms of such media spectacles were also prevalent among British dailies themselves. On January 18, 1979, the *Daily Mail* reported that four members of a flying picket had followed a lorry driver, eventually beating the driver and calling him a 'scab bastard' all the while. Christopher Hitchens investigated the report for the *New Statesman* and found that pickets had not chased the victim, nor were the words 'scab bastard' shouted at him. Moreover, there was no evidence that the perpetrators were even striking lorry drivers. The *Daily Mail* was eventually forced to admit that it could not substantiate that the story was a case of 'picket-inspired violence.'[123]

This incident was not isolated, but reflected a broader political shift in British media. In fact, 'Labour was suffering a more hostile press than any

---

[120] Fred Beach, interview with Paul Smith. See also: Glasgow University Media Group, *Really Bad News* (London: Writers and Readers, 1982), 8.

[121] Don Avery, interview in *Secret History: Winter of Discontent* (Brook Lapping Productions for Channel Four, 1998).

[122] Note of a Meeting at the Cabinet Office on Thursday, January 18 at 11:15/Road Haulage Dispute: National Liaison Group, PREM 16/2128, National Archives at Kew.

[123] Thomas, *Popular Newspapers*, 80.

time in the post-war period.'[124] Derek Jameson, the then editor of the *Daily Express*, is candid about how his paper achieved such an end. 'We pulled every dirty trick in the book to get rid of Callaghan and Labour [...] We made it look as if this [the strikes] was general, universal, eternal. In fact, it was only fragmentary, here and there. There was no big problem.'[125]

To see this series solely as a right-wing conspiracy that deceived an unwitting British public would be overreach, however. Adam Raphael, who was a journalist for *The Observer* in the late 1970s, dismissed the accusation that the press had it in for the Callaghan government. He attested that other journalists like himself considered themselves left of centre. Therefore, they were attracted to the issue not because it could be used to smear Labour, but because 'it was a fantastic story.'[126] Nevertheless, Raphael admits that anti-union feeling was present among the same journalists because of their interactions with print unions on Fleet Street. He observed that while such biases might have influenced their coverage of the Winter of Discontent, their own views not just fostered anti-union sentiment, but reflected it, too. He states frankly that 'Undoubtedly, there was an anti-union mood in the country.'[127]

By the end of January, the first settlements of the strike began to appear. On January 28, for instance, the TGWU in Hull settled for £64 a week for 40 hours. From that point until February 6, a series of area settlements were concluded.[128] In a conversation with Tony Benn, Callaghan expressed the view that 'the road haulage drivers' settlement between 15 and 20 per cent reminded him of Munich, that's to say he felt relief and disquiet in equal proportions.'[129]

Such lingering unease was becoming all the more apparent as public sector strikes began on January 22. In the *Guardian*, Peter Jenkins agreed with the Labour government's assertion that most of the claims of food shortages and massive lay-offs were unfounded. However, he pointedly argued that, 'in another sense, there is certainly a crisis.' With the onset of public sector and rail strikes, coupled with the closure of some ports, the Labour government was losing its grip on the situation, a hold which Thatcher was increasingly beginning to assert. His criticism of trade unions

---

[124] Thomas, *Popular Newspapers*, 61.
[125] Derek Jameson, interview in *Secret History: Winter of Discontent* (Brook Lapping Productions for Channel Four, 1998).
[126] Adam Raphael, interview by author, June 2006.
[127] Raphael, interview.
[128] Paul Smith, *Unionization & Union Leadership*, 154.
[129] Benn, *Conflicts of Interest*, 446.

was cutting, and he increasingly saw that Thatcher was providing a clear alternative to present situation:

> Disorganised labour, responding to no one's leadership, recognising no constraints, cannot be dealt with in this way, and cannot claim, under either a Conservative or a Labour Government, the special treatment, consistent consultation and direct influence in policy-making which the movement in its better day first came to regard as right.
>
> It is Mrs Thatcher who, in the past few weeks, has most vividly set out that choice, Mrs Thatcher who has best expressed the growing national conviction that we can't go on like this, that the balance of collective bargaining needs to be changed, and the law, which gave the unions new rights, should also give rights to the rest of society.[130]

Jenkins expresses how much had changed from early January as the lorry drivers' strike came to an end. Thatcher had now found momentum that would continue on through the winter.

Throughout the chapter I have demonstrated that while central to the broader disputes of the Winter of Discontent, the road haulage strike was rooted in specific currents within that industry, in particular work conditions and a growing rank-and-file mobilization of the workforce. These trends in the industry would harness the budding labour activism of shop stewards like Fred Beach, but frustrate Labour ministers like Bill Rodgers. Moreover, the two individuals provide a snapshot of the countervailing political trends present within the Labour Party that fed into the disputes of the winter of 1978–79.

The road haulage strike also reveals the significance of how the media helped framed the events of the Winter of Discontent. It helps to substantiate Colin Hay's view of this series of events as a manufactured crisis; however, it also demonstrates that the 'manufacturers' were at times a variety of groups, including trade unions. Nevertheless, while archival evidence indicates that most supplies were stable, some, like animal foodstuffs and the ingredients for penicillin, were under pressure from the strikes. At a deeper level, I assert that the seeming helplessness that the British public began to feel was accentuated by the extreme weather. Both the strikes and the weather fuelled the feeling of victimization and fed into the crisis-ridden atmosphere. As Hay also acknowledges, the British public's sense of crisis increasingly was pulled into a right-wing resolution not through outright manipulation, but because the Right framed the problem so that their resolutions appeared reasonable and necessary.[131] I would argue further that the Labour government's inability to take leadership of the problem, as Margaret Thatcher

---

[130] 'How We Are and How We Might Be,' op-ed, *Guardian*, January 24, 1979.
[131] Hay, 'Narrating Crisis,' 274.

deftly did, was a grave misstep on their part. However, not calling a state of emergency was not; Cabinet discussion illustrates that a state of emergency would only have made conditions worse. Hay is correct that the media was crucial at this point, but Labour's failure to frame their actions positively made them vulnerable to the media-savvy Conservatives.

As the road haulage strikes ended, public sector unions had already begun their National Day of Action on January 22, worsening the tide of discontent upon which Thatcher was riding. Moreover, the winter continued to wield its seemingly unrelenting grip on Britain. Michael Palin observes, 'Even the weather was dull harsh [and] uncomfortable, reflecting the spirit of the times.'[132] This morose sentiment would be qualified by movements of counter-memory as public sector workers engaged in a series of battles that would invigorate them and have lasting effects on their political identities for decades to come.

---

[132] Sandbrook, *Seasons in the Sun*, 740.

5

Freezers of Corpses and Sea Burials: The Liverpool Gravediggers' Strike

During a sermon in early 1979, a vicar shared his apocalyptic vision with his parishioners:

> When gravediggers will allow corpses to mount up rather than carry out their duty, I detect the undermining of the whole structure of our society. This civilization of our[s] has taken thousands of years to reach a point where the dignity of the human being has reached a high level of care and concern. I shall not witness its destruction through inertia.[1]

Such denunciations of callousness and impending anarchy characterize the overall reaction to a strike of 56 gravediggers and crematoria workers in Liverpool. The action struck such an emotive chord with the British press and public that the frenzy subsumed many of the facts of the strike, providing the myth of the Winter of Discontent with one of its most powerful and memorable images. One of the key misrepresentations is that the left-wing NUPE 'callously' rejected the government's pleas to put a halt to the Liverpool gravediggers' dispute. In Callaghan and Healey's autobiographies, both politicians decried NUPE General Secretary Alan Fisher's refusal to bring Liverpool gravediggers back to work.[2] While NUPE gravediggers outside of Manchester *did* strike, the gravediggers in Liverpool were, in fact, part of the GMWU. This is but one of several misrepresentations that have distorted what actually occurred during those 10 days in early 1979. This chapter will chart the development of the GMWU and the lives of those involved in the strikes. Finally, it will reveal how and why these relatively brief instances of industrial militancy became the focus of such intense media attention in 1979.

---

[1] 'A Sermon Preached in Saint Mary's Epiphany IV 1979,' 1979, / P95/MRY3/245, London Metropolitan Archives, UK.

[2] Callaghan, *Time and Chance*, 537; Healey, *The Time of My Life*, 463.

In order to understand how the strike occurred, it is necessary to examine the overall history of public sector unionization in post-war Britain. As noted previously, public sector trade unionism grew and became increasingly militant from the late 1960s and early 1970s. This new movement of public sector militancy first crystallized in the Dirty Jobs Strike of 1970. In the government's battle with exploding inflation, the Secretary of State at the time, Robert Carr, sought to make public sector wage restraint an example for the private sector to follow. He noted, 'If private employers do not resist excessive wage claims, the Government is certainly not going to rescue them. We are not going to treat our own employees in any way unfairly, but we are going to set an example.'[3] This extra pressure on the public sector proved fruitless when in September of that year, 65,000 public sector workers, including bin men, canteen, and sewage workers rejected a 34s pay offer[4] and won a 42s 6d for women and 50s for men. The disparity in the settlement for women and men was still seen as a victory because 'it did represent a higher percentage increase than that offered to the men, and there was a requirement under the Equal Pay Act to move towards parity.'[5] This strike also set an important precedent organizationally with the three principal unions involved, NUPE, GMWU, and TGWU, working together at the national, regional, and local level.[6] Not only was the Dirty Jobs Strike an important victory for public sector workers, but their unions would expect similar levels of support in the disputes of 1979.[7]

Growing public sector union membership did not, however, immediately translate into increased influence within the labour movement. Despite their burgeoning numeric presence, public sector unions continued to be underrepresented on TUC economic committees, leaving them especially vulnerable when issues of public expenditure cuts arose.[8] Consequently, the 1974 election of a Labour government provided an opportunity for these unions to make up for this lack of influence in the TUC by directly pressuring the government. Again, the Social Contract played a pivotal role in public sector unions' support for wage restraint. Of special interest to public sector unions was the government's promise to increase public expenditure as part of the Social Contract.

This final commitment came under fire as early as 1975, when Denis

---

[3] Quoted in Eric Wigham, *Strikes and the Government, 1893–1981* (London: Macmillan Press, 1982), 165.
[4] Williams and Fryer, *Leadership & Democracy*, 173.
[5] Williams and Fryer, *Leadership & Democracy*, 180.
[6] Williams and Fryer, *Leadership & Democracy*, 175.
[7] Larry Whitty, interview by author, September, 2006.
[8] Ludlam, 'Too Much Pluralism,' 156.

Healey proposed £1 billion of cuts in public expenditure as part of his annual budget.[9] Not only did this proposal come into direct conflict with the Social Contract, but the cuts it put forth would also have a particularly negative effect on public sector workers. First, many of the benefits set to be reduced were those same benefits that helped to supplement the low pay among these workers. Second, the cuts would result in layoffs that threatened public sector work itself. Nevertheless, the unions remained loyal to the government, and joined the TUC in 1975 and 1976 in endorsing the Labour government's spending cuts.[10]

With a membership entirely based in the public sector, NUPE's position epitomized the public sector unions' troubled relationship with the Labour government: they sought to keep a sympathetic government in office, but at the same time they knew that the same government was negatively affecting their members' livelihoods. In 1975 the NUPE Conference endorsed the Social Contract, but voted to fight the cuts in public expenditure.[11] NUPE continued to support the Labour government, but the relationship was showing considerable strain by 1976. At the TUC Conference, General Secretary of NUPE Alan Fisher announced, 'My union's particular contribution would be to warn the Government that if there are further cuts in public expenditure, although we welcome the pay policy today, we will not be bound by a contract, which is broken on the other side.'[12]

Prior to Britain's assumption of the 1976 IMF loan, the Labour government had brought local authority expenditure to a standstill and was committed to reining in the growth of the welfare state. Callaghan notes that he did not need to 'be convinced by the IMF that we ought to bring the growth of public expenditure closer to the growth of industrial output.'[13] Nevertheless, 1976 did signal a change as local authorities could no longer borrow, and the standstill in expenditure turned into real cuts by local authorities.[14]

Unsurprisingly, given Fisher's warning at the TUC Conference, public sector unions now began to respond more assertively. In 1976, NUPE and NALGO picketed the TUC Conference and launched the NSCAC. Eleven public sector unions, including NUPE, NALGO, NUT (National Union of Teachers), ASTMS (Association of Scientific, Technical, and Managerial Staffs), COHSE, and the AUT (Association of University Teachers), made

[9] Cronin, *New Labour's Pasts*, 168.
[10] Ludlam, 'Too Much Pluralism,' 156.
[11] Ludlam, 'Labourism and the Disintegration of the Postwar Consensus,' 676.
[12] Ludlam, 'Labourism and the Disintegration,' 380.
[13] Callaghan, *Time and Chance*, 442.
[14] Whitty, interview, 2006. See also: Ludlam, 'Labourism and the Disintegration,' 650.

up this group.[15] On November 17, 1976 the NSCAC organized a one-day strike against the cuts in public expenditure.[16] However, many public sector unions were still reluctant to fully endorse the fight against the cuts. For instance, the GMWU, one of the unions with the largest public sector membership in Britain, criticized the November 17 stoppages, stating that they were 'hastening the advent of the Tory Government.'[17] Once again, the GMWU's position reflects the public sector unions' need to temper criticisms of the cuts out of loyalty to the Labour government and outright fear of a Tory government.

Although divisions over cuts in public expenditure were apparent among public sector unions, by 1977, frustration with the cuts, and an underlying restlessness with the Social Contract, was becoming more acute. In one NUPE policy document, the union criticized the Labour government, citing that it had failed to pursue the economic and social objectives it had promised as part of the Social Contract. The authors further warned:

> NUPE wants to see a Labour Government in power after the next General Election, because it is only through a Labour Government that workers have any hopes of realising their aspirations. But in order for the Government to survive it must implement the alternative economic strategy as a matter of urgency.[18]

Nevertheless, political changes in 1978 compelled public sector unions to temper this frustration with the Labour government. The 'Lib-Lab Pact' was to end in July 1978; consequently, unions began to outline their strategy in regard to what they believed to be an impending October election. NUPE laid out their plan for 1978 and 1979:

> Indeed, a date in October 1978 looks increasingly likely. [...] The advent of a General Election would not necessarily change the Union's wages strategy. [...] However, the consequence for the wages campaign flowing from the abandonment of the Lib/Lab pact and the increased likelihood of an election is that emphasis must be placed in the campaign on securing a clear commitment to ending low pay in the Labour Party manifesto, and maintaining sufficient pressure to ensure that such a commitment was honoured.[19]

---

[15] Ludlam, 'Too Much Pluralism,' 157.
[16] Ludlam, 'Labourism and the Disintegration,' 372.
[17] Ludlam, 'Labourism and the Disintegration,' 584.
[18] *Fight Back!: NUPE's Policy on Pay, Prices, Jobs and the Cuts*, June 1977 (London: McDermott & Chant Ltd.) NUPE Publications, UNISON/Rodney Bickerstaffe papers, MSS 389/6/B/Box 70, Modern Records Centre, University of Warwick, UK.
[19] 'The Development of the Union's 1978–1979 Wages Campaign, Low Pay Campaign,'

As the passage indicates, by mid-1978, public sector unions were now holding out for a general election in order to have the government spell out definite promises to benefit the low paid in its manifesto.

Even Callaghan's inner circle was led to believe that the election was to come that autumn. Tom McNally, one of Callaghan's closest political advisors, admits that he was misled by the Prime Minister into thinking that the election would be held soon:

> He [Callaghan] kept [the date] entirely to himself. He [Callaghan] slightly misled me. He once took out his diary [...] and said, 'I know the date of the election. I won't tell you because I don't think it would be fair.' And it was a 1978 diary he had in his hand.[20]

Callaghan's choice of a 1978 diary led McNally and members of the press to assume that, indeed, the election would be held in October 1978. Therefore, the announcement of the delayed election came as a bombshell to public sector unions. Their strategy of obtaining a 'commitment to end low pay' in the Labour Party manifesto had been undermined. There was now little incentive for public sector unions to maintain their loyalty to the Labour government and adhere to the Social Contract.

Ford workers' defiance of the 5 per cent pay norm simply exacerbated an already volatile situation. Days before Ford workers walked out of the gates of Halewood and Dagenham, the Low Pay Committee set out that 'The Union's negotiators should be instructed to inform the employers that, they could not agree to a settlement within the Government's 5 per cent guidelines.'[21]

On December 14, all major public sector unions agreed that January 22 would be the National Day of Action.[22] Soon thereafter, the press began to report on the negotiations. The government had offered unions £86 million, a deal that would have remained within the 5 per cent limit. Local authority manuals and hospital workers wanted a 40 per cent rise on basic rates, which

---

UNISON/Rodney Bickerstaffe papers, MSS 389/6/B/Box 93 File 1, Modern Records Centre. University of Warwick, UK.

[20] (Lord) Tom McNally, interview by author, November 2006.

[21] 'Minutes of the Meeting of the National Low Pay Campaign Committee held on Thursday 14 of September 1978 at the Bloomsbury, Centre Hotel, Coram Street, London, WC1,' Low Pay Campaign, UNISON/Rodney Bickerstaffe papers, MSS 389/6/B/Box 93 File 4, Modern Records Centre, University of Warwick, UK.

[22] 'Minutes of the National Low Pay Campaign Committee held on Thursday 14, December 1978 at the Bloomsbury, Centre Hotel, Coram Street, London, WC1,' Low Pay Campaign: MSS 389/6/B/Box 93, File 4. Modern Records Centre, University of Warwick, UK.

would result in a £60 basic weekly wage, two-thirds of the national average, and a 35-hour week, which was seen as a 'token' rather than a real demand.[23]

The rejection of the offer was rooted in long-standing issues of low pay among both men and women in Britain. David Bond, working in the local parks department in Solihull, earned a basic wage of £40, and £50 if he put in overtime. After the £11 a week he paid for his council home, little was left over for him and his family by the end of the month. Again, the extremely cold weather of 1978–79 shaped Bond's dissatisfaction with the £13 he paid for electricity and heating, 'If the winter gets much harder, we shall be stumped.'[24] Therefore, when NUPE General Secretary Alan Fisher spoke to the October 1978 Labour Party Conference in support of the £60 minimum wage, he explained how the government's pay policy and subsequent offers were sorely inadequate. He jibed sarcastically, '100 per cent of nothing is bugger all.'[25]

Despite the fixed date set for the strikes, unions and the government were still attempting to avoid a head-on conflict. Larry Whitty, a GMWU researcher at the time, explained that he and Derek Labben, a regional officer of the GMWU and 'very close to Jim Callaghan,' created a deal with basically 'money on the table and an inquiry.'[26] Whitty claimed that the union secretaries involved, David Basnett, Moss Evans, Albert Spanswick, and Alan Fisher, all informally agreed to the deal. Their assent did not automatically assure acceptance among the rank and file, and he supposes that Fisher himself would not have been able to sell the deal to his membership. Nonetheless, Whitty got the deal to No. 10 on Christmas Eve, 'which meant it was going to be another month because we had already given a date for the strike. [...] So they had a month to get out of it. The word came back very early in the New Year that there was no deal.'[27] David Lipsey, Head of the Political Office and Policy Unit during the Winter of Discontent, agreed that many deals were proposed:

> There were attempts to settle the threats of strikes in local government. I was in touch with Derek Labben and the GMWU about that. I think in retrospect – I think that neither of us understood what the other one was saying. They [unions] were saying, 'We want a deal, but you'll have to give us a bit more money.' And I was hearing them say, 'We want a deal. We will settle for what is available for low settlements.' No doubt there was

---

[23] 'Stand By for Rubbish in the Streets in January,' *Economist*, December 16, 1978, 117.
[24] 'How Do They Get By On £40 a Week?' *Guardian*, January 23, 1979.
[25] Williams and Fryer, *Democracy & Leadership*, 321.
[26] Whitty, interview with author, 2006.
[27] Whitty, interview with author, 2006. See also: Steve Ludlam, 'Old Labour and the Winter of Discontent,' *Politics Review* 9 (2000), 2–5.

disagreement over what was and wasn't an acceptable settlement. I don't think communication was great on either our part or on the trade union part. There were loads of attempts to finds ways out of this. And you're right – we were in shouting distance in January of 1979, but none of them crystallized.[28]

If any compromise was in the works, Callaghan showed no such indication in his New Year's address. 'Let those who possess industrial muscle and monopoly power resolve not to abuse their great strength. Individual greed and disregard for the well-being of others can undermine and divide our society.'[29]

Nevertheless, Callaghan was facing a new force in trade unionism. A growing membership within the public sector was feeling intense frustration with wages and poor conditions, and this discontent would explode in late January. General Secretary of the TUC at the time, Len Murray, emphasized that the Labour government's fortunes had been written long before January 1979. 'In the end,' he stated, 'it was the decision to batten down the hatches in the public sector that led to the uprising, to the so-called winter of discontent.'[30]

There was a last ditch effort on the part of the government to prevent the tide of public sector strikes heading their way. In the middle of January 1979, Cabinet discussions revealed that Denis Healey proposed 'introducing permanent comparability machinery,' and underpinning the 5 per cent policy with a £3.50 increase to help 'with the impending public service claims.' The reality of the incomes policy dissolving was not lost on the Chancellor as he declared, 'It was clear that this would be a general modification of existing pay policy, applicable to public and private sectors alike.'[31] Callaghan could not mask what was obviously a retreat from the incomes policy when he announced the deal in Parliament the next day.[32] Public sector unions rejected the deal because the £3.50 was seen to represent only a 'marginal concession and was £14 short of the minimum wage set out in the claim.' Continued concerns over comparability with the private sector also made them wary of the deal.[33]

Unions' rejection of the proposal only aggravated a problem that

---

[28] David Lipsey, interview by author, September 2007.
[29] 'Callaghan Talks of "This Year of Decision,"' *Guardian*, January 2, 1979.
[30] Ludlam, 'Too Much Pluralism,' 159.
[31] 'Cabinet Minutes and Conclusions,' 15 January, 1979, The Cabinet Papers, CAB/128/65/2, National Archives UK at Kew, UK.
[32] 'Battle Order: Boost for Lower Paid, Prices Curb, Public Service Pay Link: Premier Fights Pay Fever on Three Fronts,' *Guardian*, January 17, 1979.
[33] Williams and Fryer, *Leadership & Democracy*, 327.

Margaret Thatcher was already exploiting. After Callaghan's presentation in Parliament, 'Mrs Thatcher was the star of the debate,'[34] as she savaged his retreat on pay and attacked the issue of secondary picketing prevalent in the transport strike. Those in the media, like Peter Jenkins, also began to see the end of the 5 per cent pay policy:

> Oppositions don't win elections, government's lose them and the Callaghan government was busy losing the next election with the powerful assistance of the trade union movement.
> He [Callaghan] rattled once again the money supply, dispensed carrots to the low-paid, offered comparability studies to others in the public sector, and promised a bill to bone up the Price Commission.
> But these were mere patches to sew to the shreds of his government's pay policy. For the present reality is that the cooperation of the trade union movement for any kind of effective pay policy is lacking while the Government, as it nears the end of its days, has not the authority to govern without the active consent of organized labour.
> The probable result, however, of recent events is that the legal position of the trade unions is an open question once more in British politics. It has been reopened not so much by Mrs Thatcher's zeal but by the failure in its turn of the approach adopted by Labour after the Heath debacle of 1974.[35]

Again, at least in the media, the option of Thatcher as a viable alternative to Labour came more and more into focus.

Upheaval in Liverpool

The immediacy of the public sector disputes were rooted in the specific dynamics of the relevant unions. The Liverpool gravediggers' strike in particular has been seen as the result of left-wing trade unionism and shop floor irresponsibility at its worst.[36] However, the Liverpool gravediggers' trade union, the GMWU, was renowned for its political conservatism and its resistance to rank-and-file militancy. First of all, the GMWU had a long-standing relationship with the Right of the Labour Party. Throughout the post-war era, the GMWU had used their large number of votes in the Labour Party Conference to thwart any form of left-wing challenge presented to the Parliamentary leadership.[37] Second, the union was known

---

[34] 'Guidelines on Pay Relaxed: Callaghan Seeks Fresh Deal with TUC,' *Daily Telegraph*, January 17, 1979.
[35] 'With friends like this Jim needs no enemies,' Commentary, *Guardian*, January 17, 1979.
[36] John Golding, *Hammer of the Left: Defeating Tony Benn, Eric Heffer and Militant in the Battle for the Labour Party*, ed. Paul Farrelly (London: Politico's, 2003), 1.
[37] Richard Hyman, 'Trade Unions: Structure, Policies, and Politics,' in *Industrial Relations in Britain*, ed. George Sayers Bain (Oxford: Basil West Blackwell, 1983), 58.

for being devoid of rank-and-file activism and for its 'authoritarian (and nepotistic) leadership.'[38] In 1971, for instance, an internal survey revealed that 80 per cent of shop stewards went through no form of election, and only 35 were subject to re-election.[39] Furthermore, the GMWU was one of many unions that used the 'block vote system' where members who showed up to branch meetings could use the votes of those members who failed to show up.[40] Such an undemocratic decision-making structure manifested itself in 1969. That year Halewood workers transferred their membership *en masse* from the GMWU to the TGWU after the GMWU leadership refused to back the Ford strike.[41]

While still one of the largest and most powerful unions in post-war Britain, the GMWU's conservatism appeared to become a liability in the 1970s. It was now apparent that other unions were outpacing it in growth. From 1970 to 1978, the GMWU's membership grew by 13 per cent, but that was far lower than the TGWU's 26 per cent growth rate in the same period. Furthermore, unions like NUPE and COHSE were 'more effectively' organizing public sector workers, as both unions' membership exploded during the 1970s. From 1970 to 1978, NUPE's membership grew by 91 per cent, and COHSE's membership grew by 139 per cent.[42] During the 1970s, the GMWU faced the daunting task of shedding its reputation as the conservative, 'scab union.' It now had to confront the reality of diminishing numbers in membership and, with it, its influence in the trade union movement.[43]

The election of David Basnett as General Secretary in 1973 and growing pressure from the GMWU membership sought to reverse these trends. One of his first efforts was to devolve power from the rigid leadership structure while simultaneously putting more resources into serving and mobilizing the GMWU's rank and file. The first changes occurred in 1975, when for the first time in the GMWU's history, a lay majority was placed on the national executive of the union. Basnett also pushed to commit more resources to research, education, and health and safety representation for members and officials.[44] Changes emanating from the national leadership were coupled with pressure for change from the GMWU's rank and file. Whitty noted that the influx of workers into the GMWU was becoming 'a source of great

[38] Hyman, 'Trade Unions: Structure, Policies, and Politics,' 43.
[39] Robert Taylor, 'How Democratic are the Trade Unions,' *Political Quarterly* 47, no. 1 (January 1976): 35.
[40] Taylor, 'How Democratic are the Trade Unions,' 33.
[41] Hyman, 'Trade Unions: Structure, Policies, and Politics,' 43.
[42] Marsh, *The New Politics of British Trade Unionism*, 25.
[43] Ludlam, 'Labourism and the Disintegration,' 563.
[44] Hyman, 'Trade Unions: Structure, Policies, and Politics,' 43.

militancy within the union,' placing pressure on the national leadership to take more strident stands in terms of the wages and conditions of their members.[45]

Among the local authority workers the GMWU organized were gravediggers and crematoria workers. In the 1970s, harsh working conditions and low pay fed into a restlessness among these workers who had historically never been on strike. Relying on picks and shovels, gravediggers faced a backbreaking, and sometimes dangerous, work environment. Especially when digging in the north-west of England, the weather itself could make the conditions life-threatening. One gravedigger in Liverpool explained:

> When you dig a new grave you are covered in mud and slime. I have lost count of the times when the earth around me has caved in while I've been digging. Just when you think you've finished, you find yourself up to your neck again in mud. Every day of your life you run the risk of being trapped and smothered.[46]

The dangers involved in the job were magnified by the grim realities associated with working with decomposed bodies. 'Some of the older graves we have to reopen contain coffins that are old and broken. One minute you're clearing the soil the next minute your feet are going through wood and you find yourself staring at a decomposed body.'[47]

The nature of their work was not easily forgotten when they returned home. One gravedigger described how the smell of 'body water' lingered on his clothing after working, raising questions among his children as to the source of the odour.[48] Another worker agreed:

> At the end of the day there are no facilities for showering or any arrangements for having your clothes washed. We have to drive home or take a bus each night stinking. My wife is lumbered with my dirty overalls. You carry the smell of death to your home, and it never goes away.[49]

Furthermore, the workers believed that their pay provided no real compensation for such hard work. While the gross weekly pay for a gravedigger in 1979 was £47.65, the take home pay was £35 a week. Like other local authority and health service workers, overtime could serve to increase wages. For gravediggers, take home pay could increase to £50 a week if they worked

---

[45] Whitty, interview, September 2006.
[46] 'Low Pay-For a Filthy Job,' *Liverpool Echo*, February 2, 1979.
[47] 'Low Pay-For a Filthy Job,' *Liverpool Echo*, February 2, 1979.
[48] 'Mercifully there is a Lull in the Gravediggers' Dispute: REPRIEVE?' *Daily Post* (Liverpool), February 2, 1979.
[49] 'Low Pay-For a Filthy Job,' *Liverpool Echo*, February 2, 1979.

on the weekends.[50] Such low pay affected the everyday lives of the workers and their families. One 36-year-old gravedigger married with two children explained that he had only been able to take his wife out once in the last five years, and only had one pint a week 'for recreation.'[51]

Growing dissatisfaction with these conditions fuelled a push to elect more assertive local trade union leadership. This particular group of workers was to be led by a man who had been politicized by the trade unionism of Merseyside and influenced by the flourishing political culture of the late 1960s and early 1970s. The gravediggers' convener, Ian Lowes, noted that his trade union politics stemmed from his father's trade union activism before and after the Second World War. Lowes' father worked in the building industry as a carpenter in Liverpool. The seasonal nature of the work and employers' disregard for their workforce shaped his father's stalwart commitment to trade unions. When Lowes began to work with the local authority at the age of 19, his father's influential politics and his membership in the GMWU provided a foundation for Lowes' loyalty to trade unions.[52]

At the age of 23, he was elected shop steward of the local forestry branch. The everyday politics he encountered as a shop steward incited his activism. Again, like most local authority jobs, the low pay in Lowes' department could be somewhat offset by working overtime. However, in Lowes' section, the foreman always picked the same four men, his favourites, for overtime. In the pub after work, the other workers, including Lowes, were complaining about the unfair treatment and decided that they wanted somebody to confront the foreman, forcing him to institute a fairer distribution of overtime. Lowes related:

> So I said, 'We don't have a representative, have we? There's no one to go in and speak for us.' So they all look at me and say, 'You do it.' I said, 'It's not my job. I'm younger than most of you.' [They replied,] 'Well you just made the argument here. Why don't you go in on our behalf?

Lowes then convinced the four men always chosen to reject the foreman's request for them to work overtime. When this occurred, the foreman became aware that something was awry. He then spoke with Lowes, and they instituted a rota system for overtime. Lowes' stand against the foreman was the first step in his rapid accession among the rank-and-file leadership, and by the age of 27, he was the convener for the GMWU branch,

---

[50] 'Mercifully there is a Lull in the Gravediggers' Dispute: REPRIEVE?' *Daily Post* (Liverpool), February 2, 1979.

[51] 'Mercifully there is a Lull in the Gravediggers' Dispute: REPRIEVE?' *Daily Post* (Liverpool), February 2, 1979.

[52] Ian Lowes, interview by author, October 2006.

representing local authority workers, including those in the six cemeteries and two crematoria in the area.[53]

To assume that Lowes was representative of all the political currents in the GMWU would be incorrect. Not only did the GMWU sponsor Prime Minister Callaghan as an MP, but key political advisors were also brought up through the political hierarchy of this union. One such person was David Lipsey, an advisor in Callaghan's Policy Unit, and later the No. 10's Political Office in 1978 and 1979. Lipsey grew up in the Gloucestershire countryside; his parents 'voted Conservative in the 1959 Election, and they regretted it for the rest of their lives.' His ascent into politics was inspired both by a desire to right injustice and by personal ambition. 'You get into politics to either improve the lot of the human race or to fulfil personal ambition, which I certainly had at that stage.' An opportunity to work in the GMWU arose, and he soon began his two-year stint as a researcher 'because that's what all the young, ambitious people did at the time because that's where the power lay.'[54] Within this milieu Lipsey's 'Croslandite' or 'right-wing' Labour views had a chance to develop:

> I had always taken up right-wing views: that socialism was about equality – not about who owned the means of production, distribution, and exchange. And I didn't hold what were left-wing views on national policy. The left-wing, broadly, supported the Soviet Union and hated the Americans. I neither hated the Americans nor supported the Soviet Union.

After working for Tony Crosland from 1972 to 1977, Lipsey began to work for No. 10's Policy Unit, where he continued to work very closely with Derek Labben, who became a key conduit between the GMWU in 1978 and 1979. The contrasting political identities of Lowes and Lipsey thus reveal the ideological diversity within the labour movement on the eve of the Winter of Discontent.[55]

The National Day of Action scheduled for January 22, 1979, therefore, would be an outlet for these lingering tensions within the GMWU. Union strategists, however, had to maintain a balance between having a national impact, and not 'bankrupting the unions.' Therefore, the union would pull out key groups of workers to strike, while other members in the union continued to work and paid for those called out on selective action.[56] In order to employ this strategy, all of the public sector unions involved had

---

[53] Lowes, interview, October 2006.
[54] (Baron) David Lipsey, interview by author, September 2007.
[55] Lipsey, interview, 2007.
[56] Whitty, interview, 2006. See also: Williams and Fryer, *Leadership & Democracy*, 326.

local branches propose strike action, and the membership would have to approve the action by a two-thirds majority. If the proposed action passed, it was then delivered to the GMWU's national executive, where the action would either be rejected or approved. If the national executive approved the action, it would then be reported to the Regional Co-ordinating Committee, made up of full-time officials from the GMWU, the TGWU, and NUPE, approving or rejecting the proposed actions.[57]

Set within these parameters, both at the national and local level, union organizers also wanted to bring out new groups of workers out on strike. Whitty, who operated at the national level as a researcher, and Lowes, speaking from his experience at the local level, both agreed that in the past, bin men were often the only local authority workers brought out on strike. Not only did bin men feature prominently in the Dirty Jobs Strike of 1970, but they continued to be engaged in more minor disputes throughout the 1970s. Described by some as the 'praetorian guard' of local authority workers, bin men were able to cause a maximum amount of disruption that could effectively force local authorities to settle for unions' wage claims.[58]

In January 1979, bin men complained at a strike committee meeting in Liverpool that they were 'sick and tired' of being at the forefront of all such disputes. Convener Lowes described the scene:

> I remember going to the committee meeting, and everybody sat there, and the chairman of the committee said, 'Right. Well, can we have some suggestions as to who we're going to bring out?' Nobody spoke. Nobody said a word. I'm sitting there, bearing in mind that I'm 27 years of age. That is very, very young to be a convener. I'm sitting there, and I said, 'So what are you all waiting for?' And they said, 'Waiting for you.' 'What do you mean?' 'You've got the gravediggers. You've got the [crematoria workers]. Bring them out.' And so I said, 'Well, okay,' I said, 'but we're not going out on our own.' I said, 'If I bring them out, or I go and ask them,' because I had the power to bring them out, 'If I were to go and ask them to go and take part in strike action, I expect other groups to come out as well.'[59]

In exchange for this pledge of action by gravediggers and crematoria workers, the bin men agreed to close the tips once the strike began. All that was left was for the national executive of the GMWU and the Regional Co-ordinating Committee to approve the action. Lowes explained:

> So the application first went to the Executive. I think, personally, what

---

[57] Lowes, interview, October 2006.
[58] Stuart Hill and Linda Hoffman, interview by author, November 2006.
[59] Lowes, interview, July 2006.

had happened, the Executive delegated power to the General Secretary because you couldn't be dragging the Executive to meetings every day, so I would assume that the Executive would delegate responsibility to sanction strike action to the General Secretary in conjunction with the National Officer. So, we made our application to our Executive. They sanctioned the action, and then it would be reported to the Regional Co-ordinating Committee what we were doing.[60]

Despite Lowes' initial push to have this group of workers come out on strike, he did not believe that the national leadership would accept the proposal:

This was the first strike in history involving this type of worker. So it never happened before. [...] To be quite honest with you, I was surprised that they gave us permission in the first place. Because I knew how the [...] press was going to latch onto it. And they totally underestimated the venom that headed our way.[61]

Whitty confirmed that the national leadership approved the strike because unions were counting on the public support that emerged for workers in the Dirty Jobs Strike of 1970. He pointed to an extremely important shift in public opinion towards trade unionism and/or strikes that occurred from 1970 and 1979: the public sector unions' failure to accurately gauge this change further turned the tide of public opinion against them. 'We also gave some degree of authority to workers in Liverpool not to dig the graves. We didn't realize that it was a big mistake. We shouldn't have done it. It became obvious that we didn't have the public support that we had in the early 1970s.'[62]

No. 10 advisor David Lipsey concurs that higher-ranking officials in the GMWU were 'probably' aware of what was occurring in Liverpool:

Lipsey: I forgot that it was the GMB [GMWU] in Liverpool that did this [had the gravediggers go out on strike]. In any case, I am not sure that the union leadership had much control over what was happening at the grassroots level. Indeed, the GMWU official that was responsible for much of it was Derek Labben, but there wasn't much that we could do.

Martin: In an interview with Larry Whitty [from the GMWU], he did say that it [the Liverpool gravediggers' strike] got official sanction.

Lipsey: Well, often when you are a trade union official, you give official sanction to a group in order to try to maintain some measure of control and influence even though you don't like what they're doing. I would have expected, therefore, that the striking workers would have had union

---

[60] Lowes, interview, October 2006.
[61] Lowes, interview, October 2006.
[62] Whitty, interview, September 2006.

support because, otherwise, how could you organize an orderly return to work?[63]

It is evident in the gravediggers' vote to strike, and the GMWU's official sanction of the action, that the Liverpool gravediggers' dispute was not simply the act of 'irresponsible Left wing trade unionists of the Winter of Discontent,' nor was it the result of the 'bloody-minded' rank and file.[64] Instead, the strike was part of a co-ordinated national campaign to resist wage restraint for national trade unions, and it arose out of an action to address specific grievances on the part of the workers.

In Liverpool the strike was proving effective, and by February 1, 200 bodies were awaiting burial and being stored at a factory in nearby Speke.[65] It was humiliating and distressing for mourners. One woman, Brenda Pratt, appeared on the front page of the local *Liverpool Echo* with the story of her mother who had died on January 17. She explained, 'All I want is to give my mother a decent funeral she would have wanted. It is heartbreaking to think of her body lying in a coffin with hundreds of others in an old factory.'[66] Fellow trade unionists were also affected by the strike. NUPE shop steward Robert Gregory explained:

> My mother died, and I was involved with NUPE. [...] My mother was put in a warehouse, basically. In a coffin, in a warehouse, in Speke. And they said, 'We can't bury because of the gravediggers.' I got a special dispensation to bury my mother. She wasn't buried in the end. She was cremated. I had to go cap in hand basically. I had to do that unofficially because I couldn't do it officially 'cause if the press would have found out, they would have made a good meal of it.[67]

Both instances underline the fact that the strike did indeed have a powerfully traumatic effect on those families whose relatives could not be buried.

This local strike soon attracted national attention. On February 1, the *Daily Mail* cried: 'THEY WON'T EVEN LET US BURY OUR DEAD!'[68] Even more frightening was the *Sun*'s headline: 'STRIKE CITY MAY BURY AT SEA.'[69] Liverpool Local Area Medical Officer Dr Duncan Dolton provided the *Sun* reporter with this information, but in a later interview, he explained:

---

[63] (Baron) David Lipsey, interview by author, April 2008.
[64] Golding, *Hammer of the Left*, 1.
[65] 'Let Me Bury My Mother,' *Liverpool Echo*, February 1, 1979.
[66] 'Gravediggers to Resume Work,' *The Daily Telegraph*, February 2, 1979.
[67] Bob Gregory, interview by author, October 2006.
[68] *Daily Mail*, February 1, 1979.
[69] *Sun*, February 1, 1979.

> A newspaper reporter rang me up right as I was about to go home. And I was tired and upset for all that had gone on. And he said, 'What's going on? I gather that there are lots of unburied dead bodies lying around.' And I said, 'While it is a grave affront to the next of kin, this really isn't a public health problem. We have plenty of cold storage for weeks and months, if necessary.' And he [the reporter] sort of badgered me and said, 'Come on. Come on. If this goes on for months, what will happen?' I answer, 'If necessary, we'll have to bury them at sea.' Now to me that didn't sound strange. I had been a naval officer [...] and I thought that this was a dignified and honourable way of disposing of the dead. So I was absolutely astonished the next morning with the headlines: 'BURIALS AT SEA SAY MEDICAL OFFICER.' And I have to confess; I was horrified.[70]

The media frenzy soon became global in scale. Lowes described speaking to a friend in Australia about the strike:

> I mean I got friends in Australia, who were in Australia then, and I remember a conversation with a friend of mine in Australia. 'What's going on? There's bodies, dead bodies piled up in the streets.' I said, 'No.' [Lowes' friend] 'Well, that's what it said in the *Melbourne Times*' or whatever paper. I said, 'No.' Somebody actually sent me a news clipping in Buenos Aires. It was like epidemic fear in Liverpool with all these dead bodies just lying around. It's going to be like the plague or something.[71]

As is apparent, the media took hold of a strike that would make for a good story and ran with it. Unfortunately, the furore often distorted and confused the reality of what was actually occurring among these workers.

Politicians also attacked the strikers. After the Labour government released a statement on the picketing at graveyards and crematoria, Tory Lord Chancellor Lord Hailsham demanded that the names and addresses of the gravediggers in Liverpool be published. 'Isn't it time we knew the names and addresses, that they were published so that the public could bring to bear the full force of their anger?'[72]

Other workers' reactions could be just as hostile. Alan Cemetery, where the gravediggers were picketing, was on the way to the Ford Halewood plant, and Lowes recalls the reaction of Ford workers to the strike:

> Ford, being on strike, pushed the government's pay limits, and we had Ford workers hurling abuse at our pickets when we were on strike, and there was an irony there for them to go out on strike and break the govern-

---

[70] Duncan Dolton, interview in *Secret History: Winter of Discontent* (Brook Lapping Productions for Channel Four, 1998).
[71] Lowes, interview, October 2006.
[72] 'Picket "Abomination,"' *Guardian*, February 1, 1979.

ment's pay policy, but [we were] on half the wages they were on at Fords. There were threats of physical violence against the people that were on strike.[73]

Lowes' experience sheds light on the divisions within the trade union movement during the Winter of Discontent. Not only do these conflicts reveal that the trade union movement was not a monolithic entity, but it shows how these tensions ran along the lines of private and public sectors.

One striking gravedigger noted, 'We have only been out a short time, and there is already murder about it. We are not supposed to strike, just take what we're offered. But there are people, including some on the dole getting more than us, and telling us we should be at work.'[74] The Liverpool gravediggers and their families also faced threats and ostracism:

> We are emotionally disturbed. We know it is an emotional situation. We have been attacked by the Press, the public and in some cases, our own families. Our kids have been attacked at school. We live in fear of reprisals – our homes have been vandalised and bricks thrown at our windows.[75]

Some politicians attempted to defend these striking workers. In an attack on Environment Secretary Peter Shore, left-wing MP Dennis Skinner said, 'There is no one, but no one in this House who would do the job these people are doing for a take-home pay of £40 a week.' He accused MPs with only a few exceptions of 'indulging in a bout of utter hypocrisy.'[76]

The bitter public reaction to the strike triggered the government's moves to immediately quell a politically damaging situation. On February 1, 1979, Peter Shore personally intervened in the Liverpool strike to try and convince the men to return to work. The GMWU was also putting pressure on Lowes to call off the strike:

> They [GMWU leadership] gave us permission [to strike], but obviously when it got too hot for them, they said, 'You got to go back to work.' And this was only a couple of days after the strike had begun. I said, 'You gave us permission to go out on strike. This is part of the national dispute. If we go back to work now, what message is it going to send to other people that are out on strike?'[77]

The combination of this pressure, however, was successful, and the gravediggers voted on February 2 to return to work based on 'humanitarian

---

[73] Lowes, interview, July 2006.
[74] 'Mercifully there is a Lull in the Gravediggers' Dispute: REPRIEVE?' *Daily Post* (Liverpool), February 1, 1979.
[75] 'Low Pay-For a Filthy Job,' *Liverpool Echo*, February 2, 1979.
[76] Gravediggers' Strike Deplored,' *Guardian*, February 1, 1979.
[77] Lowes, interview, July 2006.

grounds.' However, the return to work was to be conditional. The workers warned that if there were no settlement including an improvement in wages and conditions, they would come out on strike in four weeks.[78] Although they voted to return to work, Lowes noted that the hostility they had faced had actually hardened, rather than diminished, the workers' determination to continue striking. He explained that 'once they got the bit between their teeth and suffered all the abuse they suffered, they became hardened to it.'[79]

While it is unfair that NUPE has borne the brunt of criticism for the Liverpool gravediggers' strike, in Tameside, just outside of Manchester, NUPE gravediggers did go out on strike. NUPE's National Local Government Officer at the time, Rodney Bickerstaffe explained that the then Northwest Regional Secretary of the area, Colin Barnett, 'would have notified [NUPE] Head Office of the [gravediggers'] strike, and either Bernard Dix or me would have approved the strike.'[80] On February 6 NUPE workers voted to return to work, but only after much conflict with a Conservative-controlled council. Only days before, the council had decided to use contractors and non-union labour to dig graves and operate the crematoria. NUPE's Barnett saw this as an affront and was quoted as saying, 'If they want to aggravate the situation, this is the way to do it.'[81] As in Liverpool, the strike came to a halt after Peter Shore's visit to the north of England. Bickerstaffe joined Alan Fisher up north to meet with Shore. Bickerstaffe related that

> Peter Shore had asked, 'What about the dignity of the dead?' And I was quite young then – I was 33 then – I said, 'What about the dignity of the living?' We had men digging through a foot of snow, January '79, through the turf, 6 feet through gravel, re-opening graves, and it was bitterly cold, and they were being paid a pittance.[82]

The intense focus on Liverpool, however, came to obscure the growing number of gravediggers' strikes across the country. Cemeteries in Wirral, Sefton, Southport, and Crewe all reported gravediggers and crematoria workers' strikes in late January and early February.[83] Durham county gravediggers (also part of the GMWU), employed by Sedgefield Council (later Tony's Blair's constituency), had also decided to come out on strike. They voted to return to work only after two bereaved families had broken

---

[78] 'Gravediggers to End Their Strike,' *Liverpool Echo*, February 2, 1979, 24.
[79] Lowes, interview, July 2006.
[80] Rodney Bickerstaffe, interview by author, June 2008.
[81] 'Tameside Moves to End Graves Strike,' *Guardian*, February 3, 1979.
[82] Bickerstaffe, interview, May 2006.
[83] 'Go Back, Grave Men are Urged,' *Liverpool Echo*, January 26, 1979.

the strike and dug the graves themselves.[84] Nor were the disputes confined to the north of England, as reports of such strikes emerged from places like Woking and Guildford.[85] GMWU gravediggers and crematoria workers in Plymouth were aware of the negative reaction a strike could trigger, so instead they offered to proceed with burials and cremations if undertakers agreed to give their services for free. Undertakers responded to the offer as 'ridiculous.'[86]

The moral outcry that engulfed the gravediggers' strike did little to stifle the upsurge of other public sector strikes across Britain. Nevertheless, the cacophony of denunciations of 'callous' workers, oversimplified the complex nature of their action and obscured how national trade union and political leaders had played a role in the strikes. The national response of the GMWU, however, subsequently faded from view, while the conviction that it was NUPE that had sanctioned the Liverpool gravediggers' strike died hard. NUPE fit the image of left-wing union, inciting bloody-minded rank and file to take industrial action. In reality, it was the GMWU, a much more conservative union, that was involved, and not solely at the local level. However, this proved an inconvenient truth in the construction of the larger narrative. We will return to the implications of memory and the gravediggers' strike in a later chapter, but now we must turn to another group of local authority strikes in schools and care homes. These strikes, dominated by women workers, played an integral role in the Winter of Discontent.

---

[84] 'Tameside Moves to End Graves strike,' *Guardian*, February 3, 1979, 24.

[85] 'NUPE Strike Bulletin,' February 2, 1979, Working Class Movement Library, Salford, UK.

[86] 'Tameside Moves to End Graves Strike,' *Guardian*, February 3, 1979, 24.

6

Unseemly Behaviour: Women and Local Authority Strikes

Local authority strikes, like that of the Liverpool gravediggers, represented only one of the myriad actions deployed in British public sector unions' co-ordinated actions during the Winter of Discontent. One key aspect of these disputes in particular, the involvement of women, has been relatively ignored in the literature.[1] Women working for local authorities, from school meals workers to assistants in care homes for the elderly, began to reveal themselves as a robust industrial force in the midst of these upheavals. For decades, local authorities in Britain experienced a rapid growth in female employment. From 1949 to 1974, employment in local authorities had risen by 110 per cent, and by 1974, women made up 1.5 million out of the 2.5 million workers employed by local authorities in Britain. Most of the jobs women took with local authorities, however, were concentrated in low-paid, part-time, unskilled, and semi-skilled manual jobs.[2] Since half of their entire membership was based in local authorities, NUPE was one of the leading public sector unions to confront the problems facing these women.[3]

It was NUPE's mobilization of its female membership in local authorities, therefore, that profoundly shaped the nature of the strikes of the Winter of Discontent. NUPE began to energize their female membership at a time when dynamic new ideas of trade unionism, participatory democracy, and women's liberation had burst upon the political scene. The effect

---

[1] Exceptions to this trend are: Sheila Cunnison and Jane Stageman, *Feminizing the Unions: Challenging the Culture of Masculinity* (Aldershot: Avebury, 1995); Sandbrook, *Seasons in the Sun*.

[2] 'The Struggle Against Cuts in Public Services: Background note for discussion at CSE Day School on Changing Forms of Working Class Struggle' R.H. Fryer, T. Mason, A. Friclough, R. Race/Given at Economics Department, Birkbeck College, 15 February, 1977, UNISON/Rodney Bickerstaffe papers, MSS 389 Box 16, Modern Records Centre, University of Warwick, Coventry, UK.

[3] Ludlam, 'Labourism and the Disintegration of the Postwar Consensus,' 669.

these larger social and political currents had on NUPE can most easily be understood by looking at key individuals involved in the union. By examining the evolution of their political identities in NUPE at this time one can begin to see that many of the changes in the union were rooted in broader shifts in the economy and political culture of 1970s Britain. National and local union leaders and activists alike were articulating a wider process of social transformation. This, in turn, shaped the local authority strikes of the Winter of Discontent. Again, the exceptionally frigid winter would not only underline the impact of these strikes, but would help to crystallize the resonance of this series of events in British collective memory.

The ability not merely to recruit, but to actively mobilize, working women required a radically new approach to organizing. NUPE had to contend with entrenched stereotypes of women workers as undercutting the male 'breadwinner' or simply earning 'pin money,' making many unions reluctant to organize them. Even when women workers were recruited into unions, they often became passive members, while their male counterparts took control of grassroots and more influential forms of leadership. This was a troubling problem for the union, especially in schools where male caretakers dominated union branches. This phenomenon 'created a tendency for hierarchy in the job relationship to carry over into union activity, to such an extent that the majority of the membership had difficulty in overcoming the dominance of supervisors in the union context.'[4] In the mid-1970s, the union would institute reforms to remedy this inequity with an eye on broader change in the labour movement. As Bernard Dix, Assistant General Secretary of NUPE, 'Once NUPE does it, others will rapidly follow suit. We will then be doing something not just for NUPE but women in the trade union movement in general.'[5] This vision for the union and society made NUPE distinctive among unions in this era. A trade union officer in another union once told NUPE trade union official Tom Sawyer that 'The trouble with NUPE is that is not a union: it is a campaign.'[6] Indeed, it would take more than a union, but rather a campaign to overcome the engrained and powerful obstacles to female activism in the trade union movement.

At the helm of this movement for change was NUPE General Secretary Alan Fisher, who took both the criticism and credit for leading one of the most powerful left-leaning unions in Britain. Prime Minister Callaghan, for instance, saw Fisher as a particularly 'appalling' leader and 'a Left-wing

---

[4] Williams and Fryer, *Leadership & Democracy*, 234.
[5] Williams and Fryer, *Leadership & Democracy*, 240.
[6] (Lord) Tom Sawyer, interview by author, June, 2006.

windbag.'[7] Such disdain for Fisher and NUPE was also tangible within the trade union movement. Frank Chapple, General Secretary of the EEPTU, 'spoke with justifiable contempt of Alan Fisher, adding that "most his members have never done a single fucking day's hard work in their lives."'[8] However, the intense focus on Fisher has obscured the pivotal role Bernard Dix played. Dix was the 'brilliant political bureaucrat'[9] behind all of NUPE's changes in the 1970s and the source of many of its left-wing politics and associations. The combination of Fisher and Dix created a very distinct dynamic that one *Guardian* journalist described as the 'Tweedledum and Tweedledee of the movement' in which Fisher was seen as the 'aggressive mouthpiece' and Dix 'the grand strategist.'[10] Robert Fryer, the academic who eventually led the study of the union's reorganization, notes the complex interaction of politics that came with Fisher and Dix's leadership:

> [The NUPE leadership] was a very pragmatic Left, deeply influenced by Bernard Dix and his own commitment to Marxism. But he had a very, very special relationship with the General Secretary [Alan Fisher], who was not a Marxist, who was on the Left of the Labour Party – Reformist – who was pushed more to the Left by the events of the 70s – certainly more than he had been in the early '70s.[11]

Dix's Marxism was not that of the Communist Party, however, but an 'independently-minded' Marxism inspired by the ideas of participatory democracy of the New Left with which Dix sought to infuse NUPE.[12] In his first speech to the TUC Congress in 1968, Dix outlined what he saw as the unique role unions played in society:

> More than at any time in our history, the trade unions are the centre point around which the labour movement operates. We can demonstrate to the workers of the world that trade unions can act as a mainspring of social and economic change and of a radical transformation of society.[13]

At the TUC General Council Meeting in 1974, Dix was much more succinct: 'We see trade unions not simply as fruit machines in which workers put tanners to get the jackpot; we see trade unions as agents of social change.'[14]

---

[7] James Callaghan quoted in Donoughue, *The Heat of the Kitchen*, 309.
[8] Frank Chapple quoted in Donoughue, *The Heat of the Kitchen*, 309.
[9] Judy Mallaber MP, interview by author, October, 2006.
[10] 'As action by local government workers looms, KEITH HARPER examines the reality behind NUPE's public image: The justified grievances of Britain's low paid workers,' *Guardian*, January 2, 1979.
[11] Robert Fryer, interview by author, June 2006.
[12] Stuart Hill, interview by author, September 2008.
[13] Williams and Fryer, *Leadership & Democracy*, 157.
[14] Bernard Dix quoted in Robert Taylor, *The Fifth Estate: Britain's Unions in the Seventies*

His approach to trade unionism marked him as a visionary to some, but as a 'political leper' to others as his ideas of change ran up against deep-seated attitudes in the labour movement.[15] Consequently, these currents pushed NUPE more and more in opposition to the political mainstream of the Labour Party and British trade unionism.

The project of infusing NUPE with new ideas resulted in the national leadership bringing on board a new generation of trade union officers from working-class communities. Fisher and Dix made a concerted effort to hire full-time officials who mirrored their progressive politics and were dedicated to NUPE's campaign ethic. The full-time officers entering NUPE at this time were seen as an 'awkward squad' of trade unionists because they were devoted to the labour movement, but they also had a desire to infuse the movement with new ideas, especially in regard to women workers.[16] The two men who would eventually come to lead NUPE in the 1980s and 1990s, Rodney Bickerstaffe and Tom Sawyer, embodied a new kind of 'enthusiasm.'[17] Their roots were in the new kinds of working-class communities in post-war Britain from which both had derived a critical awareness of both class and gender.

Bickerstaffe was only 19 years old when he began working as a NUPE officer in 1966, but his ties to NUPE ran deep. His mother, a NUPE activist, often took him to meetings when he was a young:

> My mum was a single parent mum, and I went wherever she went, and she was an activist in the union. So since childhood days, I knew NUPE branch meetings, area conferences and the lot. So when I came out of college, I either wanted to be the Prime Minister or the General Secretary of NUPE.[18]

Bickerstaffe's deeply personal connection to the British labour movement was transmitted through his single, service sector-employed mother. From an early age, he was acutely aware of the misperception that women's earnings were merely 'pin money':

> And people used to say it is only 'pin money' anyways, isn't it? These are women workers. The man is the breadwinner, so the woman should be pleased that she has a little bit to do during the day, instead of being bored stiff. It wasn't like that. But the view that women workers were

---

(London: Routledge & Kegan Paul, 1978), 87.

[15] Stuart Hill, interview by author, November 2007.

[16] Godfrey Eastwood, interview by author, May 2007.

[17] (Lord) Tom Sawyer, interview by author, June 2006. Sawyer repeatedly used the word 'enthusiastic' to describe himself and Rodney Bickerstaffe at this time.

[18] Bickerstaffe, interview, May 2006.

really second-class, third-class citizens was rife in the forties, fifties, and sixties.[19]

Sawyer's commitment to trade unionism, like Bickerstaffe's, was also steeped in personal experience. Born in north-east England, in Darlington, Tom Sawyer came from a tight-knit, working-class community:

> My mother was a domestic cleaner for rich people, you know. I didn't really like that much personally. My father was a labourer in a factory. No aspirations. No real quality of life, so I thought it was just a bit unfair, really. And I think that's what made me interested in trying to do something about it really. In a very broad sense.[20]

The acknowledgement of *both* his mother's and father's experiences of class underlines the significance of the evolving role that working-class women played in forming Sawyer's political identity. He soon followed in his parents' footsteps, and at the age of 15 he began to work in a factory. In the early 1960s, the factory closed, and Sawyer was made redundant. He and his family then settled in Coventry, where he found a job in the car industry at Jaguar. It was there that Sawyer came into contact with a Communist shop steward at the factory. 'And I used to watch him arguing with the boss, you know, and I thought, "This is interesting." I kind of liked the idea of having a go at the boss. It seemed like a good thing to do.'[21]

This shop steward played a key role in Sawyer's political development, and he began to 'devour' political books that the shop steward provided him. Still in his mid-20s, Sawyer returned to the north-east to work for Chrysler, but now he desired to act upon the political ideas he had been forming down in Coventry. While at Chrysler, he saw an advertisement in a magazine for full-time organizers for NUPE. He described his experience:

> I was ready to explore, really, with ideas and things, you know? I looked at the head of my union, and it was a lot of older men, and I thought, 'Well, I am never going to be able to fulfil my enthusiasm for like say working for a union.' Then, by chance, there was this union called NUPE that had been growing really rapidly and had been doing really well. And it was a newish type union. It had a new leader. He was recruiting lots of people [...] who hadn't been recruited in the union before. Mainly, they were women and part-time.[22]

Opposition to 'traditional mainstream' unionism dominated by these 'older

---

[19] Bickerstaffe, interview, May 2006.
[20] (Lord) Tom Sawyer, interview, June 2006.
[21] Sawyer, interview, June 2006.
[22] Lord Tom Sawyer, interview by author, November 2006.

men,' combined with the excitement of being involved in an active union, fuelled both Bickerstaffe's and Sawyer's nascent activism.

Gendered understandings of working-class politics were further emboldened by the strength of the Women's Movement in the early 1970s. Not only was the movement bringing attention to gender inequality affecting all women, but activists, many of whom were also influenced by socialism, were beginning to pay particular attention to the position of working-class women. Sheila Rowbotham described this reworking of feminist ideas:

> When women's liberation re-emerged as a movement in the 1960s, an optimistic liberal assumption that work, or more specifically, a career, was in itself emancipatory, prevailed. [...] The new movement opposed these ideas as having no relationship to the lives of working-class women, especially women with children.[23]

Socialist feminists began to develop a combined critique of inequality at work and the need for changes in domestic life and in the community. They supported women on strike, efforts to unionize unorganized women, and also pushed both issues of equality and social demands within the labour movement. Feminist artists also began to infuse their own work with issues affecting working women. Kay Hunt and Mary Kelly, for instance, documented work in a London factory in an exhibition called *Women and Work: A Document of the Division of Labour in Industry, 1973–1975*. One particularly salient image from the show in 1979 juxtaposed a woman in the middle of her shift, staring directly at the camera, with boldface print below exclaiming: 'We are 40% of the Workforce.'[24] This message resounded politically, too. From 1974, the Working Women's Charter presented a coherent front. The group's purpose was to unite women from the wider community and women in trade unions to 'improve the pay and conditions of low paid women and to make the Women's Liberation Movement relevant to their lives.'[25] Included in the Charter were ten points covering equal pay, improved day care, free contraception and abortion, and an overall call to 'to campaign among women to take an active part in the trade unions and in political life so that they may exercise influence commensurate with their numbers and to campaign among men trade unionists that they may work to achieve this aim.'[26] Obviously, these demands dovetailed with the outlook of many activists in NUPE.

---

[23] Rowbotham, *The Past is Before Us*, 182.

[24] Hackney Flashers, Poster from Women at Work show 1979, in Hatje Cantz, *Goodbye to London: Radical Art & Politics in the 70s*, ed. Astrid Proll (Germany: Hatje Cantz Verlag, 2010), 162.

[25] Cunnison and Jane Stageman, *Feminizing the Unions*, 29.

[26] '10 Points of Working Women's Charter' quoted in Boston, *Women Workers and the Trade*

As a result, many of the women who became involved in NUPE during the 1970s were influenced by this commitment to both class and gender equality. Among them was Linda Perks, who began her work with the union during the Winter of Discontent. She explained how her exposure to ideas from the Women's Movement shaped her approach to trade unionism. During the early 1970s, she was 'very influenced by the Women's Movement – not as a political party – [it was] more just the climate of the time.' Trade unionism was also part of her family heritage. Perks' father was the chairman of the local Post Office and Engineer's branch in Bradford where she was raised. Not only the conversations she had with her father about his involvement in the union, but her entire family's loyalty to the labour movement influenced her to become involved in the local trades council in Durham when she was a student at Durham University. Perks described how her family background intersected with a 'social climate' permeated by ideas from the Women's Movement. Her activism during the Winter of Discontent, and deepening involvement in NUPE, would bear the mark of an awareness of both class and gender.[27]

The influence of the Women's Movement further provided a badly needed framework to address the issue of gender inequality in NUPE. Although the membership was predominately female, its male minority dominated positions of leadership both locally and nationally. NUPE shop stewards in Middlesbrough Stuart Hill and Jeane Hall noted how male caretakers of the schools dominated the branches that were made up primarily of women workers. Hall, a school cleaner, was the only female shop steward in those branches:

Hill: When you became involved, I seem to remember that there were quite a number of [male] caretakers that were shop stewards.

Hall: Oh yes. Caretakers were.

Hill: But there was only you [as a female shop steward]. Caretakers, as a rule, there was one in each school, but in the bigger schools, there might be a couple. But the number of [female] cleaners was always bigger than the number of caretakers. And [female] school meals workers, there were big groups of school meals workers, and there were no school meals workers amongst the shop stewards at all!

Hall: No. No. We [cleaners] used to do it for the school meals as well.[28]

Unions, 299.

[27] Linda Perks, interview by author, September 2007.

[28] Jeane Hall and Stuart Hill, interview by author, March 2007. Cunnison and Stageman also detail the disproportionate dominance of male caretakers in NUPE and the GMWU at the time in *Feminizing the Unions*, Chapter 5.

Male caretakers' dominance of branches was prevalent throughout NUPE nationally, not just in the north-east of England. In north London, male caretakers dominated branch meetings because they were 'in a relatively privileged position vis-à-vis other groups of workers because of bonus payments, and rent-free and rate-free accommodation.'[29] As a result of the disproportionate numbers of men in positions of leadership, feudalistic relationships developed between the male shop stewards and the female lay membership. At one union meeting in Darlington, for instance, a male shop steward explained that his members were not going to take any strike action. When others pressed how his members voted, 'He just said, "I haven't had a meeting with the women because [I] knew what [my] women would do and what [my] women wouldn't do."'[30] These examples illustrate how the mere fact of attempting to mobilize more women in NUPE would also have to disentangle the underlying power structure that stifled women's activism.

Fisher and Dix's reorganization of NUPE in 1974 made the union better able to respond to this systematic problem of gender inequality in the union. The two leaders employed an academic research team from the University of Warwick to restructure the union, with the 'aim of widening and deepening membership participation in the union.'[31] The question of democratizing representation was inextricably intertwined with gender subordination. In the *Warwick Report*, the lack of participation among women that made up the majority of NUPE's membership assumed a central focus. The study showed that although women made up 65 per cent of the lay membership, they represented only 26 per cent of all NUPE shop stewards.[32] Women were similarly outnumbered at the regional and national level. In 1974, out of the 100 branch secretaries in the country, only ten were women, and of the 93 area conference delegates in 1974, only 16 were women.[33] The study did not assume that women's inactivity in the union was a result of 'women's nature.' Instead, the *Warwick Report* asserted that such under-representation

---

[29] John Suddaby, 'The Public Sector Strike in Camden: Winter '79,' *New Left Review* 116 (July–August 1979): 84.

[30] Anne Gardiner and Stuart Hill, interview by author, November 2006.

[31] *Progress on Reorganization*, 1976, MSS.389/6/B/Box 16/, UNISON/Rodney Bickerstaffe Papers, Modern Records Centre, University of Warwick, UK.

[32] Bob Fryer, Andy Fairclough, Tom Manson, Brenda Waller, *NUPE ReOrganisation-*Warwick University Research Project, Department of Sociology, Statistical Appendix II: *Union Stewards* (based on a survey taken between May and June 1974), MSS.389/6/B/Box 16, UNISON/Rodney Bickerstaffe Papers, Modern Records Centre, University of Warwick, UK.

[33] *1981 Survey of Branch District Committees: 1st Report*, MSS.389/Box 5, UNISON/Rodney Bickerstaffe Papers, Modern Records Centre, University of Warwick, UK.

had 'to do with the position of women in the wider society and at work.'[34] If the broader vision of democratic control had inspired union restructuring, the report also raised issues of gender and democracy in society at large.

Obstacles to mobilizing NUPE's rank and file were obviously numerous and complex; therefore, the leadership's changes had to be similarly concerted and multifaceted. This strategy included increasing women's influence at the national and local level; transforming the union culture to encourage women's activism; and bringing on key, politicized women into the union. The first of these changes was institutional. In 1974, there were no women on the Executive of NUPE, so, as a result of the findings of the *Warwick Report*, five spaces on the Executive were reserved for women. Furthermore, encouraging women to become more active members, shop stewards, branch secretaries, etc. now became an integral part of paid officers' job.[35] After 1974, NUPE began to produce union literature specifically targeted at women members; created women-only education courses; and began education courses for part-time workers.[36] Such structural changes were complemented by efforts to recruit politicized women at the national level of NUPE. One such person was 24-year-old Judy Mallaber, who began to work as a research assistant to Bernard Dix in 1975:

> I joined at the phase also when the union had been undergoing restructuring – to try to integrate – to try to get activists more involved and try to get the activists more active. And positive discrimination to try to get more women involved – to try to bring more women at the national and local level.[37]

Mallaber brought with her a very politicized personal background, in which the Women's Movement played a key role:

> I was brought up in an argumentative household. My dad was a solid Labour man. He had been a Labour Party agent in 1945 after the war. He had been a conscientious objector during the war. [...] I wasn't active when I was growing up, but I was always a solid Labour person. My grandparents – you know – were very political. My mother came from the Welsh borders, which was [...] Liberal territory. [...] I grew up with arguments around the news. My sister was very argumentative, so I grew up with the assumption at the time that I would always be a Labour supporter. And then I supposed I got consciously involved through the

---

[34] *Organization and Change in NUPE*, 1974, MSS/389/Box 5, UNISON/Rodney Bickerstaffe Papers, Modern Records Centre, University of Warwick, UK.

[35] Wrigley, 'Women in the Labour Market and the Unions,' 60. See also: Cunnison and Stageman *Feminizing the Unions*, 70.

[36] Cunnison and Stageman *Feminizing the Unions*, 70.

[37] Mallaber, interview.

Women's Movement – when I was young and bold and involved in various Women's Liberation campaigns.[38]

The changes that occurred at the institutional level in NUPE were the result of a combination of different political influences. Out of this mix, two consistent themes arise. First, 1960s and 1970s social movements infused NUPE with a new political energy that shaped their approach to trade unionism, refocusing 'traditional trade unionism' upon issues of gender and democracy. Second, while emanating from different social and cultural contexts, personal ties to trade unionism and Left politics were significant in shaping the labour politics of these NUPE officials. These influences further fuelled NUPE's momentum, which only grew in force with an equally impassioned and politicized rank and file.

A new generation of local activists was emerging who were shaped by the distinctive shifts in working-class communities in post-war Britain. One such woman was school meals worker Betty Hughes, who became a NUPE shop steward in 1968. Hughes' gradual move into activism had its roots in her upbringing in the north-eastern city of Middlesbrough soon after the Second World War. Like many people, her first experience with politics came from her parents. Hughes recounted that her father was not political, but that when working in the United States as a member of the Canadian Merchant Navy, he was galled by the treatment of an African-American friend:

> And he used to stock the boilers for my father because my father was an engineer, you see? So he was a friend because they worked together. And he went to get on one of the buses in – Oh, I don't remember where he said it was. And they wouldn't let the lad on. So my father said, 'If he's not getting on, then I'm not getting on.' You know? [...] He used to say, 'They're just the same as us. They got the same colour blood as us.' Because he mixed with them, you see? So, that's as much as I knew of how my father was motivated.[39]

The effect of her mother's politics was also apparent at an early age. 'My mother – she was a bit like me: she stood her ground. But she wasn't political. The only thing political about her was when the voting came. She used to warn us. She used to say, "Don't you dare vote Conservative. You're Labour."'[40]

In her late teens, Hughes began to work fusing wires on telephones at the local General Electric Company and continued to work there part-time after

[38] Mallaber, interview.
[39] Betty and Joe Hughes, interview by author, March 2007.
[40] Betty and Joe Hughes, interview.

she got married. The marriage, unfortunately, was an abusive one; however, it was pivotal in shaping her politics:

> He busted my nose no end of times because he was violent! And he would come in, and, funny enough, it was a Saturday when the break eventually came. And he'd been out, and he'd come in, and he just swiped everything off [the mantlepiece]. Ornaments. Everything. Then started on me. By then, I was cooking his tea, wasn't I? I had a frying pan, so he got the lot. And the frying pan as well. [...] Then, he just went berserk. The two neighbours saw out at the back because he had me outside on the drive. And that was the end of that, and I divorced him.[41]

After she divorced, she found part-time employment as a school meals worker and later joined NUPE. At the time, school meals workers made up the largest occupation group in the union.[42] Hughes believed the divorce and the social ostracism she later endured for being a single mother emboldened her activism in NUPE:

> And I think that's why I got involved in the union, because I would stand up for myself. I wouldn't let anybody put me down. Because when you're on your own [...] in a one-parent family years ago, they put you down. The officials. The workplace. Everything. And if you weren't strong enough to stand up for yourself, you just went under. But by then, I stuck up for myself and thought, 'Nobody's gonna try and put me down.'[43]

Her divorce was also part of changes that were affecting British society in the late 1960s. For example, divorce rates between 1970 and 1979 tripled for people under the age of 25, and doubled for people over the age of 25. This high divorce rate had a direct impact on the rise of lone motherhood in Britain, a trend that more than doubled from 1970 to 1990.[44] Circumstances as well as feminist pressure were changing attitudes to childcare. Working mothers were speaking up for themselves. Letters to the editor in British newspapers in the 1960s and 1970s reflect this mood. One wife and mother wrote to the *Manchester Evening News*:

> I love my husband and son very much but for financial reasons, I have to work. Nurseries are not places to 'stick children' – the children are exceptionally well cared for [...] Life is not that easy for working mothers.

---

[41] Betty and Joe Hughes, interview.
[42] Williams and Fryer, *Leadership & Democracy*, 258.
[43] Betty and Joe Hughes, interview.
[44] Rowbotham, *A Century of Women*, 432. See also Jane Lewis and Kathleen Kiernan, 'The Boundaries between Marriage, Nonmarriage, and Parenthood: Changes in Behavior and Policy in Postwar Britain,' *Journal of Family History* 21, no. 3 (July 1996): 372–387.

> We have to cook, clean, shop, wash, iron and run the home in the same way as any other housewife, but with less time in which to do it.[45]

Although the north-west had a long tradition of women working, similar shifts in divorce, parenthood, and work were evident in the lives of working-class women in other parts of Britain, too. Betty Hughes' experiences were part of this larger picture.

She eventually remarried Joe Hughes, a shop steward in the TGWU from a nearby steel factory, ten years later. Betty Hughes' resilience and her husband's encouragement of her activism allowed her work as a shop steward to flourish. Her responsibilities then began to develop. In order to counterbalance the preponderant influence of professional people, NUPE officials nominated manual workers to the courts, and in 1977, NUPE put her name forward to become a magistrate. Being a magistrate provided Hughes with an unprecedented opportunity for leadership in her community, but it also exposed her to the lingering class prejudices that persisted in Britain:

> One of the Magistrates said to me she didn't know I worked in the school kitchen. And she was talking in the cloakroom, and she said she'd only been appointed, maybe a couple of months she'd been appointed. And she said to me, 'What job did you do, Betty?' I said, 'I worked on the school meals.' 'Oh, so you're a cook supervisor?' 'No,' I said, 'I used to peel potatoes, cook 'em, chip 'em, fry 'em. Any job (*laughs*) you did.' She said, 'Ohhh.' She said, 'Ohhh. Well that's strange. How did they appoint *you*?'[46]

During the 1970s NUPE women and men were more active within the union and in the outside community. These experiences were sometimes painful, but they also contributed to a much greater confidence that was essential to increasing their influence in NUPE.

In nearby Darlington, Anne Gardiner became a shop steward in NUPE later in 1978. Like Betty Hughes, many of Gardiner's family traditions were important to her political development. Although Gardiner's father was Conservative, Gardiner followed more in the footsteps of her grandmother, who was a Labour supporter:

> I was a political person because my grandma had been brought up in Durham. [My grandmother's] father was a miner, and she was very political. [...] If there were any jumble sales, my grannie used to bake for

---

[45] N.A. Gladstone, 'Postbag' (letter to the editor), *Manchester Evening News*, January 15, 1979.

[46] Stuart Hill, Betty and Joe Hughes, interview by author, November 2006.

them – for the Labour Party. And she used to always have the Labour stickers in the window.[47]

After Gardiner left school, she began working in a nearby factory, but stopped working when she was 17 years old and married. She returned to paid employment at the age of 34 as a care assistant in a care home for elderly people. There she was forced to work under a matron who constantly terrorized the staff. The interpersonal relations among the women at the home shaped her consciousness:

> I wasn't particularly mouthy in those days. I was quite quiet, but I couldn't – I couldn't appreciate how grown women could work with a woman they were terrified of. She [the matron] would get women in their 50s crying, shaking. You know. And I couldn't appreciate that. When she went, we used to talk about her and everything, but when she sat and carried on, they all used to run! You know! Put down their tea. Sometimes you never got a tea break. You used to get a cup of tea made, and she used to come down, and they all used to scatter. And I couldn't understand how women – grown women – would let somebody like that reduce them to nothing![48]

Gardiner describes when she fought back against this matron:

> One day I just flipped! And she [the matron] started. And you know after you've said your piece, you usually back down, don't you? But I didn't back down this day. [*laughs*] And I followed her. No! She followed me, and she kept going on. And I was giving her hell all the way. I wouldn't back down. And all the girls, it was a talking point for weeks how I mastered her! They said I mastered her! She had to walk away. She had to go upstairs into her flat. But I thought, 'If I'd given in, she would have broken me as well.' But she didn't. She tried – two or three times.[49]

The way she had 'mastered' the matron impressed Gardiner's co-workers, and they eventually voted Gardiner as shop steward. Like Hughes, the union became a means for Gardiner to articulate an underlying desire for respect and dignity in the workplace. Dorothy Sue Cobble notes a comparable impetus among American women forming clerical unions in the 1970s: they 'wanted their personhood acknowledged.'[50] Cobble's observation applies equally to British women in the public sector in the same period. 'Personhood' for these women was not confined to the workplace. Their

---

[47] Anne Gardiner and Stuart Hill, interview by author, March 2007.
[48] Gardiner and Hill, interview.
[49] Gardiner and Hill, interview.
[50] Dorothy Sue Cobble, '"A Spontaneous Loss of Enthusiasm": Workplace Feminism and the Transformation of Women's Service Jobs in the 1970s,' *International Labor and Working Class History* 56 (Fall 1999): 31.

personal and public lives were interconnected. In Hughes' case, her first marriage contrasted starkly with her second. Gardiner, on the other hand, found that her nascent activism at work led to domestic conflict. She recalled how the fight with her husband to be an active shop steward constituted a major challenge for her. 'The battle with my husband [was also important] because I wanted to be a shop steward. I wanted to go out and about and do things that he didn't really approve of. You [as a woman] didn't really go out and do things.'[51]

Hughes' and Gardiner's accounts give an indication of how union restructuring created important openings for women. They also provide a glimpse of how these structural changes were accompanied by myriad acts of individual defiance. Both help to explain women's participation during the strike of January 1979.

Therefore, multiple dynamics coalesced within NUPE, making it a cutting-edge union, bursting with new politics and groups of workers eager to find their footing in the labour movement. As the end of January 1979 came around and public sector action against the government's policy commenced, this restlessness would soon find expression. Nevertheless, this budding militancy would also make NUPE a target for those opposed to their politics and methods.

Strike

Spurred on by the numbers and solidarity demonstrated on January 22, school workers began to take part in thousands of strikes across the country. By January 30, strikes by caretakers and school meals workers were instrumental in closing 170 schools in the London boroughs of Barking and Waltham Forest, and in the north east strikes closed 1,300 schools in places like Newcastle and Sunderland.[52] In Birmingham, school meals worker Maureen Groves noted the reasons for this massive show of force. As the wife of a lorry driver and the mother of four children, she revealed the gendered character of the desperation that led many women to rebel. 'Women would work for next to nothing because it's a little bit extra. The authorities know that. We couldn't afford to give up the job even if we are low paid. That's why they don't bother about our jobs [in local authorities].'[53] While inspired by the numbers of school meals workers involved in the January 22 demonstration, and in the number of strikes across the country,

---

[51] Anne Gardiner, interview by author, November 2006.
[52] 'Government Promised "Hammering" on Pay,' *Guardian*, January 30, 1979.
[53] 'No More Making Do … We Want a Living Wage,' *Women's Voice* 26 (February 1979): 10.

Groves pointed to the challenge of maintaining enthusiasm among women who had never taken industrial action. 'As long as we keep together, we've got a chance of winning. They're always underestimating women, saying they won't stick together. I hope we stick together in our school.'[54]

When the strikes began, public sector unions established strike committees made up of representatives from the public sector workers involved in the dispute, the TGWU, the GMWU, and NUPE, to be in charge of the planning of industrial action. These committees wielded significant power. For instance, the Cleveland county strike committee alone brought out up to 7,000 manual workers on strike by the beginning of February 1979.[55] On January 22, Middlesbrough's *Evening Gazette* reported that talks between fire and police chiefs and local unions broke down over the chiefs' insistence that, despite the strike, the local authority work of road clearing and gritting be maintained 'to keep open major routes needed in the event of disaster.' The unions refused to grant this request, so the strike committee became the 'Dispensation Committee,' which would consider requests for local authority work on an individual basis.[56] NUPE shop steward and Communist Party member Stuart Hill describes the strike committee:

> You have to imagine that the headquarters was the 'command centre' of the strike, you know. So messages would be coming in from the different picket lines. [...] And we had a *massive* system of intelligence gathering. [...] It was amazing. It's very, very difficult for people to understand the extent to where if people saw anything they thought might be trying to undermine the strike, they'd be on the phone to us. And some of the people that were ringing us up for information: they were police officers, fire officers, people from the NHS service. You know. We'd get, 'We got to take our ambulances to so, so, and so because the road's going to be gritted. We just thought you should know just in case they're trying to get blacklegs to grit the roads.'[57]

Hill's account provides an important counterpoint to the image of the Winter of Discontent as a chaotic upsurge of militancy. Instead, his description of the strike committee reveals that striking workers not only developed a highly sophisticated level of co-ordination, but also received support from the wider community.

It was Betty Hughes' work on the Dispensation and Strike Committee that provided her the unprecedented opportunity to exert leadership in the

---

[54] 'No More Making Do ... We Want a Living Wage,' 10.
[55] 'Unions to Bring in Guerrilla Tactics,' *Evening Gazette* (Middlesbrough), February 10, 1979.
[56] 'Chaos as Services Grind to a Halt,' *Evening Gazette* (Middlesbrough), January 22, 1979.
[57] Hill, Betty and Joe Hughes, interview.

union, and gave her the nickname 'Battling Betty.' Late one evening, in the middle of a blizzard, the Chief Executive of Cleveland county banged on the door of the Strike Committee, demanding that they have the roads gritted:

> Hill: She [Betty Hughes] wouldn't let the Chief Executive in, and there was a blizzard going on.
>
> Martin: What did you tell him when he tried to come in?
>
> Betty Hughes: 'No! You're not coming in! This is *our* place. If you want anything, just tell me, and we'll go back and decide.' I never got into trouble for that, though.
>
> Joe Hughes: That's when you got stronger.[58]

Hughes' confrontation with the Chief Executive was a transformative opportunity for her to simultaneously exert and develop more confidence in labour militancy. The extraordinary circumstances of the Winter of Discontent allowed for this overturning of customary relationships of hierarchy and power.

Such demonstrations of new-found confidence, however, resulted in the services not being delivered, evoking ire among some members of the public. One individual from Bristol wrote to Prime Minister Callaghan, 'I am an old age pensioner and cannot get out through the roads not being gritted and the risk of falling and breaking a limb and probably no ambulance service available.'[59] Mrs Clark from Billericay, Essex, explained that her family had been socialist their entire lives, but she 'vowed to never to vote for you (Labour) again.' She decried Labour's lack of action, in regard to the strikes, while, 'Here we are, our everyday lives in disruption, with no services, no goods in the shops, no rubbish collections, no paper, no ambulance men, no hospital services.'[60] Hughes' experience and the responses of the public reveal the sometimes conflicting perspectives of the strike.

Newly elected shop steward and Strike Committee member Anne Gardiner in Darlington led strike action in an even more delicate work environment: elderly care homes. Gardiner took this lead for a variety of reasons. She was encouraged by paid officials in NUPE who were providing women like Gardiner with more chances to become active. Also, a leadership void was

---

[58] Hill, Betty and Joe Hughes, interview.

[59] Mr Ripley, Wallingford, Oxon., *NEC Minutes Part 10: Apr. 1974–Dec. 1983* (Microfiche), Archives of the British Labour Party, Labour History and Archive Study Centre, Manchester, UK.

[60] Mrs Clark, Billericay, Essex, *NEC Minutes Part 10: Apr. 1974–Dec. 1983* (Microfiche), Archives of the British Labour Party, Labour History and Archive Study Centre, Manchester, UK.

appearing because seasoned officers and shop stewards were reluctant to take industrial action:

> Hill: It's no use having – they weren't falling over themselves to get the position [on the Strike Committee]. And there was a certain kind of feeling – I would say – from the older, more experienced branch officials, some of them were sort of fairly lazy or didn't want to fall out from the Council. They were coming up to retirement. All that sort of thing.
>
> Gardiner: They took a back seat. Didn't they?
>
> Hill: I think that there was also a fear that after the strike there would be retribution.[61]

On the Darlington Strike Committee, Gardiner and the other members decided that they would only have three men from the local depot come out on strike. Therefore, with the three key people pulled out on strike, the union would have a maximum amount of effect without bankrupting the union or pulling out service workers upon whom patients depended:

> They organized a Strike Committee and because I was the only woman that was involved with the social services, their representative, I became involved in the Strike Committee. I got really into that. I enjoyed the hassles and the fighting. Then, of course, I think I proved myself, with the men.[62]

Gaining more confidence from her work on the Strike Committee, and because of increased pressure from the branch to have women in social services come out on strike, Gardiner sought to figure out a way to mobilize these women. Her efforts were aided by Linda Perks, then an activist on the local Durham Trades Council, who was volunteering with NUPE during the Winter of Discontent. Perks explained that the branch wanted the social service workers to 'just strike.' Gardiner and Perks, however, refused to call for action that could potentially harm patients. Gardiner, therefore, forewarned care home managers that assistants were coming out on a one-day strike, so emergency cover could be made for the elderly in the homes. Darlington's local newspaper, the *Northern Echo*, quoted the Chairman of the County Council, Roy Robinson in regard to the emergency cover to be provided. 'There will be difficulties in homes for old people and children but the staff not on strike will do their best to maintain a normal level of care for the residents. Voluntary organizations and relatives of residents are being contacted to help.'[63] Gardiner reflects that many of the

[61] Gardiner and Hill, interview.
[62] Gardiner, interview.
[63] 'Schools Hit Again By NUPE Strike,' *Northern Echo* (Darlington), January 17, 1979.

patients themselves supported the strike. 'The old people were telling us to go. They would say, "No, go. Go. You've come this far." Because they came from the harder times, of course. They had been in the war, the First World War, so they were saying, "No, go. Just go."'[64]

Perks stated that creating new ways for these women to strike was key to sparking a new era of labour activism:

> That sort of microcosm reflected a whole new approach in how you would approach organizing women workers who were caring for people because we had to import thinking from people who were working in the hospital branch. And it was probably key in developing a more assertive union organization amongst the women in local government because the union began to realize that you couldn't have the standard male tactics all out. You had to be more subtle and sophisticated.[65]

Some shop stewards in the branch opposed the strikes in the care homes and laid the blame directly at Gardiner's feet. Fellow Darlington shop steward Brian Whattam observed:

> As I say – she [Anne Gardiner] wanted to make a name for herself, in my opinion, and that was my opinion, and that was the way she was going to do it. She conned George [Branch Secretary] into going up one morning, assuring us that all the staff were going out on strike and going to leave the old people. And what a publicity stunt it would be! The Branch Secretary cooking the breakfasts. And I told George, 'I'm not going to the home!' I didn't want to be involved in it. I sat in the car, and I didn't go in. And none of the staff had any intention of going out at all.[66]

The opportunity to take a more central role in the strikes also made these women more visible targets for public backlash. Any such disputes, no matter how carefully planned, would inevitably make a negative impression on the public. The antagonistic response was not simply a matter of being anti-union. Mrs Pierce from Greater Manchester wrote in a letter to the editor of the *Manchester Evening News*:

> Why do such workers expect as their right, more money than is sufficient to provide them with three meals a day and a roof over their heads?
>
> It would seem to me, from my own humble position in society, that the humbler-positioned NUPE members could be quite satisfactorily substituted by robots, or parallel devices, were this country not so Neolithic in employing real Government tactics.

---

[64] Gardiner, interview.
[65] Interview with Linda Perks, September, 2007.
[66] Brian Whattam, November 2006.

The infamous four words, 'Let them eat cake,' seem peculiarly justified here – I wonder why? They were once quite undeserved.[67]

At times, members of the public would take matters into their own hands and defy the strikes. In the London borough of Haringey, for example, a group of parents tried to make their way into Creighton Comprehensive School while it was closed due to a caretakers' strike, but ran into a counter-demonstration of caretakers, school meals workers, and teachers who thwarted their efforts.[68]

Action among local authority workers also provided challenging situations for Labour councils. Their sympathies with the labour movement had to be balanced with assuring that essential services were provided to the public. Alf Illingsworth, who was the Chief Personnel Officer for Middlesbrough Council, describes such difficulties:

> The intensity of the action was taking place [...] in the majority of Labour councils. And the Labour councils used to say, 'Hey, Alf, how is that here we are, a Labour-controlled council, with all the relationship and sympathy that we have with the trade union movement, yet we're getting the sticky end of the stick. Why is that?' And I said, 'Because you're living in a culture – You're living in an environment where the majority of people are Labour, and they believe in the trade union movement. They believe in the labour movement.' It was like a religion. And it was all-powerful because it transmitted itself through the family. The whole family believed in the Labour Party, and, therefore, it was right, or this is what the trade union thought we should be doing, a bit like the coal mining culture: very collective, very community organized. So I knew that most of the people I was working with were Labour people anyway.[69]

Sometimes the backlash would be directed specifically at individuals who had come out on strike. Anne Gardiner noted that 'older fellas' at clubs would shout at her and other striking women, 'You should be ashamed of yourselves as women. The way you're carrying on! It wasn't right! Women don't do things like that.'[70] On one occasion during the strike, Tom Sawyer, Regional Officer in the north east by that time, was confronted with hostility. While at a nearby corner shop, one man spat at him and yelled, 'You are calling these strikes! You are ruining the country!'[71]

---

[67] Mrs Pierce, 'Postbag' (letter to the editor) *Manchester Evening News*, January 23, 1979.
[68] 'As Teachers and Pupils Side with Caretakers, Parents Protest against School Closure,' *Guardian*, January 30, 1979.
[69] Alfred Illingsworth and Stuart Hill, interview by author, November 2006.
[70] Gardiner and Hill, interview, March 2007.
[71] (Lord) Tom Sawyer, interview by author, June 2006.

Criticism of media bias was voiced in a letter to the *Guardian* headed 'How the Media are Sowing a Wind of Ill Will':

> Sir – Working people do not strike and stand on picket lines in cold and nasty weather out of sheer bloody-mindedness. In the present difficulties, it is clear that their case has not been adequately or fairly presented to the public.
>
> It is perfectly legitimate for Conservative proprietors and editors to try to win an election, but they should remember that if they attain that goal at the cost of irrevocably alienating the trade unions, it will be the nation which will reap the whirlwind.[72]

Media reports on the chaos caused by local authority strikes were based on fact, even if the negative aspects were stressed rather than the strikes' motives. Moreover, reports of disruption were two-edged and not simply a Tory press conspiracy. Although photos of rubbish piles in Leicester Square and striking caretakers made NUPE vulnerable to public criticism, they were also visible signs that the strikes were successful. A NUPE strike bulletin issued in early February encouraged its members by stating that 'Screaming headlines in the press and daily statements by Government Ministers show that the action by the four public service unions is now really biting hard.'[73] Rodney Bickerstaffe admits that not all of the media attention was unwanted:

> What we did do – there is no doubt about this – we made the best in PR terms in regards to what action was going on. And I think nowadays they call it 'spin.' […] Whilst it may have looked like that entire country was in uproar for six or seven weeks, it wasn't quite like that. Certainly, in parts of London, if rubbish was as high as this roof, and there were rats running around, that was clearly high profile. That may not have happened in a village 18 miles away. So it was both sides for their own reasons were happy to see it look bigger and more devastating than it actually was. The right-wing to use it as a 'whiplash' so they could say, 'They [unions] are bringing the country to its knees.' And the unions, who wanted to show that although there was a lot of industrial action going on, 'It was everywhere!' because that would put the pressure on the negotiators and the government.[74]

Bickerstaffe admitted that unions were not merely passive victims of an unsympathetic media. Rather, the images of the strikes were used to inflate

---

[72] Lord Ayleston, Lord Wigg, John Ellis MP, Neil Kinnock MP, letter to the editor, *Guardian*, February 2, 1979.

[73] 'Strike Bulletin' National Union of Public Employees, 2 February, 1979, Working Class Movement Library, Salford, UK.

[74] Bickerstaffe, interview, May 2006.

the real size and power of the actions in order to put more political pressure on the Labour government to abandon their stance on the 5 per cent wage limit.

Public sector strikes added to the debate on trade union reform. For decades, the idea of trade union 'barons' ruling Britain had been an idea often touched upon in the press. In 1977, the *Sun* printed an article with the headline 'Move over, Jim Callaghan. It's Jack Jones [General Secretary of the TGWU] and his men who really run Britain.' The poll the paper cited revealed that 80 per cent of the British public 'thought that union leaders have "a lot" of power and influence in governing the country,' while Cabinet ministers placed third.[75] Whether or not this was an accurate assessment of trade union influence at the time, conflicts between unions and the government during the Winter of Discontent, where the British public was often adversely affected, intensified this mood that unions were too powerful. Especially in the case of the public sector strikes that were meant to put pressure on the government, it was the British public who bore the burden of the everyday inconveniencies the strikes created. Even if exaggerated in the press, ordinary people could not help but be made aware of trade union power in a negative manner.

Margaret Thatcher's long-term plans to make trade union reform central to Tory policy now found an increasingly receptive audience among the public. The 'Stepping Stones Steering Group' now had the opportunity to propel their ideas to the forefront of policy debate:

> What rejuvenated the Stepping Stones initiative was the collapse of the [Labour] Government's 5 per cent pay policy that autumn [of 1978]. [...] Even though Party opinion had begun to shift in my direction, no amount of discussion between Shadow ministers, advisors and MPs would have sufficed to persuade the Shadow Cabinet of the need to think seriously about trade union reform, had it not been for the industrial chaos of the 'Winter of Discontent.'[76]

Thatcher's January 17, 1979 'Three-point Plan,' which focused on what were seen as the excesses of striking lorry drivers, also emphasized the need to reform industrial relations in the public sector. One such reform included the creation of 'no strike agreements' among employees in 'vital services' such as hospitals and water works in return for increases in pay.[77] The rhetoric of this 'Three-point plan' continued to be evoked throughout the

---

[75] 'An Exclusive Marplan Poll Reveals the Public's View of Union Power in Britain: Jack's in Charge,' *Sun*, July 25, 1977.

[76] Thatcher, *The Path to Power*, 422–423.

[77] 'Battle Rejoined,' *Economist*, January 13, 1979. See also: '3 Points "To Avoid Anarchy,"' *Daily Telegraph*, January 18, 1979.

public sector strikes, but couched in an approach that aimed to appeal to 'responsible trade unionists.' Thatcher's proposals were echoed throughout the party. Deputy Leader of the Conservative Party, William Whitelaw emphasized how Thatcher's proposal was created with the purpose of 'strengthening the moderates' in trade unions. Whitelaw promised, 'We will confront the militant wherever he seeks to undermine traditional standards and the rule of law – and in doing so we will defend the position of respectable workers and trade union leaders.'[78] This political strategy would be increasingly important during the campaign in the general election. Conservatives would position themselves on the 'moderate side' of the trade union movement, effectively sidestepping allegations that their planned legislation was in any way a direct confrontation with the trade union movement.

Labour failed to deflect the Conservatives' charges in their own Party Political Broadcast (PPB). On January 24, 1979, Labour released a broadcast in which a Manchester councillor made a case for council houses rather than addressing how the government was going to deal with the industrial disputes. The conspicuous omission was not lost on the British public, leading a Mr Ripley to write to the Prime Minister stating, 'How weak and pathetic was your Party Political Broadcast on television last night. How could you possibly avoid the important national interests about which everyone was expecting an announcement, namely the strikes?'[79] Another member of the public wrote:

> As a voting member of the public I expected to hear a senior member of the government speaking about the current industrial troubles and how your government will act to put the country back on an even keel. It is the government's duty to govern and I believe that means taking action and not abdicating your responsibility to trade unions. (I am a trade union member but feel the unions have too much power.)[80]

These two reactions illustrate how Labour's silence on the Winter of Discontent provoked ire and outrage among the public. Also, the second letter indicates that Labour could not simply depend on trade union loyalty for votes; it was quite possible to be a trade union member and yet still believe that politically unions were too powerful. Anger flourished within

---

[78] 'Tories "Will Confront Militants,"' *Guardian*, February 10, 1979.

[79] Mr Ripley, Wallingford, Oxon., *NEC Minutes Part 10: Apr. 1974–Dec. 1983* (Microfiche), Archives of the British Labour Party, Labour History and Archive Study Centre, Manchester, UK.

[80] A.T. Harland, Haywards, Heath. *NEC Minutes Part 10: Apr. 1974–Dec. 1983* (Microfiche), Archives of the British Labour Party Labour History and Archive Study Centre, Manchester, UK.

the party ranks, too. James Micholl, a 'life-time Socialist and member of Stechford C.L.P. since 1945' worried about the effects of the PPB on the Party:

> Dear Comrade,
>
> I listened with disgust at the feeble effort put out to-night which was called 'A Labour Party Political Broadcast'. Here we are, with this country in absolute turmoil looking for someone of standing in the Government, if not the Prime Minister at least someone of the Cabinet rank to give us some re-assurance that everything possible was being done to resolve our present problems. How do you think that we the Party workers are going to go out and seek support if this is the best that we can expect from you people at Transport House? Get someone else to write your script – it would have been much better at this moment in time to have had no broadcast at all than this rubbish – it was pathetic! It left me feeling that you must either be completely out of touch with grass-root feelings, or that perhaps you are just bowing out to that Thatcher woman.[81]

Mr Micholl aptly points to the bind that the Labour government found itself in as the strikes of the Winter of Discontent were appearing to dissolve the government's tie to unions and with members of their own party. If they acted against the unions, they would undermine their base, but if they failed to address the problem, as they did in the PPB, the public would feel left adrift in the midst of what appeared to be mounting chaos.

This chapter sought to go beyond the vilification of the strikes to unearth the reasons why people engaged in industrial action. First of all, a new generation of trade union officers infused NUPE with emerging ideas of participatory democracy and women's liberation at a time when NUPE's membership was increasing dramatically. These concepts helped to open spaces for working-class women to take leadership roles in the union. Structural changes that resulted from the 1974 *Warwick Report* instigated efforts to recruit and mobilize the female majority of NUPE's membership. However, trade union women were not passive in this process. Women took advantage of the spaces that opened up in the union. Many of these women who had assumed local positions of leadership in NUPE engaged in their first major and national strike during the Winter of Discontent. Their rejection of the 5 per cent limit was rooted in political and social changes in working-class communities in the late 1960s and

---

[81] James Micholl, Taunton, *NEC Minutes Part 10: Apr. 1974–Dec. 1983* (Microfiche), Archives of the British Labour Party, Labour History and Archive Study Centre, Manchester, UK.

throughout 1970s, in particular the rise of lone motherhood and the service economy. Only be ancillary workers in the NHS strikes of the Winter of Discontent would match the transformative effects achieved by women like Anne Gardiner and 'Battling Betty.'

7
'Celia's Gate' and the Strikes in the NHS

With disputes among Ford workers and lorry drivers in the immediate recesses of memory, public sector strikes like those among gravediggers and school meals workers added to the continuing pressure on the British public and the Labour government. All of these disputes, nevertheless, came to a resounding crescendo with action taken in the NHS. Already emboldened by her attacks on secondary picketing, Thatcher appeared on the *Jimmy Young Programme* on January 31, 1979, directly challenging the striking workers in the health service. 'Some of the unions are confronting the sick [...] If someone is inflicting injury, harm, and damage on the sick, my God, I will confront them.'[1]

Thatcher's bold assurances, however, obscured a more complex dynamic of accumulative factors within the health service since its foundation. Acute staff shortages and the government's need for cheap labour created low-paid, working-class vocations within the NHS. Three major groups were recruited: men left redundant from de-industrialization; white working-class women who were primary and/or essential breadwinners, and overseas workers, particularly from the West Indies, restricted to such work partly by racism. NUPE was one of the major unions to mobilize this workforce. During the Winter of Discontent, as the workers pushed for improved wages and conditions, they were also reshaping new forms of industrial militancy.

Although the NHS was a key beneficiary of increasing public expenditure under both Labour and Conservative governments, two major problems developed: budgets and staffing. From its inception in the Beveridge Report, politicians assumed that there was a 'fixed quantity of illness in the community,' so as people became healthier, their need for a health service would taper off, and expenditure on the NHS would as well.[2] Politicians

---

[1] Margaret Thatcher quoted in Beckett, *When the Lights Went Out*, 473.
[2] Christopher Ham, *Health Policy in Britain: The Politics and Organization of the National*

failed to foresee that the number of individuals seeking health care would actually increase. Therefore, from 1950 to 1958, the NHS' budget grew by a modest 12.8 per cent, but in both periods 1958 to 1968 and 1968 to 1978, governments more than doubled the NHS budget by 26 per cent.[3]

Governments could not prevent the number of patients being served by the NHS, but they could control staff wages. Therefore, 'unskilled' ancillary grades were created in order to help the hospital with essential work such as cleaning and cooking. By the early 1970s, the basic wage of women ancillary workers was £17.88 a week and that of male ancillary workers £19.48.[4] Despite the low wages, vulnerable sections of the working class took up this work.

Among them were men who lost their jobs as a result of de-industrialization. From 1966 to 1979, of the 2.9 million jobs lost in production, three-quarters of them lost by men.[5] Moreover, from 1966 to 1982, industrial employment declined by over 4 million, with 3 million of these jobs lost in manufacturing. During the 1970s, increases in service work in the public sector came to absorb some of the workers left redundant by this economic restructuring.[6] When Peter Ellis in Sheffield, for instance, lost his job as a steel worker, he entered the public sector as a lavatory attendant. Although there was a dramatic drop in his wages, it was 'better than being out of work – just.'[7]

The NHS, in particular, benefited from these fluctuations in the workforce. After working in the Liverpool docks as a shipwright for seven years, Robert Gregory was laid off. Just before he lost his job, Gregory fell into a deep tank of diesel oil and was forced to spend the next six months in hospital. Without a job, Gregory answered the local hospital's call for staff and began studying to become an ancillary nurse or State Enrolled Nurse (SEN).[8] Outside Liverpool in nearby Prescott, Mike Donovan had worked in various industries, from British Rail to window cleaning. In 1974, he became a porter at Whiston Hospital and continued to work there until he retired in 2005.[9]

Donovan and Gregory's trajectories point to a wider influx of working-class men from traditional industries who began to assume jobs in the health

---

Health Service, 3rd ed. (1982: London: Macmillan, 1991), 17.

[3] Rudolf Klein, *The Politics of the National Health Service*, 2nd ed. (London & New York: Longman, 1989), 67.

[4] 'Strike – Whittington Hospital April 1973,' *Red Rag* 4: 10.

[5] Cronin, *Labour and Society*, 194.

[6] R.L. Martin, 'Job Loss and the Regional Incidence of Redundancies in the Current Recession,' *Cambridge Journal of Economics* 6, no. 4 (1982): 375.

[7] 'How Do They Get By On £40 A Week,' *Guardian*, January 23, 1979.

[8] Bob Gregory, interview by author, May 2006.

[9] Mike and Lorraine Donovan and Celia Newman, interview by author, October 2006.

service. As one of the largest unions to recruit in the health service, NUPE often recruited shop stewards who had prior trade union experience in manufacturing or mining. NUPE trade union officer Tom Sawyer described the contribution these workers made to the union:

> It's about a group of people who hadn't really done things before. Where I came from in the engineering industry, everyone was organized, so there was a high level of competency amongst the engineers about how you take on employers. In the health service [...] no one knew what to do. [...] So I would say almost every union rep you engaged or enrolled [...] had probably never done it before, except you very often would find a porter who had been in the shipyards, so you would say to a group of people, 'Alright – we need somebody to be a union rep. Anybody interested?' And somebody would say, 'What about Jimmy? You were a rep in the shipyard,' and he would say, 'Yeah, I was' [...] So there were a lot of people like that coming out of the old industries, like mining. A lot of shop stewards were ex-miners or ex-miners' wives. There were a lot of people who had experience with unions, and there were a lot who had never done it. So you were organizing people to do things for the first time. And the same with the strike: they had never been on strike before, so they had to kind of learn about it. It obviously had pros and cons, but mainly I think it was a good thing because [...] people were so open minded about it.[10]

Sawyer aptly articulates how the influx into NUPE of a distinct combination of people with varying degrees of trade union experience at the time began forging a new type of militancy within the NHS.

White working-class women were also part of this movement into ancillary work. The unskilled and often part-time nature of this employment provided opportunities for women in dual-earner households and for single mothers. Lorraine Donovan explained that the seasonal nature of her husband's work as a bricklayer made the year-round salary she earned as a switchboard operator at the local hospital crucial to maintaining the family:

> I had two children, but my husband was a bricklayer. And in the summer, you could earn a reasonable wage, but in the winter [...] there would be weeks when he would earn nothing, so it was very sort of unreliable. And my going to work part-time, gave us that sort of comfort of knowing that there was one regular wage. The building trade then was pretty poorly paid anyway. [...] So his income was never steady. And I had two children at school, and my taking that job meant at least we had a regular income. And that's why I was happy to take it because it meant every week I had – it was 50p an hour – but I had that money coming in.[11]

---

[10] (Lord) Tom Sawyer, interview by author, November 2006.
[11] Mike and Lorraine Donovan, and Newman, interview.

The supplementary role of Lorraine Donovan's salary would assume an even more central role after her husband left. Since her ex-husband provided no child support, her work at the NHS became essential:

> I'd been married at 18, so I had married very young, had children very young. [After my divorce] I thought, 'Crikey, how am I going to manage?' But I did. The relief that I had when I moved in [my own home] was knowing what bills were generated. And I had to pay them, and I didn't have to worry about whether I would get any money from him or whatever.[12]

Celia Newman's story resonates with Lorraine Donovan's:

> Celia: I went to work at Whiston Hospital on 17 February 1974.
>
> Mike: [...] to get a new telly. [*laughs*]
>
> Celia: [...] To buy a new telly. [*laughs*] Basically. It's the truth. Yeah. I am newly married, young wife, woman, two children, and I wanted to start, you know, get things around me. I wanted a television, and my husband said, 'Well, we can't afford one. Go and get yourself a job!' So I did! And I went to Whiston, and I was 22 years of age, washing dishes on a ward.[13]

Donovan and Newman's motivations to work in the health service illustrate that the women's wages played a key role in maintaining working-class households. Either their wages became their sole basis of financial security for single parent households, or they supplemented their husbands' pay.

Workers from abroad were also recruited into the health sector. After the Second World War, the Irish immigration that had previously helped to fill staff shortages tapered off. Consequently, the British government began to look to the Commonwealth and poorer European nations to staff the fledgling NHS. The Colonial Office established selection committees to recruit hospital staff from Nigeria, Sierra Leone, British Guiana, Mauritius, Trinidad, and Jamaica.[14] This campaign was successful, and in 1959 6,000 nurses from the West Indies, Hong Kong, Malaysia, and Ireland arrived in Britain; by 1970, that number had increased to 19,000.[15] These women were representative of the increasingly diverse workforce recruited to meet the labour needs of the NHS.

The opportunity to acquire some form of social mobility through such work, however, did not materialize because the NHS directed overseas

---

[12] Mike and Lorraine Donovan, and Newman, interview.

[13] Mike and Lorraine Donovan, and Celia Newman, interview.

[14] Lesley Doyal, Geoffrey Hunt, and Jenny Mellor, 'Your Life in Their Hands: Migrant workers in the National Health Service,' *Critical Social Policy* 1, no. 2 (1981): 55.

[15] Ramdin, *The Making of the Black Working Class*, 310.

recruits into obtaining ancillary nursing qualifications (i.e. State Enrolled Nurse qualification or SEN) that provided little opportunity for promotion and were qualifications recognized only in Britain.[16] With limitations placed upon all overseas nurses, West Indian nurses were at a particular disadvantage because they were disproportionately concentrated in ancillary grades deemed 'less glamorous positions.' The auxiliary nurses dealt with common illnesses, caring for elderly patients, the chronically, physically, and mentally ill.[17] For instance, when Patricia Matthews left Barbados for Britain in 1962, the hospital she worked in immediately relegated her to auxiliary nursing tasks. 'They said I would have to work as an auxiliary first because of my age. I now know this isn't true; they could have taken me on as a cadet. So I worked as an auxiliary doing bedpans, washing babies' woollies, cleaning lockers, etc.'[18] For West Indian women like Matthews, the lack of advancement available was shaped by barriers rooted in larger problems of racism in British society. Instead of a career, auxiliary nursing became a 'black working-class vocation.'[19]

Ancillary work in the NHS thus attracted a unique combination of working-class people into its ranks. While part-time hours and regular pay benefited women like Lorraine Donovan, the nature of the work had its limitations, as evidenced by the case of Patricia Matthews. By the 1970s, this workforce would come together collectively to address grievances with their employment.

By the early 1970s, unionization in the NHS had expanded greatly. In 1948, 40 per cent of all NHS workers belonged to trade unions. In 1974, unionization in the health service was 90.5 per cent, compared to 61.9 per cent in education, and 60.9 per cent in local government.[20] Ancillary workers increasingly joined the major unions in the health service: COHSE, GMWU, and the TGWU. There was some overlap in the types of worker recruited among these unions. COHSE, for instance, recruited from the 'least prestigious professional qualifications,' such as ancillary nurses in mental health and long-stay hospitals.[21] NUPE also became one of the leading unions for hospital ancillary workers, who comprised one-third of

---

[16] Ramdin, *The Making of the Black Working Class*, 310–311.
[17] Mick Carpenter, *Working For Health: The History of COHSE* (London: Lawrence & Wishart, 1988), 317.
[18] Black Women's Group, 'Black Women and Nursing: A Job Like Any Other,' *Race Today* (August 1974): 229.
[19] Katherine Holden, 'Family, Caring and Unpaid Work,' in *Women in Twentieth-Century Britain*, ed. Ina Zweiniger-Bargielowska (Harlow: Longman, 2001), 140.
[20] Beaumont, *Public Sector Industrial Relations*, 44.
[21] Klein, *The Politics of the NHS*, 112.

its membership,[22] the majority of whom were porters, ward orderlies, and cooks.[23]

Behind the external facts of trade union expansion, it is possible to glimpse an extraordinary fusion of diverse influences upon the individuals who became involved in the Winter of Discontent. Some such influences were handed down through the family. Robert Gregory, first of all, explains that his family's commitment to the labour movement was shaped by the poverty they endured after the Second World War:

> When he [Gregory's father] came home, he was very, very bitter because he was injured. He got no help at all from the state. So that made him more and more on the Left because he was fighting for his country. And he said, 'I came home from the war, and I couldn't even get myself a pair of boots off the, you know, off the government.'[24]

It was such experiences of privation that crystallized his family's intense ties to trade union and Labour Party politics:

> My father was a postman, and he bred in us the philosophy of socialism, Labour: 'Labour was for the working man. Tories were for business and people who were well off, better than us.' So my family, my sisters and I all vote Labour. Always have done and always will do till we die. We vote Labour because it was brought into my family going back to my father's father, who was born and bred in Liverpool. My mother's father was born in Shropshire, voted Labour. So we all voted Labour.[25]

The experience of Lorraine Donovan's father provides striking similarities to that of Gregory's:

> When he [Donovan's father] came back [from the war], he was a broken man. He couldn't get his job back as a baker. That had gone. He couldn't get any kind of a job, until he was able to get a job working for the local council. And it was brushing the streets, and it was extremely poorly paid. [...] He used to say about going to war: 'If I had my time over again, I wouldn't join my hands in prayer for them,' which translates into he would have been a conscientious objector [...] They used to talk about a land 'Fit for Heroes,' and these men came back to nothing. And so the poor were still poor, if not poorer than before the war. So then as I was growing up, we were well looked after because my father was resourceful. [...] But it was a hard, a very hard existence. [...] And he used to talk about the

---

[22] Ludlam, 'Labourism and the Disintegration of the Postwar Consensus,' 669.
[23] Klein, *The Politics of the NHS*, 112.
[24] Gregory, interview, August 2006.
[25] Gregory, interview, August 2006.

injustice, and, for me, I think that's where it [interest in politics] came from.[26]

The striking parallels between Gregory and Lorraine Donovan's accounts reveal that the common effect of the poverty servicemen faced when they returned from the Second World War not only reinforced their commitment to Labour Party politics and trade unionism, but left an indelible mark on their children like Gregory and Lorraine Donovan, who would eventually join trade unions in the 1960s and 1970s.

NHS workers from Europe also brought the political traditions of their native countries into their trade unionism. London hospital worker Jonathan Neale noted how many of the Spanish porters in his hospital chose unions based on political cleavages prevalent in Spain. According to Neale, royalists joined the GMWU, and left-wing Spaniards aligned themselves with NUPE.[27] Personal conflicts also influenced workers' choice of union. In the same hospital, Neale remarked that Sicilian kitchen workers who got along with the head chef became part of the GMWU, and those who harboured some form of animosity towards the chef were quickly recruited into NUPE.[28] Political traditions from their homelands and personal antagonisms also fed into emerging trade unionism among ancillary workers.

Some of those who played key national roles had been also politicized by a combination of class and radical politics. Prime Minister Callaghan's political advisor, Tom McNally, was also from a working-class background in the north west of England. His father, a factory worker, encouraged the family to talk about politics. Seeing himself as 'one of Attlee's children,' McNally saw Labour as the party that opened up avenues of social advancement denied to working-class youth of a previous generation. When he arrived in London in the 1960s to study at University College London, he describes it as 'a good time to be a Northern, working-class Labour Party supporter.' It was the belief that the 'Labour Party was a vehicle for political and social change' that would profoundly affect his later political trajectory. McNally was eventually drawn into politics at the national level because he believed that 'Democracy needed democrats for it to work,' and he began to work for Jim Callaghan in 1970.[29]

The local activists I interviewed had a more chequered experience in work, and this shaped their labour politics. Porter Mike Donovan details his own transition from trade unionism in 'traditional' industries to that of the NHS:

---

[26] Mike and Lorraine Donovan and Newman, interview.
[27] Jonathan Neale, *Memoirs of a Callous Picket* (London: Pluto Press, 1983), 43.
[28] Neale, *Memoirs of a Callous Picket*, 43.
[29] (Lord) Tom McNally, interview by author, May 2008.

> I always had a leaning to trade unions even before I worked at Whiston Hospital because I didn't like to see people being treated badly. I always want to say I leaned towards trade unionism [...] You name it. I've done it. Cleaned windows. Sold insurance. [...] British Railways. There wasn't always a union there, or if there was, you joined it, but you didn't really know what it was about. It was just sort of, 'I'm a member, and that was it.' And it was probably in my later years, probably a year before I started in the hospital, I got more interested. And when I started in the hospital, on the 30th of November 1974, I remember Dave Mill, who was the steward, came to me from the union [...] A couple of days later [he asked me], 'You want to become a steward?' I said, 'Sure.' So it was sort of a bit that way. And I never looked back since then. I was into it, then, really full time.[30]

In addition to the influence of family on his trade unionism and politics, Gregory's membership in a union in the Liverpool docks attracted him to trade unionism in the health service. When Gregory first began working as an ancillary nurse, he was shocked by the dramatic cut in pay that he experienced. Instead of the £85 a week he earned at the docks, Gregory was now earning £33 for his work as an ancillary nurse. He, along with six or seven other male nurses, harnessed their previous trade union experience and began to organize workers in their hospital:

> When I worked in a hospital, and I started working as an auxiliary nurse, I'd seen the way auxiliary nurses worked, and I'd seen the way the cleaners worked, and I'd seen how the nurses worked, and I said, 'There's an injustice here. These people are working bloody damn hard, and they're getting peanuts.' And that was an injustice. And I said, 'Where is the trade union?' We'd have meetings with six or seven male nurses and say, 'Where is the trade union in here?' 'There isn't a trade union in here.' 'Right, so we'll form one.'[31]

Part of the militancy amongst NUPE activists was fuelled by previous experience with trade unionism in industry and manufacturing from whence they came.

Not all those who took part in the strikes of the Winter of Discontent had such long lasting formal political and trade union ties. Whiston Hospital cleaner, and later NUPE shop steward Celia Newman describes how her mother was a stalwart Conservative voter. '[My mother] voted Conservative. I used to tell her, "You were poor, mum, what did you have to conserve?" She said, "I don't know, girl. I think it was just family tradition."'[32]

In addition to her lack of strong Labour Party ties, Newman had little

---

[30] Mike and Lorraine Donovan and Newman, interview.
[31] Gregory, interview, August 2006.
[32] Mike and Lorraine Donovan and Newman, interview.

experience with trade unions. Although her father had been a union member when he worked on the docks, Newman, on the other hand, lacked such experience when she began to work after she left school. She was a window dresser at a children's clothes company where there were no unions, so, she explained, 'I never really heard of trade unions. I never had to.'[33]

The loose ties she had to formal institutions like unions and political parties, nevertheless, did not prevent women like her from taking a public role in her community:

> I think I got drawn into politics before I went to work at Whiston. [... My husband] always wanted to put things back into the community [...] and we used to do an awful lot of it. [My husband] ran a Pensioners' Club off the estate. They would run the Bingo. [...] It grew into politics for my husband. It went into politics for me. [...] I looked after the girls in the estate. I used to teach them to play netball. Take them to play netball. [...] When we came to live up here [in Prescott], I got a job at the hospital, and then [my husband] sort of brought that knowledge or experience he had with him.[34]

Unions organizing in the NHS, like NUPE, had to utilize members' very diverse backgrounds to create a strong collective force in the health service. 'Informal' forms of workplace leadership played an important role in NUPE's effort to organize and mobilize hospital workers, especially the previously inactive female majority in the union. Historians Laura Frader and Sonya O. Rose argue for historians 'to dissolve the oppositional categories of public and private [sphere]' for by doing so we can understand the underlying force of politics in activities that lack the title of a political party or a trade union, like those exemplified with Celia Newman and her husband.[35]

At Whiston Hospital in Prescott, NUPE Assistant Branch Secretary at the time was the first to encourage Newman to become a shop steward. At a meeting where bonus schemes were being explained to the membership, Newman's assertive and questioning actions made her the perfect candidate for shop stewardship in NUPE:

> And she [Assistant Branch Secretary] is trying to explain to us about this bonus scheme. Obviously, with all sorts of us looking dumb, I thought, 'What the hell are you talking about?' [...] And in the end, I just popped my hand up, in this hall and I just said, 'I haven't got a clue what you're talking about! Can you explain it in simple terms? Because we're all sitting

---

[33] Mike and Lorraine Donovan and Newman, interview.
[34] Mike and Lorraine Donovan and Newman, interview.
[35] Frader and Rose, 'Introduction: Gender and the Reconstruction of European Working-Class History,' 23.

here. We're all nodding, like dogs, going "um, um."' And, obviously, we didn't know anything. So one thing led to another, and she was saying, 'You need to get yourselves organized. You need to get people that will speak for you.'[36]

Not only the multitude of individual influences, but a collective memory of previous action over the course of the 1970s contributed to industrial militancy in the health service. On March 1, 1973, the four unions representing ancillary staff, the COHSE, NUPE, GMWU, and the TGWU, struck against the Conservative government's pay policy, calling for a wage increase of £8 for ancillary workers.[37] This strike was an important precursor to the Winter of Discontent because the unions sought to mount an effective campaign that would put pressure on the government while maintaining 'services which are essential to the saving and sustaining of life.'[38] In an attempt to dissuade workers from such action, Secretary of State for Social Services, Keith Joseph, issued a letter to all ancillary staff stating:

> The people who would suffer [from the strike] would be those least able to defend their standards of living – the elderly, the sick, and the low paid. [...] I ask you to consider the facts and the suffering which would result from the disruption of hospital service if any form of industrial action is taken.[39]

Joseph's plea points to the dilemma that would eventually plague all strikes in the hospital services: a withdrawal of labour amongst this workforce could present a risk to people's lives, making striking an ethical as well as an industrial issue. Hence, ancillary workers would have to strategize delicately around patient-related issues while seeking to further their claims.

As a result, one of the crucial sites of industrial disruption would be laundry services since they posed no risk to human life, yet a stoppage in cleaning linens would cripple hospitals. On March 6, 1973, the *Guardian* reported that strikes in laundries had hit more than 150 hospitals. By the next

---

[36] Mike and Lorraine Donovan and Newman, interview.

[37] 'Strike Whittington Hospital April 1973,' 10.

[38] Letter From Department of Health and Social Security to Regional Hospital Boards, 23 February 1973, Records of Carlton Hayes Hospital, Narborough (Formerly Leicestershire and Rutland Mental Hospital and Leicestershire and Rutland Lunatic Asylum, Leicester), DE 3533/113, Leicestershire County Council, The Record Office for Leicestershire, Leicester and Rutland, Wigston Magna, Leicester, UK.

[39] Letter From Keith Joseph, Secretary of State for Social Services to Each member of Hospital Ancillary Staff, February 1973, Records of Carlton Hayes Hospital, Narborough (Formerly Leicestershire and Rutland Mental Hospital and Leicestershire and Rutland Lunatic Asylum, Leicester), DE 3533/113, Leicestershire County Council, The Record Office for Leicestershire, Leicester and Rutland, Wigston Magna, Leicester, UK.

day, the paper reported that this number had increased, and the strikes had caused shortages of laundry in 500 hospitals across Britain.[40] Not only did ancillary workers win an increase of £1.64,[41] but their strikes in the laundry services were so effective that the Department of Health and Social Services advised regional hospital boards of governors to 'reconsider having laundry services centralised because it makes it more vulnerable to such action even though it is cost effective.'[42]

The impact of the ancillary strike of 1973 helped to inspire unionized workers' organizational confidence. First, the strike 'destroyed the assumption that people in the NHS simply did not take industrial action – that their responsibilities to the patients necessarily imposed a self-denying ordinance on them.'[43] Second, the strike made workers aware of their own abilities to take action. London hospital worker Jonathan Neale described the effects:

> The strike in itself was no great victory. But it changed the way workers felt. [...] Now, they had been on strike for the first time in their lives. Militants discovered themselves on picket lines up and down the country. At the end of the strike, they went back to the hospitals and got themselves elected stewards. They took up one case after another. If the head porter had previously dished out overtime in return for drinks in the pub, he was now held to a proper rota. The cleaner who hadn't had a mop in three years got one. The porters got a fridge in their restroom. Now, nobody could be fired out of hand because their face didn't fit. Management had been unnerved by the strikes.[44]

One West Indian female auxiliary echoed the confidence gained from the strike. 'It was a wonderful experience striking. We marched and shouted. From 1972 to today, we have had to fight for everything we have since won.'[45]

Assistant General Secretary Bernard Dix agreed that during this strike in 1973 ancillary workers 'found a political commitment and an awareness which over spilled onto the following years.' Commenting on hostile media

---

[40] 'Strike Halts Cancer Operations,' *Guardian*, March 6, 1973 and 'Hospital Strikers Deny Putting Life in Danger,' *Guardian*, March 7, 1973.

[41] 'Strike Whittington Hospital April 1973,' 10.

[42] Letter From Department of Health and Social Security to Secretaries of Regional Hospital Boards of Governors, November 1973, Records of Carlton Hayes Hospital, Narborough (Formerly Leicestershire and Rutland Mental Hospital and Leicestershire and Rutland Lunatic Asylum, Leicester), DE 3533/113, Leicestershire County Council, The Record Office for Leicestershire, Leicester and Rutland, Wigston Magna, Leicester, UK.

[43] Klein, *The Politics of the NHS*, 111.

[44] Neale, *Memoirs of a Callous Picket*, 67.

[45] Race Today Women, 'Caribbean Women and the Black Community,' *Race Today* 7, no. 5 (May 1975): 108.

coverage of the strikes in the *Daily Telegraph*, Dix asserted that, 'In disputes with ancillary staff, newspapers always comment when they are West Indian and foreign.'[46] This remark not only indicated the increased crucial presence of West Indian and immigrant workers in the labour force, but it also revealed how this diversity could be portrayed as a supposedly negative aspect of their union. Moreover, the comment points to the dynamic workforce that would eventually take part in the strikes during the Winter of Discontent.

Ancillary workers' victories were tempered, however, by governments' increasing willingness to cut ancillary staff in the face of larger economic problems. By 1974, OPEC 1 and OPEC 2 had already rocked international markets, sparking rampant inflation around the world, especially in Britain. With inflation at an all-time high of 25 per cent in 1975, combined with Britain's assumption of an IMF loan, the Labour government at the time saw cuts in the NHS' budget as one way to stave off further economic crisis.[47] From 1970 to 1974, under Heath's Conservative government, the NHS' budget grew by 4.3 per cent, but from 1974 to 1979, under the Labour government, it grew by only 1.5 per cent, and in the years 1976 to 1977 and 1979 to 1980, the NHS was subjected to 'severe cash limits.'[48] Eliminating the numbers of ancillary workers employed was one way in which hospitals dealt with these financial constraints. Between 1974 and 1977, ancillary staff working throughout the NHS in Britain fell by 10 per cent.[49]

Compounding these cuts were changes in the way NHS workers were supervised and paid.[50] Both Conservative and Labour governments introduced bonus schemes to increase productivity amongst ancillary staff.[51] In 1975, 40 per cent of the NHS' ancillary workers were covered by a bonus scheme, but additional revenue did not pay for these bonuses. Instead, reduced services and not replacing staff were to fund the bonus scheme. One West Indian ancillary worker in a London hospital complained that

---

[46] Valerie Kaye, 'Inside Engine Room of NUPE Powerhouse,' *Health and Social Services Journal*, July 15, 1977, p. 1043 in UNISON/Rodney Bickerstaffe Papers, MSS 389/B/Box 25, National Health Service Dispute Correspondence, Modern Records Centre, University of Warwick, UK.

[47] Cronin, *New Labour's Pasts*, 168.

[48] Klein, *The Politics of the NHS*, 109.

[49] 'British Health Spending Low,' *Financial Times*, November 26, 1978.

[50] Nicholas Bosanquet, 'The Search for a System,' in *Industrial Relations in the NHS: The Search for a System*, ed. Nicholas Bosanquet (London: King Edward's Hospital Fund, 1979), 4.

[51] Bosanquet, 'The Search for a System,' 4.

'we work harder than before because after 1974, they introduced the bonus system – where there were four of us to a ward, now there are only two.'[52]

Lorraine and Mike Donovan reveal how such changes simply exacerbated the chronic problems of low pay rife amongst ancillary workers. 'We couldn't afford a mortgage. [...] The majority of us, although we were working, were entitled to some form of extra benefit because we were so poorly paid.'[53] Mike Donovan explained that it was this 'extra benefit' that became a particularly important issue in triggering the hospital strikes in the Winter of Discontent:

> The money was so low that the NHS realized that it was low and gave us a weekly supplement. And what actually made the strike [of the Winter of Discontent] occur [was] the offer they made to us that year [...] to transfer part of the supplement onto your basic wage. [...] That brought it to a head.[54]

His experience was not an isolated case. By 1978 the average gross hourly earnings of local authority workers and NHS ancillaries had fallen since 1976, and many were forced to claim Family Income Supplement to make up for the shortfall in their family budgets.[55] Penny Hibbins, a 34-year-old divorcée with four children, was a domestic worker at Starcross Hospital in Devon, and exemplified the constraints on these workers. Although she sometimes made £48.29 a week when doing overtime, she still qualified for a £12-a-week family allowance from the state.[56]

The effects of the cuts in ancillary staff, as a result of public expenditure cuts and/or the introduction of the bonus scheme, had effects on all hospital staff. London hospital worker and NUPE steward Jonathan Neale explains:

> Nurses found the cuts particularly galling. In the end, it was the nurses who had to deliver the cuts to the sick. If the laundry was short staffed and didn't do the patients' clothes, the nurses watched the patients in last night's pajamas all day. If the canteen and food budget were cut, the nurses had to feed fattening stodge to the patients. If the porters couldn't bring the drugs, it was the nurses who tore their hair out. They were busier and busier making tea and mopping floors and doing the other things the domestics who used to be there do.[57]

By December 1978 NUPE was already teeming with these various influences

---

[52] Race Today Women, 'Caribbean Women and the Black Community,' 108.
[53] Mike and Lorraine Donovan and Newman, interview.
[54] Mike and Lorraine Donovan and Newman, interview.
[55] Williams and Fryer, *Leadership & Democracy*, 319.
[56] 'How Do They Get By On £40 A Week?' *Guardian*, January 23, 1979.
[57] Neale, *Memoirs of a Callous Picket*, 82.

and pressures, both longstanding and immediate, which would affect the dynamics of these strikes in early 1979.

With the National Day of Action set for January 22, 1979, health service workers joined local authority workers in their rejection of Labour's 5 per cent wage limit. Reports of hospital strikes immediately exploded across the pages of Britain's major newspapers. On January 24, the *Guardian* reported that workers in 172 hospitals across the north east of England and in Cumbria were causing disruptions by 'controlling' the activities of laundries, post rooms, and refuse disposal, yet maintaining emergency services all the while.[58] By February 1, there were reports of 320 ancillary staff banning overtime work at Queen Elizabeth Hospital in London. That day they vowed to 'step up action' by picketing non-essential hospital supplies such as furniture.[59] The flash of such industrial action during the Winter of Discontent would expose this emergent form of militancy, fuelled by frustration with lingering problems of low pay and executed with innovatory creativity.

Years of accumulated discontent were immediately apparent when workers justified taking action. At one laundry that serviced 30 hospitals around Northampton, 73 workers, the majority of whom were married women, went on strike in early February, stopping the flow of clean linen to hospitals. One of the pickets, Mrs Pam Clemens, complained that the pay of £35 a week, plus a £10 bonus for output, was insufficient. Clemens asserted, 'Most of the workers here help to pay mortgages and buy food, but it's hardly worthwhile. And if you use the crèche, it's £9 a week for each child.'[60] Russ Oakley, a porter for 22 years, noted his inability to achieve financial independence on his pay. He stated that it was 'lucky' he had got his mortgage ten years before because he would not be able to pay it on his present earnings.[61]

Neale observed that many workers were also willing to strike because they continued to harbour bitterness towards the Labour government for its cuts in public expenditure. This disaffection was further exacerbated when Ford workers, oil tanker, and road haulage drivers settled for wage increases in excess of the Labour government's 5 per cent. Neale noted the poignancy of the hospital workers' justification to strike. Hospital ancillary workers 'were bitter over the cuts, and they weren't willing to settle for a lower deal than

---

[58] 'Hospitals hardest hit as disruption goes on,' *Guardian*, January 24, 1979.
[59] 'Hospital workers set to step up action,' *Guardian*, February 1, 1979.
[60] '"We know that we are hitting our relatives, friends and neighbours": Hospitals strikers with red faces,' *Guardian*, February 3, 1979.
[61] '"We know that we are hitting our relatives, friends and neighbours": Hospitals strikers with red faces,' *Guardian*, February 3, 1979.

other workers just to save the Labour Government's face.'[62] In an interview with Nigel Fountain in 1993, ancillary and COHSE Assistant Branch Secretary Jeanette Roe emphasized that it was a Labour *not* a Conservative government that was attempting to restrict workers' wages. The 5 per cent wage limit was such a shock for Roe because 'you expect to be bitten by something that isn't friendly, and it went beyond pale.'[63]

Upon closer examination, striking hospital workers across Britain had to negotiate how to strike effectively enough to achieve their ends, while maintaining emergency cover to avoid risking lives in the process. Therefore, as in the ancillary workers' strike of 1973, laundry services once again became a critical site of disruption. NUPE area officer Robert Gregory, who was charged with co-ordinating many of the hospital strikes in Liverpool, recounted how zealously pickets maintained one of their few effective tools of industrial militancy – the laundry service:

> I remember there was a picket line at the top of the hospital, by the gate, and I remember the porters stopping the nursing management, the nurses' officer, and he had two big canvas bags in the boot. 'Open your boot, let's have a look of what's in your boot.' We open the boot. 'Oh [...] you got two laundry bags!' The laundry bags were full of shitty sheets. He was taking them to the launderette to be washed. 'We're not having that', so we take the bags, and he buggers off [...]. He has his allocation of sheets, which are paper sheets, but he's trying to get more by trying to take them off to the launderette.[64]

The crippling effect of such laundry stoppages was apparent as the *Liverpool Echo*'s headline screamed in a state of panic: '"WASH OUR LINEN!" Plead Hospitals.'[65] Administrators' desperation for clean linen was also apparent outside Manchester when administrative staff raided the laundry at Bolton General Hospital.[66]

Those who did not work in the laundry, however, had to find other ways of showing solidarity with the strikes. This task proved especially difficult for Brenda Tredwell, a nursing auxiliary in South Wales, and other members in the branch because they worked with individuals with special needs. In line with NUPE directives to provide essential services and their own dedication to their patients, they would not stop providing them with medication,

---

[62] Neale, *Memoirs of a Callous Picket*, 83.
[63] Nigel Fountain, 'A Long Hot Winter,' *Guardian (Weekend)*, September 19, 1993.
[64] Gregory, interview, May 2006.
[65] '"Wash Our Linens," Plead Hospitals,' *Liverpool Echo*, February 3 & 4, 1979.
[66] 'NUPE Promises Retaliation in North-west after Management Raid Moves Linen from Laundry: MPs to Raise Nurses' Pay in Commons Debate,' *Guardian*, March 15, 1979.

food and other essentials. The only way to strike, then, was to not take the patients swimming one day, or to not do the patients' hair on another.[67]

As a hospital switchboard operator, Lorraine Donovan was in a similar quandary about how to show solidarity with the strikes. She had been a member of NUPE since 1972, but it was not until the Winter of Discontent that she desired to become active in the union. However, her department could not go out on strike because it was an emergency service. Donovan and one other switchboard operator, therefore, took turns on the picket line, while the other answered emergency calls. The two also devised other ways to show solidarity with their co-workers:

> My department didn't go on strike because we were an emergency service. If a patient had a cardiac arrest in the hospital, we got the teams out. [...] And then the management came in and treated us so insultingly. Basically, they said that they could bring some of their people in. And they brought in typists, even one of the midwife tutors came in. She'd worked during the war in the army or something like that. And they brought them in, and they operated the switchboard two operators. Two of us stuck behind them, working for nothing. And when an emergency came in, we took over, and then sat back. [...] And we threatened to withdraw our service. We didn't in the end because we felt, at the end of the day, the patients had to come first. And we maintained cover throughout the strike. And in between covering, we were on the picket lines.[68]

Outside of Whiston Hospital, cleaner Celia Newman was charged with deflecting any deliveries coming in to the hospital, while simultaneously directing in ambulances. Planning and co-ordination was needed because the hospital had several entrances:

> We did have to organize because there were so many entrances to Whiston at the time. [...] They used to bring the stores in. We knew when the stores came in, but the management would try to get one up on us, so we'd have lookouts all around the roads, and they'd shout: 'Stores are coming!' And we'd all belt down to that gate and go, 'You're not going in, are you? You're not going in.' And the drivers would be going, 'Oh.' Then we'd say, 'We're on strike. Don't be taking stores to them! We're on strike! We're on strike!' 'All right.' They'd all turn around in their lorry.[69]

Humour did ensue, too:

> Celia: Yes, it was sad, funny sometimes. We had some laughs. We'd all be outside. [...] I always say, 'We were on the gate.' We don't have any gate!

---

[67] Brenda Tredwell, interview by author, February 2007.
[68] Mike and Lorraine Donovan and Newman, interview.
[69] Mike and Lorraine Donovan and Newman, interview.

There was no gate at Whiston Hospital. I said, 'We were on the gate!' And one of my friends said, 'Oh, here we go, again! What is this gate?! Whiston Hospital never had a gate!'

Mike Donovan: After that it was 'Celia's Gate.'[70]

Gregory needed similar ingenuity in his efforts to unite ancillary workers with nurses in the strike:

> We used to use passwords. When we were calling out people on strike, we would have a password. We'd have passwords [...] if we needed to call out domestic or catering staff. We'd ring up and say to the steward: 'Nice day it is. Isn't it?' 'It's a lovely day.' The phone would go down. Because if we'd said, 'Today's the day we go out on strike,' the girl on the switchboard would tell the management. Another password was: 'Did you pick up those polo mints we left for you?' [...] We'd call out the ancillary staff in the canteen that were cooking 300 meals for 500 people. We'd have them cook all the meals. Come 12 o'clock, you'd say: 'We're saving all of the meals till 3. We'd cook all the meals [...] All the nursing staff would then get free meals because they would serve themselves. There was nobody on the tills to take the money, so they used to throw polo mints in the honesty boxes.[71]

Bringing ancillary workers together with other hospital workers was also an important goal for workers at Whiston Hospital. Therefore, during the Winter of Discontent, workers like Celia Newman and Mike Donovan helped to create the Joint Negotiating Committee, which included COHSE, NUPE, NALGO, GMWU, and RNC members. Ancillary workers sought nurses' support, but they also realized that nurses could not simply leave their posts, especially those from the RNC, who pledged not to strike. Newman explained that 'not loads of nurses' wanted to support the strikes, but those who did would 'come out on their lunch hours and their breaks and stand with us and show solidarity.'[72]

Not all efforts to lead health service strikes without endangering people were so successful. In early February 1979, the government led an enquiry into a crew of striking ambulancemen in London. The crew was accused of refusing to retrieve a woman who was dying of a brain haemorrhage because her house was outside their area. Instead, they made a call for an ambulance in Surrey to pick up the woman, delaying her treatment.[73] A week later,

---

[70] Mike and Lorraine Donovan and Newman, interview.
[71] Gregory, interview, May 2006.
[72] Mike and Lorraine Donovan and Newman, interview.
[73] 'NUPE orders strict adherence to emergency code as nurses hold one-day strike in London: Ambulance crews decide to get tougher,' *Guardian*, February 7, 1979.

after ambulancemen stepped up pressure by vowing to hold an unofficial strike, national leaders of their own union all warned the ambulancemen to 'not damage their own cause.'[74] The ambulancemen did little to allay fears the next day when their leader Bill Dunn was quoted as saying, 'If it means lives are lost, that is how it must be.'[75] Abrupt calls for militancy regardless of the human consequences were to trigger the most vehement denunciations of the strikes. Health workers faced a wider ethical problem common to public sector trade unionists when they took action. This would also become a political issue in the longer run because of the unavoidable impact these strikes would have on the British public at large.

Although the Labour government was supposedly allied with the unions through the Social Contract, some of the most scathing criticisms of the strikes came not from Conservatives, but from Labour Party leaders themselves. Soon after the strikes began, Prime Minister Callaghan labelled the disputes forms of 'free collective vandalism.'[76] Political advisor Tom McNally was quickly 'disillusioned' at how the 'trade union movement acted towards the Labour Government both nationally and locally.'[77] At one Cabinet meeting, Minister Joel Barnett commented, 'The NHS auxiliaries are well-paid unskilled people, and the trade union leaders have raised the expectations of people on £60 a week, who do not starve, and anyway 50 per cent of their wives work.'[78] What is especially interesting about Barnett's comment is that he put his finger on how many hospital workers made a living: having both partners work. In an era of exploding inflation, it was Labour, a government that was supposed to support workers' rights, who as the employer was trying to keep public sector workers' wages in check.

The severity of the strikes eventually led the Health and Social Services Secretary David Ennals to call for volunteers to help out hospitals during the strikes.[79] The *Daily Mail* framed volunteering in hospitals as an extension of one's patriotic duty. The newspaper's headline cried on February 5, 1979, 'Welcome the volunteers [...] Callaghan must back them and hospitals must use them: TIME TO STAND UP AND FIGHT.' The subsequent article stated, 'At last the British people have a chance to show what they feel about the wreckers who hold the sick, the suffering – and even the

---

[74] 'Joint union warning to Ambulancemen,' *Guardian*, February 19, 1979.
[75] 'As Hopes Rise in One Dispute, The Country Faces Another Crisis: NO MERCY!,' *Daily Mail*, January 20, 1979.
[76] 'Callaghan Condemns 'Free Collective Vandalism': Hospitals Now Face All-Out Strike Action,' *Guardian*, February 2, 1979.
[77] McNally, interview, May 2008.
[78] Benn, *Conflicts of Interest*, 450.
[79] 'Ennals calls on the volunteers,' *Guardian*, March 16, 1979.

dead – to ransom in their scramble.'⁸⁰ At a children's hospital in London, administrator Ted Hayward covered strikers' work by throwing hospital waste in the furnace. Nevertheless, he expressed sympathy with the strikers. 'It's a stinking helluva job. I wouldn't do it by choice or for their money.'⁸¹

Yet striking hospital porter Mike Donovan noted that volunteers often vilified strikers as committing an immoral act. 'On the first day of action, hundreds of volunteers streamed into the gates, telling the strikers, "You ought to be ashamed of yourselves!" After a few weeks, the volunteers dropped off because they realized that jobs weren't romantic.'⁸² The moral ramifications of striking in the health service eventually ignited a media storm of condemnation for the actions. When David Ennals asked striking hospital workers, 'What kind of morality is this?'⁸³ headlines from the *Daily Mail* sarcastically announced: 'Ambulencemen lift emergency ban. Cheer up – It Could Be Worse (But Not Much!).'⁸⁴ The strike at Queen Elizabeth Hospital for Children in London provoked the headline: 'Target for Today – Sick Children.'⁸⁵ Finally, NUPE workers' strike at a hospital in Birmingham inspired the *Daily Mail* to declare: 'Patients Sent Home – "Some Will Die."'⁸⁶ Despite union efforts to provide emergency cover, much of the criticism revolved around the ethics of the strikes, an element that would re-emerge in the mythologized reworking of the Winter of Discontent.

By early February the government and unions began negotiations in order to end the public sector strikes. The result of the discussions became known as the 'Valentine's Concordat' whereby the government offered unions a 9 per cent rise for workers, an enquiry into comparability, and a payment 'on account' for those individuals working at least 35 hours a week.⁸⁷ Local authority and hospital workers from all the major unions voted to accept the offer by early March 1979. The only workers to vote to reject the 9 per cent offer were NUPE health workers. On March 8, 1979, commenting on his members' rejection of the settlement just days earlier, NUPE General Secretary Alan Fisher said, 'It is true that the other three unions have said yes to the offer. The fact remains that my union has the vast majority of

---

⁸⁰ *Daily Mail*, February 5, 1979.

⁸¹ 'Longbridge downs tools in bitter bonus row – NUPE strike gets sympathy in Gt. Ormond Hospital chief stoke for strikers,' *Guardian*, February 8, 1979.

⁸² Pat Corr and Mike Donovan, interview by author, June 2006.

⁸³ 'Minister tells unions: providing emergency cover cannot justify Health Service action: What kind of morality is this, asks Ennals,' *Guardian*, March 6, 1979.

⁸⁴ *Daily Mail*, January 22, 1979.

⁸⁵ *Daily Mail*, February 2, 1979.

⁸⁶ *Daly Mail*, January 25, 1979.

⁸⁷ Williams and Fryer, *Leadership & Democracy*, 336.

membership – 124,000 ancillaries in NUPE voted against the offer. That is almost 50 per cent of the total ancillary staff in the country.'[88] Not only were NUPE workers dissatisfied with what was seen as the low 'own account' offer, but 'hundreds of thousands of women workers' were excluded from this Concordat since they did not work the requisite 35 hours outlined in the deal.[89]

The blame for the prolongation of the strikes in the health service has been laid squarely on the shoulders of NUPE General Secretary Alan Fisher.[90] However, in negotiations with his members, he presented the government's offer as 'an honourable settlement' to the chagrin of NUPE leaders like Bernard Dix and Reg Race.[91] After the NUPE Executive had rejected the government's offer, Fisher considered resigning. 'If I thought that it would help solve the present dispute, I feel it would be my duty to go.'[92]

One of the most notable branches that vowed to carry on was that at Westminster Hospital, led by shop steward Jamie Morris. He began to assume a 'maverick'[93] image even within his own union when he refused to acknowledge a code of conduct that NUPE headquarters submitted to striking health care workers. When asked about the code, Morris replied, 'I hope it's been sent in the post to my home address because it won't get to me here. Our pickets are stopping the mail.'[94] The national leadership's apparent lack of control over these strikes was embodied in Morris' attitude towards negotiations. He reflected on his relationship with the national leadership almost two decades later. 'Senior officers in the union would have liked to have had control of the strike. My view was that they weren't on strike. Therefore, it was none of their business. And I was taking my orders from my members not trade union officials.'[95]

Journalist Andy Beckett asserts that 'Since the early stages of the Winter of Discontent, the right-wing papers had been looking for union ogres,' and the cocky 26-year-old 'with puppy fat in his face, flicked and styled longish

---

[88] 'Ancillaries urged to increase disruption in hospitals: NUPE to fight alone against 9 pc health deal,' *Guardian*, March 8, 1979.

[89] Williams and Fryer, *Leadership & Democracy*, 339.

[90] Sandbrook, *Seasons in the Sun*, 756.

[91] Williams and Fryer, *Leadership & Democracy*, 337.

[92] 'Fisher Prepared to Resign if NUPE Members Reject Offer: Public Service Workers Begin Voting on Deal,' *Guardian*, February 26, 1979.

[93] Terry Roberts, interview in *Secret History: Winter of Discontent* (Brook Lapping Productions for Channel Four, 1998).

[94] Beckett, *When the Lights Went Out*, 472.

[95] Jamie Morris, interview in *Secret History: Winter of Discontent* (Brook Lapping Productions for Channel Four, 1998).

hair and handsome young man's beard,' fit that mould.[96] For some his flair evoked begrudging respect, but as NUPE activist Stuart Hill asserted, Morris was an 'articulate demagogue, which went down fine in terms of sound bites, and he then blew up and got too arrogant with the media pretention.'[97] NUPE National Health Services Officer Robert Jones, on the other hand, had a very different view of Morris. For Jones, Morris 'was a good man' who 'became the victim of the event.'[98]

The recalcitrant image of Morris holding the country virtually to hostage became all the more glaring when David Ennals was admitted to Westminster Hospital for thrombosis on March 6. Morris found this a key opportunity to highlight the dispute in front of the press, and proclaimed that Ennals too was a 'legitimate target' for strike action, which included not delivering papers to the minister.[99] While his face would be emblazoned on the myth of the Winter of Discontent, the female faces of his branch members standing behind him would fade into historical obscurity.

While the Labour government was in the midst of attempting to broker a deal with public sector unions, the Conservatives were capitalizing on Labour's inability to control the strikes. This pervasive feeling that ordinary British people were under siege by a trade union onslaught of strikes played into Conservative leader Margaret Thatcher's longer-term plans of realigning her own party and the country to undercut trade union power. The hospital disputes fuelled the momentum she gained after the lorry drivers' strike. Industrial action in the health service, on the heels of a winter of strikes, opened a crucial window for Thatcher to implement policies that even her own party was reluctant to endorse:

> [In January 1979] [t]he balance of opinion in the Shadow Cabinet, following rather than leading opinion in the country, was now that we could and should obtain a mandate to clip the wings of the trade union militants. Similarly – though I was to be less successful in dispensing with this unwelcome aspect of my political inheritance – the collapse of Labour's pay policy made it easier to argue that the whole approach of prices and incomes controls, both 'voluntary' and statutory, should be abandoned. Above all, I was sure that there had been over the winter a sea-change and that our manifesto had to catch that tide.[100]

The opportunity to 'catch that tide' appeared in mid-March, when Wales and Scotland voted on a referendum on devolution: the results were inconclusive

---

[96] Beckett, *When the Lights Went Out*, 472.
[97] Stuart Hill and Peter Doyle, interview by author, June 2010.
[98] Robert Jones, interview by author, May 2013.
[99] Beckett, *When the Lights Went Out*, 473.
[100] Thatcher, *The Path to Power*, 435.

as Wales rejected the proposal, while Scotland accepted it by a slim majority. Soon after the elections, Donald Stewart, leader of the Scottish National Party (SNP), warned the government that if Callaghan refused to pursue an early Commons debate, the SNP would table the motion of no confidence in the government.[101]

The Conservatives now had the chance to call for a vote of no confidence. Margaret Thatcher, however, remained cautious:

> Many of our backbenchers wanted an early confidence motion, but initially the Shadow Cabinet held its fire. One reason was that we would need the support of anti-devolution MPs to make absolutely sure that the order repealing the Devolution Acts went through; we did not quite trust the Government on this question. Moreover, unlike previous occasions when there seemed a probability of bringing down the Government in a vote in the House of Commons, we were extremely reluctant to put down a Motion of No Confidence until we were assured of its likely success. A Government victory would strengthen it at a bad time. When we considered the matter at the Shadow Cabinet on Wednesday 21 March we decided, indeed, that we would move such a motion until the SNP, the Liberals, and, if possible, the Welsh Nationalists gave firm assurances of support. But there was still no question as far as I was concerned, of doing deals which would tie my hands in government.[102]

Everybody in the Labour government, especially Michael Foot, was acutely aware that a vote of no confidence would easily play into the Conservatives' hands. Therefore, Foot advised Callaghan to put forward a motion to delay the vote by inviting 'all parties in the House' to talks on devolution that were to end in late April. The move would effectively sidestep the vote the government knew it would lose. However, Callaghan rejected Foot's offer, appearing to welcome an election. 'It seemed to me then, as it did on a number of other days afterwards, that his [Callaghan's] patience had suddenly snapped. [Callaghan] wanted to invite the election and the decision that would lead to it. It was, in my opinion, a considerable error.'[103]

According to Callaghan, Foot's plan to delay the election was unfeasible because the Prime Minister believed that the move would simply exacerbate the already growing problem of the government's unpopularity and further deal the Conservatives more political leverage. If Callaghan did not exactly

---

[101] 'Callaghan is given election ultimatum by SNP,' *Guardian*, March 14, 1979.

[102] Thatcher, *The Path to Power*, 431–432.

[103] 'Correspondence With Jim Callaghan Re. 1979 Defeat' *How The Government Fell a Few Brief Notes* – Michael Foot dictated 'very hastily just after the event' later sent a copy to Callaghan on April 15, 1986, Michael Foot Papers, C11/1, Labour Party Archive and Study Centre, Manchester UK.

believe he had 'snapped' at that point, he did admit the futility of maintaining an unpopular, minority government in office any longer:

> Michael [Foot] is a fighter, and he still thought the day could be saved. Why not, he said, lay the Repeal Order before Parliament, but invite the House to reject it? This would leave the Scottish Act on the statute book in accordance with the wish of the majority of those who had voted. But it would not come into force until the second Order, known as a Commencement Order, was laid, and this should be postponed until after the general election. [...] I reasoned that we would have a hard job to recover from our unpopularity without handing a further stick to our opponents. In fairness to Michael [Foot], I promised to consider the idea although he detected a lack of enthusiasm.[104]

Nevertheless, the Labour government still had a chance of winning the vote of no confidence by a very narrow majority. The government appeared to be using all the cards remaining in its deck to swing the vote their way. Labour advisor and *Daily Mirror* reporter Geoffrey Goodman recounted:

> MP Clement Freud was tracked down in Liverpool and [...] contacted by 'someone in No. 10' and, despite Callaghan's injunction, he was confidentially offered a safe passage for his Freedom of Information ('Private Members') Bill if he 'accidentally missed the train back to Westminster'. But Clement Freud, whose vote was to go against the government, decided *not* to miss the train.[105]

Despite such manoeuvres, the Labour government lost the vote of no confidence on March 28, 1979 by one vote. Foot reflected:

> What defeated us in the end was the double blow – first, that Dr. Broughton would not be able to get to the House, which we finally learnt on the Wednesday once the information was clear about his medical condition, no risks whatsoever, I am glad to say, were taken; and, the blow from Gerry Fitt. He had not misled us in any way; we had always thought he was likely to abstain. We did retain hope at the end that he might be swayed, and we retained the hope also that Frank McGuire would vote with us, but Gerry's speech effectively kiboshed that.[106]

Labour's feeling of disappointment contrasted starkly with the Conservatives, infused with the feeling that they were poised at the precipice of their time to act. With all the votes counted, Thatcher writes, 'Ayes, 311. Noes,

---

[104] Callaghan, *Time and Chance*, 559.
[105] Goodman, *From Bevan to Blair*, 223.
[106] Michael Foot Papers, 'Correspondence With Jim Callaghan Re. 1979 Defeat.'

310. So at last I had my chance, my only chance. I must seize it with both hands.'[107]

The next day NUPE called off industrial action among its hospital workers still out on strike. The NUPE leadership cited the reason for the return to work as the result of a recent settlement negotiated with the Ancillary Staffs' Council. The leadership also 'took into account the fact of a pending general election.'[108] This series of strikes crystallized currents of militancy amongst hospital ancillary workers that reflected larger shifts occurring amongst the British working class in the late 1970s. The convergence of men left unemployed by the effects of de-industrialization and white and overseas working-class women providing financial support for their households created a novel form of industrial militancy in the health service. Not only did varying levels of trade union and political experience make trade unionism amongst ancillary workers distinct from more 'established' forms of trade unionism, but the risk industrial action could have on human life presaged the challenges such workforces would have as the economy became dominated by service work. The industrial muscle women, especially West Indian women, began to flex during the Winter of Discontent also signalled an important shift economically and within the labour movement. Finally, as we shall see later, it was the experience of striking during the Winter of Discontent that inspired many of these hospital workers to further activism in the British labour movement.

The meanings of the strikes for those involved were almost immediately subsumed in the general election campaign. Thatcher had seized her 'only chance' to take power based on a mandate to undercut trade union power, and her use of the memory of the hospital strikes would eventually play a key role arousing negative opinion against both unions and the Labour Party. The following chapter will, therefore, explore how Thatcher not only used the hospital disputes, and other strikes of the Winter of Discontent, to win the 1979 general election, but how she continued to perpetuate a specific myth of these strikes. This strategy would eventually help make the Thatcherite neo-liberal agenda appear to be the only legitimate option for Britain's long-term economic and political future.

---

[107] Thatcher, *The Path to Power*, 433.
[108] 'Top civil servants vote to join strike, NUPE call off hospital action,' *Guardian*, March 29, 1979.

8

Crosscurrents: Myth, Memory, and Counter-Memory

'We should not allow ourselves to lose a vivid memory of what happened [during the Winter of Discontent], and the reversion to barbarism that took place.' – Margaret Thatcher, July 6, 1979 speech[1]

In 1991 Conservative author Eamonn Butler remarked that the Winter of Discontent was so traumatic for the British public that 'the awful details [...] are often blotted from people's memory.'[2] He spoke too soon. They would continue to be evoked. Almost 20 years after Butler declared the memory of the Winter of Discontent a disturbing event securely relegated to irrelevance, historian Niall Ferguson opened *The Shock of the Global* in 2010 with an introduction titled 'Crisis, What Crisis?' before detailing James Callaghan's media blunder upon returning from Guadeloupe in 1979. Ferguson took the headline as expressive of the apparent chaos of the decade. 'The seventies are indeed still popularly remembered – in the English-speaking world at least – as a time of crisis.'[3]

Outside of Conservative circles, the Winter of Discontent also continues to be resonant, in an especially personal way for some. When posed the question 'Why was the [Liverpool gravediggers'] strike approved when it appears an obvious strike not to approve?' Larry Whitty, who had been a GMWU researcher at the time, began to answer, but stumbled mid-sentence.

---

[1] Speech to Conservative Political Centre Summer School ('The Renewal of Britain'), July 6, 1979. Margaret Thatcher Foundation Online. http://www.margaretthatcher.org/document/104107.

[2] Eamonn Butler, foreword to *Taming the Trade Unions: A Guide to the Thatcher Government's Employment Reforms, 1980–90* (London: MacMillan, 1991), xvi.

[3] Niall Ferguson, 'Introduction: Crisis, What Crisis?: The 1970s and the Shock of the Global,' in *The Shock of the Global: The 1970s in Perspective*, ed. Niall Ferguson, Charles S. Maier, Erez Manela, and Daniel J. Sargent (Cambridge: The Belknap Press of Harvard University Press, 2010), 1.

He averted his gaze for the first time in the interview; his eyes misted over; and the articulate and poised flow of speech became an awkward trickle of words.[4] My interview with Whitty in 2006 made me realize how the process of remembering the strikes was not simply a historical endeavour, but the choices individuals had made were still a source of profound emotion personally as well as politically. Not only for participants like Whitty alone, but for the British public at large, the memory of the Winter of Discontent has taken on a life of its own and continued to have a profound effect on British political culture.

As mentioned in chapter one, the emphasis sociologist Maurice Halbwachs places on the 'framework of collective memory' as a binding force is particularly apposite in understanding how the reiteration of the dreadful memories that enveloped the strikes of the late 1970s came to have an impact on through the 1980s and '90s. Not only did the memory become shared, but it assumed a mythic quality during the general election and afterwards. As Paul Cohen observes, mythologization 'achieves its effect typically not through out-and-out falsification but through distortion, oversimplification, and omission of material that doesn't serve its purpose and runs counter to it.'[5] The development of the myth of the Winter of Discontent, as has been shown in the previous chapters, contains key emphases and exclusions that do not always align with its history. Moreover, neither myth nor history has sought out the experiences of a wide range of participants, some of whose views embody a force of counter-memory. As George Lipsitz argues, counter-memory incorporates elements both of myth and history, 'but it retains an enduring suspicion of both categories. Counter-memory focuses on localized experiences with oppression, using them to reframe and refocus dominant narratives purporting to represent universal experience.'[6] The strikers, local and national trade union leaders, and politicians interviewed reveal how memories of the strikes are contested and far from uniform. They also demonstrate how a nuanced resistance has persisted. Many of my interviewees expressed memories that went against the grain of the dominant discourse. Remembering is a highly charged political issue and the way in which memories have been held has contemporary significance. The differences, divergences, and contradictions amidst these memories of the Winter of Discontent disclose key insights not only into the social landscape of power, authority, race, class, and gender of the late 1970s, but into how people who participated understand themselves and politics today.

This is a complex process; so we must once more return to the development

---

[4] Larry Whitty, interview by author, September 2006.
[5] Cohen, *History in Three Keys*, 213–214.
[6] Lipsitz, *Time Passages*, 213.

of the myth of the Winter of Discontent and how it evolved in three stages. During the general election campaign, the Conservative Party and the right-wing press focused on the Winter of Discontent because the industrial disputes underlined what was seen as the Labour Party's incompetence, proving instrumental to the Conservatives' electoral victory in 1979.[7] The next stage was in the 1980s, when the Conservative Party used general election campaigns as commemorative events where they strategically revisited the Winter of Discontent to portray the labour movement and social democracy as bankrupt of vision.[8] Underlying this view was an apparent justification for the Thatcherite project. As Thatcher wrote, she and the Conservative Party had brought Britain out of its 'dark days which would precede tangible success,' reigniting Britain's 'faith in freedom and free markets, limited government and a strong national defence.'[9] Then, despite the election of Labour in 1997, the memory of the Winter of Discontent remained unchanged. Instead of upsetting the negative perception of this series of events, Labour's modernizers left the negative associations undisturbed, and the Winter of Discontent became a bulwark between 'Old' and 'New' Labour. The end of the Winter of Discontent thus marked the initiation of the 1979 general election and of an enduring myth.

General Election 1979

With the drama of the vote of no confidence behind them, Callaghan and Thatcher immersed themselves in campaigning. Although the Prime Minister appeared rejuvenated by the call for an election, the party as a whole could not shake the spectre of the Winter of Discontent, and the Conservatives would not let them. As historian Dominic Sandbrook has argued about the general election of 1979, 'Overshadowing everything was the Winter of Discontent.'[10] The Conservatives deftly exhumed the recently buried strikes of the winter, and bludgeoned Labour with them. With headlines 'DON'T EVER FORGET: VOTE TORY,' above a photo of the previous winter's hospital strikes, memory was not only of media focus, it was also a central rallying point throughout the general election.[11] The Conservatives frequently referred to the Winter of Discontent as emblematic

---

[7] Quoted in Butler and Kavanagh, *The British General Election of 1979*, 168.

[8] Patrick Hutton, 'Recent Scholarship on Memory and History,' *The History Teacher* 33, no. 4 (August 2000): 537. Hutton defines 'commemoration' as 'a calculated strategy for stabilizing collective memories that are otherwise are protean and provisional.'

[9] Thatcher, *The Downing Street Years*, 15.

[10] Sandbrook, *Seasons in the Sun*, 789.

[11] *Scottish Daily Express*, May 3, 1979.

of the supposed failings of the Labour government. In this process they began to develop a standard narrative that would be reiterated for decades to come, solidifying the mythic status of the strikes.

The Conservative election campaign sought to fuel the momentum Thatcher had built up after the lorry drivers' and public sector strikes. Its focus on the disputes of the previous winter was strategic. Two days after the vote of no confidence, Thatcher rebuffed a *Weekend World* proposal to take part in a televised programme with Jim Callaghan and David Steel. Not only was there fear about a Liberal 'electoral bump' that could take votes away from the Tories, but overall, polls showed that Callaghan was personally more popular than Thatcher.[12] While Callaghan's jovial disposition did, indeed, shape this perception, her advisers were also wary of stoking latent and/or overt sexism amongst the electorate. While her sex garnered Thatcher attention as a politician, it could also make her the target of derision. Leicester machinist Betty Poynton succinctly articulated this current, 'I don't fancy a woman as Prime Minister. It's a fellow's job.'[13] The rejection, therefore, side-stepped several complications, and confirmed the overall focus of the campaign. As one Conservative operative put it, 'We wanted the election to be about the winter, not a TV programme.'[14]

This single-mindedness characterized her campaign throughout the general election. On April 19, she told a crowd in Birmingham, 'All of you have suffered under the rule of pickets and the strikes this winter. We all saw at first hand that power and felt our own powerlessness.' Her populism and reference to memory were apparent. 'Well, you are not powerless now. This is a time when the ordinary people of this country in their tens of millions hold the future of our country in their hands. And when you come to decide that future on May the third, remember last winter.'[15] Thatcher set the tone of the election and began to shape a narrative of the Winter of Discontent. At the heart of this nascent legend was that idea the British public was a neglected electorate, 'powerless' and victimized by trade unions. Juxtaposed to the grim backdrop was the Conservative Party; the contrast would become embedded in the developing myth of this series of events.

The Conservatives' media campaign effectively served to emphasize this populist strategy. They specifically targeted working-class housewives and

---

[12] Butler and Kavanagh, *The British General Election of 1979*, 168–169.
[13] Sandbrook, *Seasons in the Sun*, 785.
[14] Butler and Kavanagh, *The British General Election of 1979*, 168.
[15] Cited in Sandbrook, *Seasons in the* Sun, 789. See also: Margaret Thatcher, Speech to Conservative Rally in Birmingham, April 19, 1979, Transcribed by Harvey Thomas, Margaret Thatcher Foundation Online, http://www.margaretthatcher.org/document/104026.

the skilled working class in their messaging and advertising.[16] For instance, the campaign released an advertisement in women's magazines in the form of popular quizzes. The quiz titled 'Do This Quiz to Find Out if You're Labour or Conservative,' included questions such as:

> Which of these people is more likely to know what it's like to do the family shopping?
> a. James Callaghan
> b. Your husband
> c. Mrs Thatcher[17]

Another advertisement headed 'Why Every Trade Unionist Should Consider Voting Conservative,' was followed by a litany of reasons to vote Tory.[18]

An unprecedented shift towards the Right among British newspapers helped to bring these key voters into the Conservative fold. On May 3, the *Sun* to ran a 1,700-word editorial that called on the reader to 'VOTE TORY THIS TIME.' The *Express* went one step further. The editors produced a paper with the headline 'DON'T FORGET LAST WINTER' against a picture of a pile of rubbish outside Labour's headquarters. So explicit was the connection to the Conservative campaign that the *Express* editor declared that the headline and picture was 'nothing more than a Tory election poster – so much so that it was framed and put up on a wall at Conservative Central Office.'[19]

The push towards the Conservatives would prove worthwhile on election day. Despite conjecture that Labour's gain in the polls might lead to a slim victory, on May 3 the results were definitively in the Tories' favour. The swing to the Conservatives was a post-war record 5 per cent.[20] The Conservatives had won 339 seats to Labour's 269. Key voting blocks, such as the skilled working class or the C2s swung 11.5 per cent to the Tories. The Tory vote among women 25 to 34 years of age who were part of the C2s increased by 12 per cent.[21] Unskilled working-class women (35–54 years), however, voted Labour, 41 per cent to 38 per cent. Women overall supported the Tories by 9 per cent.[22]

The media influence on the government's reaction to the strikes and the

---

[16] Sandbrook, *Seasons in the Sun*, 787–788.
[17] Figure 2.2 in Bell, 'The Conservatives' Advertising Campaign,' 17.
[18] Figure 2.4 in Bell, 'The Conservatives' Advertising Campaign,' 20.
[19] Thomas, *Popular Newspapers*, 82.
[20] Sandbrook, *Seasons in the Sun*, 800.
[21] *British Public Opinion: General election 1979* (Market & Opinion Research International, 1979), 2.
[22] *British Public Opinion: General election 1979*, 4.

electoral defeat has also been a focus of academic attention. Colin Hay's examination of the media's role during the Winter of Discontent provides a thorough analysis. He asserts that the Winter of Discontent was a moment 'in which the influence of the media, perhaps more than at any other point in post-war British history, was crucial. For it was predominantly through media discourses through the process of *informediation*, that the crisis was initially constituted *as a crisis*.'[23] Instead of viewing the British public as an audience of passive dupes, Hay argues that headlines such as 'THEY WON'T EVEN LET US BURY OUR DEAD,' readers were 'recruited through interpellation' as victims of the striking gravediggers, interjecting readers' own experiences of bereavement, allowing the public agency to view the strikers as antagonistic to the community of victims.[24]

His analysis helps to understand, for instance, that while support for Labour remained around 50 per cent, Conservatives increased their support among the *Sun* readers from 27 per cent in November 1978 to 38 per cent by April 1979. As James Thomas explains, 'This tentatively suggests that, while the paper made few inroads against its traditional supporters, it may have had rather more effect on the undecided and politically apathetic.'[25] The effect of the media, therefore, is apparent here.

However, other factors must be also considered in regard to the media coverage of the Winter of Discontent. First of all, as previously observed, even among trade unionists themselves, press spectacles were also used to the advantage of striking workers. Second, an underlying reality of anxiety and want had to exist for readers to be pulled into side with the victims of the strike, some of whom were fellow trade unionists. Finally, attitudes were changing, for instance, among the young. As a key election study concluded: 'Young people generally were attracted to the Tories.' The youth vote, those 18 to 24 years of age, in particular, middle-class women and skilled working-class men, doubled their vote for the Conservatives from 24 per cent in 1974 to 42 per cent in 1979.[26]

Nick Tiratsoo and Dominic Sandbrook both stress the rising tide of middle-class discontent that factored into the electoral results of May 1979. Tiratsoo asserts that in 1979, 'The middle class was flattered back into the Conservative fold.'[27] While the memory of the Winter of Discontent did, indeed, shape voting behaviour in 1979, the middle-class vote for Labour

---

[23] See Hay, 'Narrating Crisis,' 253–277; Hay, 'The Winter of Discontent Thirty Years On,' 545–552; Hay, 'Chronicles of a Death Foretold,' 446–470.
[24] Hay, 'Narrating the Crisis,' 262–263.
[25] Thomas, *Popular Newspapers*, 86.
[26] *British Public Opinion: General Election, 1979*, 2.
[27] Tiratsoo, 'You've Never Had It So Bad,' 189.

actually increased in 1979.[28] If anything, it was trade union discontent, with a surge of trade union votes for the Tories from 23 per cent in 1974 to 33 per cent in 1979, that indicates the real shift in 1979.[29] Moreover, despite the role of female trade unionists in key unions like NUPE, women trade union members demonstrated a 14 per cent bias towards the Conservatives in 1979 compared with 12 per cent in 1974.[30]

As the bookend to the Conservative victory appears the British public's unequivocal rejection of not only the Labour government's failings, but of Keynesian economics. Historians have contested this view. In particular, some, such as Nick Tiratsoo and Colin Hay, argue that after 1976, the economy did improve, evidenced by the Labour government's quick repayment of the IMF loan and the decline of inflation from 30 to 8 per cent. Moreover, while the government has been maligned by its supposedly failed Social Contract with trade unions, the policy was remarkably successful, the first three phases keeping wages in check.[31] Also cited by others is the decrease in public spending as a proportion of GDP, from 46 per cent of GDP in 1975–76 to less than 42 per cent two years later.[32]

The more positive evaluation of the Callaghan government's economic policy leads to another thread in the argument about the Keynesian nature of this government. Dominic Sandbrook asserts that Healey and Callaghan's adoption of money-supply targets and cuts in public expenditure revealed their true nature as, in the words of former governor of the Bank of England Gordon Richardson, 'practical monetarists.'[33] The implication of this argument is that even ardent Keynesians saw the limits of their economic policy, and partially reaffirming the idea that the Winter of Discontent represented the bankruptcy of this economic model.

On the other hand, Colin Hay develops an entirely different conclusion based on the same premise. He argues that monetarist techniques were being employed prior to 1976. However, he points out, 'One might argue, then, that the Winter of Discontent, was as much a crisis of monetarism as it was of Keynesianism.'[34]

James Cronin rejects this assertion, and argues that the Callaghan government continued to act in 'the social democratic tradition.' For Cronin the government's policies after 1976 represented a momentary breach in

---

[28] *British Public Opinion: General Election, 1979*, 4.
[29] *British Public Opinion: General Election, 1979*, 3.
[30] *British Public Opinion: General Election, 1979*, 4.
[31] Tiratsoo, 'You've Never Had It So Bad,' 172; Hay, 'Chronicles of a Death Foretold,' 452.
[32] Cronin, *New Labour's Pasts*, 186; Sandbrook, *Seasons in the Sun*, 690.
[33] Sandbrook, *Seasons in the Sun*, 691.
[34] Hay, 'Chronicles of a Death Foretold,' 453.

'party orthodoxy,' but Callaghan and Healey's later effort to expand social provision revealed that they had never 'fully abandoned their faith in Keynes or their commitment to the welfare state.'[35]

It is indisputable that the 1974–79 Labour government did, indeed, institute monetarist reforms. Especially in the case of public expenditure cuts, it appears that key figures such as Denis Healey were not entirely wedded to unfettered public expenditure. However, as detailed in chapter two, those in the Parliamentary leadership tended to have a Revisionist interpretation of Labour Party policy. While public expenditure cuts did severely compromise this interpretation for central figures like Tony Crosland, overall, the Revisionist belief in a restrained form of socialism remained in place. Moreover, state intervention like the Sex Discrimination Act of 1975 indicates a commitment to state intervention as a force for common good. Furthermore, Healey restored the cuts 'when it seemed safe to do so' by bringing the PSBR to £9 billion in 1978–79.[36] Therefore, while some monetarist strategies were used, I would agree with James Cronin that the 1974–79 government 'remained in the social democratic tradition,' albeit one seen through a Revisionist lens.

While the election of 1979 left lingering uncertainty over its causes and implications, the Conservatives obtained an unquestionable victory. Furthermore, throughout their time in power, the Winter of Discontent became a key rhetorical device deployed from their political arsenal, allowing the series of events in 1978–79 to transform in scale and magnitude.

Afterlives

Kristin Ross has argued that the subsequent reconfiguration of memory takes the form of 'afterlives,' or 'traces of political climate and memory.'[37] This is certainly the case with the Winter of Discontent. While the general election of 1979 provided a key moment when this series of events began to assume a mythic status, its solidification as a myth really took root afterwards. As James Thomas argues, the 'media memory of the Winter of Discontent' was 'the single most effective propaganda theme develop by the Tories and their press allies in the 1980s.'[38] The reiteration of this political legend was an effective weapon for the Conservatives not only in the 1980s, but also in the 1990s.

Thatcher quickly initiated this process of mythologization in a July 1979

---

[35] Cronin, *New Labour's Pasts*, 187.
[36] Burk and Cairncross, *'Goodbye, Great Britain,'* 432–433.
[37] Kristin Ross, *May '68 and Its Afterlives* (Chicago: University of Chicago Press, 2002), 7.
[38] Thomas, *Popular Newspapers*, 108.

speech on 'The Renewal of Britain' at Trinity College, Cambridge. As she came to the body of her oratory, she recounted how the Labour government had left Britain 'disillusioned and dispirited.' She described how during the previous winter, 'Children were locked out of school; patients were prevented from having hospital treatment; the old were left unattended in their wheelchairs; the dead were not buried; and flying pickets patrolled the motorways.' Appropriating the language of care, Thatcher established the standard narrative of the Winter of Discontent that was to be employed in subsequent decades. She placed emphasis on remembering when she pleaded, 'We should not allow ourselves to lose a vivid memory of what happened, and the reversion to barbarism that took place.' Furthermore, she explicitly stated that the Winter of Discontent represented the failings of any alternative to the policies of the Conservative Right. 'The events that we witnessed, mark, I believe, the failure of [...] collectivist approaches.'[39]

Conservative campaign advertising would mirror this approach. In a 1983 Party Election Broadcast (PEB) narrated victoriously over footage of Thatcher receiving a standing ovation, the narrator declared that this was the woman who 'believed that our country, our people, could do more than we dreamed possible for many years.' Suddenly interjected into the glory is a picture of a dreary and snow-covered Westminster, with copy below reading: 'Winter 1979.' As the music became increasingly foreboding, the narrator then asked, 'Do you remember what it was like during the Winter of Discontent?' Footage of striking lorry drivers, dustmen, hospital ancillaries, and gravediggers then followed. The PEB's litany of strikes placed in juxtaposition to a glorious present would be a key aspect in the standard Tory narrative. The frigid cold helped to collapse the supposed feeling of despair and chaos into one resonant symbol. The contrast of the Winter of Discontent with Thatcher's Britain underlines the message that Thatcherism is *the only* alternative to socialism. The effect is to present Thatcherism 'as the anti-thesis and nemesis of a series of negative alternatives. Social Democracy, consensus, corporatism, and decline.'[40]

In 1987 and even in 1992, the Winter of Discontent was once again brought up in the Conservative press. The *Sun*, *Daily Mail*, *Express*, and *Sunday Express* all made some reference, for example, to 'Lest we forget' the Winter of Discontent. Interestingly enough, focus groups in 1992 revealed that the memory of the Winter of Discontent was more vivid among the young who were not yet born in 1978–79 than among older individuals who

---

[39] Speech to Conservative Political Centre Summer School ('The Renewal of Britain'), July 6, 1979. Margaret Thatcher Foundation Online, http://www.margaretthatcher.org/document/104107.
[40] Thomas, *Popular Newspapers*, 109.

directly experienced the strikes of that winter.[41] Such resonance among those without direct experience further emphasizes how the myth grew in scale after the series of events had occurred.

The impetus to no longer challenge, but to incorporate and move on from the memory of the Winter of Discontent, therefore, became especially important to New Labour. By 1997, Tony Blair underscored this impetus to disassociate Labour from the past and forge New Labour in an editorial for *The Times*.

> I have staked my political reputation and credibility on making clear that there will be no return to the 1970s. Indeed there is little appetite among trade unions for such a thing. [...] Naturally the Tories want to refight the election of 1979, rather than fight that of 1997. All they have left now is to try to scare people, to terrify them out of doing what otherwise people know to be right.[42]

Consequently, by the end of the twentieth century, the myth of the Winter of Discontent became fully entrenched in both Conservative and New Labour rhetoric as a poignant symbol of socialism and trade union excess.

Counter-Memory

Although the myth of the Winter of Discontent grew more powerful throughout the 1980s and 1990s, substrata of memory amongst participants themselves continued to be resilient. In returning to those who participated in the events, it is possible to see how the dominant narrative, personal memory, and counter-memory have fused, converged, and/or disconnected since 1979.

For some Ford workers, the political ramifications of the strike were discouraging. Shop steward Rod Finlayson noted that many of the Labour supporters he knew at Ford had become 'tremendously disillusioned' because after a life of supporting the party, they were forced to fight it in the strike.[43] Dagenham convener Dan Connor observed how one of his shop stewards withdrew his political levy from the Labour Party soon after the strike. Connor noted with prescience, 'I think it is right to say now that we are going to have a very difficult job, notwithstanding the end of this strike, to get these people to continue to support the Labour government.'[44]

John Bohanna was one such 'disgruntled' Labour supporter. For Bohanna

---

[41] Thomas, *Popular Newspapers*, 108.
[42] Tony Blair, 'We Won't Look Back to the 1970s: Opinion,' *The Times*, March 31, 1997, 20.
[43] Rod Finlayson, interview by author, June 2007.
[44] 'The Ford Strike: Where does it take us? An Interview with Dan Connor,' *Marxism Today* (February 1979), 39.

the 1978 strike constituted a 'serious political awakening.' He had perceived how the trade unions collaborated with the Labour government against the Ford rank-and-file movement. The experience led him to break with the Labour Party for what he describes as 'examined revolutionary politics':

> To me, socialism equalled the Labour Party. And I thought, 'Ditch that then!' And I began to discover that it meant a lot, lot more than that. Some people see socialism as a system. I see it as a way of life, with a more human feeling and understanding than any other system. And those elements of socialism were just wonderful. Just absolutely wonderful! It's just a different way of life.[45]

By contrast, Ford Dagenham worker Roger Dillon remained loyal to the Labour Party. Nevertheless, he did not reject all the changes offered by Thatcher's Conservatives. Of particular importance to Dillon were Thatcher's calls for the sale of council homes. His mother owned a council home that she eventually purchased under Thatcher, and he argues, 'If people have pride in what they own, they improve their communities.'[46] The experience of the strikes, and the subsequent political fallout, would propel those involved in dramatically different political directions.

This could also be seen in those involved in the road haulage strike. When the tumult of the lorry drivers' strike and the general election subsided, Bill Rodgers felt increasingly disgruntled with unions and the left-ward shift in the Labour Party. As he would state, 'Unions were damaging throughout whole [sic] of my political life.'[47] Roy Jenkins' Dimbleby lecture in 1979 which set out the contours of the 'radical-centre,' 'calling for an innovative free-market economy coupled with the maintenance of public services like health and education,' provided an opening for the establishment of a new political party where Rodgers would have a key influence.[48] He soon became a founding member of the Social Democratic Party (SDP), but cutting ties with the Labour Party was not easy:

> I never thought of leaving the Labour Party, never crossed my mind. I was fighting, I'd done it before, I'd fought in support of Gaitskell in 1961–62, although it was going to be a much, much tougher proposition to deal with the far Left by that time through the 1970s […] Once the Election was over in 1979 I assumed I would have to play a hard part and rather a tough time trying to save [the] Labour Party. But I suddenly began to

[45] John Bohanna, interview by author, June 2007.
[46] Roger Dillon, interview by author, September 2007.
[47] William Rodgers, transcribed interview by Mike Greenwood, *The History of Parliament* website, http://www.historyofparliamentonline.org/volume/oral-history/member/rodgers-william-1928.
[48] Rodgers, *Fourth among Equals*, 198.

feel that there were too many shifting away. I remember when I made a speech outside and it was well reported in the newspapers and I very well remember walking along the library corridor and in the distance I saw a Labour Member of Parliament, and I knew where he was going to go, he was going towards the Library, and he saw me, and he turned away, not to disagree with me, but to avoid being seen talking to me. He was a moderate man. [...] That was the weakness of my part of the Party [...] they were running away from the hard Left. [...] Right to the last moment really I just didn't know [if I should leave the party] and [I had a] bad back and I really couldn't move and I had to lie in bed. And this sounds imaginative, but over that Christmas of 1980–81 I made up my mind and within a few days, I began to walk.[49]

When the SDP merged with the Liberal Party to form the Liberal Democrats, Rodgers continued to be politically involved as the Leader of the Liberal Democratic Peers in the House of Lords until 1998.[50] With the transformation of Labour into New Labour, Rodgers comprehended some values embodied in this shift:

> The middle England to which Tony Blair had appealed was very like the provincial suburbia in which I had grown up, frightened by strikes and trade unions, hostile to scroungers on the welfare state, unimpressed by the performance of nationalised industries, often prejudiced and sometimes smug but capable of imagination and generosity and offering a source of comfort and security that no-one should despise.[51]

However, an undercurrent of criticism of the New Labour project is also present in his political outlook:

> And yet, underlying much of the discussion of 'welfare to work', and how to deal with benefits, there is a tendency to treat the poor not as victims but as perpetrators. The Blair Government has not created a political climate sympathetic to the poor. They are somehow an embarrassment.[52]

Fred Beach, on the other hand, did not shed his allegiance to Labour:

> What we did in many ways and on many occasions, I've regretted it. But it was effective. We stopped everything. The employers, they were so humiliated. Humiliated! Some of them were country people, so of course

---

[49] William Rodgers, transcribed interview by Mike Greenwood, *The History of Parliament* website, http://www.historyofparliamentonline.org/volume/oral-history/member/rodgers-william-1928.
[50] Rodgers, *Fourth among Equals*, 288.
[51] Rodgers, *Fourth among Equals*, 289–290.
[52] Rodgers, *Fourth among Equals*, 293.

rank Tories [...] I wasn't feeling sorry for 'em. Later on in life came more realization about what we'd done. It was the world turned inside out.[53]

The immediate resolution of the strike in Liverpool in early 1979 did nothing to ameliorate the profound and long-standing political fractures it had created. Larry Whitty and Ian Lowes' divergent paths after the strike reveal how deep these divisions cut. Such differences are apparent in their overall assessment of the strike. Whitty regretted the decision to approve the Liverpool gravediggers' strike, which he believes was a 'serious mistake.' When I interviewed him in 2006, he added that,

> It probably turned the whole of propaganda against us. Whereas the rest of it, there was a balance against us, but it wasn't [...] It came out in the press as if the whole country seemed to be on strike, so it seemed like a prelude to revolution and 'This is the end of society as we know it.' But the gravediggers, it was a very emotional thing. [...] It's just entirely wrong, and you wouldn't anticipate it.[54]

By contrast, Ian Lowes was unrepentant:

> I also get asked the question, 'Would you do it again knowing what you know now? And I would have to say 'yes.' Because we had no choice. Because of the circumstances surrounding the strike. If I had said at that committee meeting that the strike would cause a public backlash, so gravediggers shouldn't go out on strike. That would have gone down like a lead balloon.[55]

These starkly different assessments of the dispute would propel the two men down opposing political trajectories. In Whitty's case, he put all of his energy into Labour's re-election campaign. Once the general election was called, Whitty headed the organization Trade Union for Labour Victory (TULV) operations. He commented that 'I was running trade union support for the Government. So I switched tack. I spent all that election on election work.' Despite both Conservative and Labour efforts to deem the unions as treacherous, Whitty emphasized the fact that 'the unions did try to support the party effort quite substantially.'[56] Over the course of the 1980s, Whitty and the TULV came to be seen as part of the overall bulwark against hard left-wing overtures in the Labour Party, creating a '"Labour loyalist" infrastructure within the unions.'[57] His 'centre-left'[58] politics of the 1970s

---

[53] Beckett (includes interview with Fred Beach) in *When the Lights Went Out*, 489.
[54] Larry Whitty, interview by author, September 2006.
[55] Ian Lowes, interview by author, July 2006.
[56] Whitty, interview, September 2006.
[57] Minkin, *The Contentious Alliance*, 498.
[58] Whitty, interview, September 2006.

started to shift more to the 'centre' in 1985, when Neil Kinnock appointed him General Secretary of the Labour Party in accordance with Kinnock's 'unspoken aim [...] to reduce the [power of] the NEC and the Left.'[59] He immediately began to reform the structure of the Labour Party, placing 'modernizers' in key positions. One such change that would presage the arrival of New Labour would be his appointment of Peter Mandelson as Director of Communications for the Labour Party. After being replaced by another Winter of Discontent veteran, Tom Sawyer, in 1994, Whitty retained stalwart loyalty to the leadership of the party.[60]

Whitty's regret over the gravediggers' strikes resonates with the Labour Party's assessment of the event. The blame was placed upon some Left trade union leaders and with the striking workers who were seen as acting against the interests of Labour. The awkward fact that the Liverpool gravediggers were part of the GMWU union led by David Basnett, a close ally of the Labour government, was muffled. Former Prime Minister Callaghan argued that the strike was actually the responsibility of the left-wing NUPE, laying the blame squarely on the shoulders of its leader Alan Fisher. Callaghan wrote that the Liverpool gravediggers' strikes:

> Appalled the country when they saw pictures of mourners being turned away from the cemetery. Such heartlessness and cold-blooded indifference to the feelings of families at moments of intense grief rightly aroused deep revulsion and did further untold harm to the cause of trade unionism that I, like many others, had been proud to defend throughout my life. [...] My own anger increased when I learned that the Home Secretary Merlyn Rees had called upon Alan Fisher [...] to use his influence to get the gravediggers to go back to work, and Fisher refused.[61]

Former Chancellor of the Exchequer Denis Healey also inaccurately laid the blame at Alan Fisher's feet. 'In Liverpool, the grave-diggers refused to bury the dead. Their union leader, Alan Fisher, refused to ask them to go back to work.'[62] Others in the Cabinet joined in the chorus of denunciations against Fisher. In a memoir about his time at No. 10, Policy Advisor Bernard Donoughue complained that 'Members of Fisher's National Union of Public Employees were refusing to carry the sick to hospitals or to bury the dead. This had nothing to do with trade unionism as Jim Callaghan or I had known it. It was just greedy capitalism with a union card.'[63]

By contrast, Labour Party loyalist GMWU General Secretary David

[59] Cronin, *New Labour's Pasts*, 277.
[60] Cronin, *New Labour's Pasts*, 278.
[61] Callaghan, *Time and Chance*, 537.
[62] Healey, *The Time of My Life*, 463.
[63] Donoughue, *The Heat of the Kitchen*, 312.

Basnett, whose union *did* approve the strike, emerged as one of the cohort of victims. In his autobiography, Roy Hattersley, then Secretary of State for Prices and Consumer Protection, described an encounter with Basnett:

> Nothing happened to me during my three years in the Cabinet to cause me more anguish than the sight of David Basnett [...] in tears at the thought of the way in which his members were behaving.
>
> [Basnett]: Who could have believed that Liverpool Parks and Cemeteries Branch would behave like this?[64]

While national leaders like Basnett never directly made decisions to have workers' execute such actions, according the Larry Whitty, 'they did authorize particular groups' to do so.[65] Therefore, at least in this specific case, the Liverpool gravediggers' strike cannot be solely seen as an unofficial rank-and-file action. Departing from the Conservatives' narrative of the gravediggers' strike as the Labour government's inability to control its trade union allies, the story becomes one of betrayal. By extricating David Basnett and the more centrist trade union, the GMWU, and falsely blaming the left-wing NUPE, the government is made to appear a victim of external, 'extremist' elements in the labour movement.

Some national trade union officials have, over time, come to re-evaluate their support of the gravediggers' strikes in general. NUPE North West Divisional Officer at the time Colin Barnett approved the gravediggers' strike in Tameside, outside Manchester. From the beginning the strike, he explained that the gravediggers' dispute was but one of many actions to alleviate low pay in Britain. In 1979 Barnett asserted that the strikes would escalate and admitted that the British public would bear the brunt of these strikes. 'This will undoubtedly cause more suffering and inconvenience, but until society is prepared to deal fairly with the needs of the low paid, we will continue our action relentlessly.'[66]

On February 3, when the local council attempted to use contractors and non-union labour to break the strike, Barnett rejected the intervention and

---

[64] Hattersley, *Who Goes Home*, 202.
[65] Larry Whitty, interview by author, June 2010.
[66] 'Unions Ready to Escalate Strike,' *Manchester Evening News*, January 26, 1979. For further detail of NUPE's and Barnett's involvement in the Tameside gravediggers' strike, see: 'Strikers Put the Block on Funerals,' *Manchester Evening News*, January 23, 1979; 'Union Warning Over Burials,' *Manchester Evening News*, January 24, 1979; 'Bid to Spread Grave Strike,' *Manchester Evening News*, January 26, 1979; 'Four Unions in Paralysis Plan,' *Manchester Evening News*, January 27, 1979; 'Strikers Let the Bodies Pile Up,' *Manchester Evening News*, January 30, 1979.

was quoted as saying 'If they want to aggravate the situation this is the way to do it.'[67] However, in 2006, Barnett reflected that

> Even though I was prepared to play every trick in the book. I suspect [...] I would have done everything to get them [striking gravediggers] back to work on the grounds that you shouldn't have somebody's personal grief to be used in terms of advancing your claims.[68]

He also stated that the gravediggers who took the strike action in the region were members of the GMWU, not NUPE. Rodney Bickerstaffe, on the other hand, refused to waver in his support for the strikers, regardless of whether they were GMWU or NUPE members. 'There were two places [where they weren't burying the dead]: Liverpool and Manchester. Our lot were in Manchester.'[69] He continued to hold the belief that the gravediggers who went on strike during the Winter of Discontent had a legitimate right to reject the harsh conditions and low pay of the job. Therefore, even within the contours of counter-memory, myth is not only challenged, but, as Barnett's case illustrates, 'counter-myth' also developed.

Bickerstaffe's solidarity with the strikes provides little consolation for Ian Lowes, who has borne much of the blame for the strikes. The GMWU's about face and the Labour government's attack on the strike undermined Lowes' loyalty to Labour, and he gravitated to the Trotskyite political group Militant:

> I started reading [*The Militant*] newspaper during the Winter of Discontent because [...] if there's anything going on, you have the paper sellers from here, there, and everywhere. And I got *The Militant* one time, when they were outside one of our meetings, selling it. Then, I read it, and I thought, 'I agree with that.'[70]

Right after the Winter of Discontent, Lowes joined Militant:

> Martin: So do you think it [Winter of Discontent] was influential in you joining Militant?
>
> Lowes: Yeah. And my experience with the Labour Government. And my experience with the trade union leadership. So them betraying us in conjunction with the Labour Government to try to sabotage the effectiveness of what you were trying to do.[71]

---

[67] 'Tameside Moves to End Graves Strike,' *Guardian*, February 3, 1979. See also 'Hope For Peace in Graves Row,' *Manchester Evening News*, February 2, 1979.
[68] Colin Barnett, interview by author, May 2006.
[69] Rodney Bickerstaffe, interview by author, May 2006.
[70] Ian Lowes, interview by author, October 2006.
[71] Lowes, interview, October 2006.

Lowes became involved in Militant, supporting its call for fundamental social change. He split with the party in 1986, when the Militant-controlled Liverpool council began to bring in private contractors to do the work of local authority workers, a move that Conservatives were making across the country. Despite Lowes' disavowal of Militant, Kinnock's inquiry in the mid-1980s into Militant in Liverpool led to Lowes' expulsion from the party. Bereft of any political outlet, Lowes continued to focus on his work in his local union and rejected any overtures to get him involved politically.[72]

The year 1997 provides a crucial historical marker in the political future envisioned by these individuals whose histories are so inextricably intertwined with the Winter of Discontent. The election of Tony Blair signalled the beginning of another era of politics, one characterized by its own set of opportunities and limits for its supporters. In 1998, Whitty became a member of the Cabinet and later became a Peer in the House of Lords. Nevertheless, he admitted that he was not entirely convinced by all of the aspects of New Labour. 'Some of it I agree with, but most of it is too stuck in the mainstream economic policy rather than the traditions of social democracy.'[73] By contrast, a political vacuum emerged for left-wing, working-class activists like Lowes as the scope of the local labour movement contracted. Lowes confessed that he voted for Labour in 1997, but he did so 'under no illusions.' He grimly added 'I remember where I was when Kennedy was shot, and I remember where I was when Tony Blair was elected.'[74]

The election of new political represented a point of no return for Ian Lowes; his outlets for political expression were now completely reconfigured, not only by the continuing resilience of the myth of the Winter, but by the defeat of the miners' strike, Thatcher's trade union reforms, and the shift to the Right in the Labour Party. While men like Rodgers, Whitty, Barnett, and Bickerstaffe had a combination of authority and resources to establish themselves within this New Labour paradigm, left-wing working-class men like Beach and Lowes, bereft of political and economic influence, were left without such outlets, and with it was lost an important form of trade union politics to the apparent 'irrelevance'[75] of history.

---

[72] Lowes, interview, October 2006.
[73] Whitty, interview, June 2010.
[74] Lowes, interview, October 2006.
[75] In 2006, the Confederation of British Industry asserted that unions in Britain have become 'increasingly irrelevant.' 'The History Woman,' *Guardian*, September 6, 2006.

Gender, Class, and Memory

The NUPE strikes provide yet another important point where one can examine what James Fentress and Chris Wickham refer to as the 'kaleidoscope of difference' that exists amongst the currents of memory.[76] The countermemory of the Winter of Discontent for some, especially among some female activists, framed this series of events as a transformative point in their involvement in the labour movement. Furthermore, the momentum gained after the Winter of Discontent helped to fuel further gendered reforms in NUPE that would help to crucially reshape the trade union movement.

If we begin, however, with the uppermost reaches of political influence, we can see the similarities and contrasts of all these currents. Prime Minister Callaghan's political adviser, Tom McNally, found his work in government from 1974 to 1979 especially formative. By the beginning of 1979, two events influenced his drift away from the Labour Party. First of all, the pact between the Liberal Party and the Labour government revealed that political parties could, indeed, work together. Second, the fall of the Social Contract during the Winter of Discontent made him 'increasingly disillusioned' with the ability of the trade union movement and the Labour Party to work together. The tipping point for McNally came soon after the Winter of Discontent when he was speaking to Dave Worberton of the GMWU. When attempting to allay McNally's concerns over what he saw as the disproportionate influence of the trade union movement on the Labour Party, Worberton stated, 'Don't worry Tom; we'll pay the money. We'll call the shots.' In addition to what he saw as the 'vicious and intolerant' conflicts between the Left and Right of the Labour Party in the early 1980s, McNally joined the Social Democratic Party and is currently a member of the Liberal Democrats.[77] The shifts in party affiliation over the course of two decades betray what McNally sees as an unshakable loyalty to the Labour Party:

> Martin: What about personally? When do you think you changed politically?
>
> McNally: I don't think I ever changed politically. [*Laughs*] I left the Labour Party in '82 partly because of its reaction to all of this with a violent swing to the Left. [...] My view is that it was a complete misresponse, and it took the Labour Party a decade to adjust.
>
> Martin: Do you think you feel more at ease with the Labour Party [in 2006] now that they have adjusted?

---

[76] Fentress and Wickham, *Social Memory*, 126.
[77] (Lord) Tom McNally, interview by author, May 2008.

McNally: With their domestic policy: yes. With their foreign policy: no. I think that's one of the great tragedies. I think that a government that's had the economic opportunity to do a lot of social good has embarked on a mad foreign policy. But I have no regrets![78]

McNally was the Minister of State for Justice in the coalition government until his resignation in December 2013. Despite feeling marginalized within the Labour Party partly due to the Winter of Discontent, McNally was able to find outlets of political expression, but only outside the realm of the Labour Party.

While McNally was able to evade the ghosts of the Winter of Discontent, Rodney Bickerstaffe, on the other hand, decries how the continued backlash against NUPE 'for bringing in Thatcher' '[...] has been around [his] neck ever since.' Bickerstaffe became the General Secretary of NUPE soon after the Winter of Discontent in 1981, and although he helped push the union in efforts to modernize the Labour Party during the 1980s, he refuses to ally himself with New Labour and its disavowal of the strikes of 1978 and 1979. Bickerstaffe asserts that the strikes were actually the fault of the Callaghan government and its obstinacy with unions, which resulted in the disputes and the subsequent electoral debacle. He further argued, 'There are those who say because Thatcher came along – "we lost the war as well as the battle" – I would have to say if I had to do it all over again today, I would do it all over again.' His refusal to apologize for the Winter of Discontent has had a profound effect on his identity as a staunch defender of workers' rights, an identity he maintains in what he sees as unanimous opposition.[79] In an interview in 2007, Bickerstaffe proudly asserted that he had refused a peerage in the House of Lords. So proud was he of this fact that he showed me the newspaper article on his rejection of the peerage, which he regularly kept on his person to show to anybody who inquired.[80] No better act could symbolize how his assessment of the Winter of Discontent shaped his present understanding of himself and the world around him.

The Winter of Discontent had quite a different effect on Tom Sawyer. Sawyer articulated in 2006 the opposing political trajectories he and Bickerstaffe took:

> It's a bit like a bad experience in a relationship. Sometimes you don't really bottom it out. You move on. It's painful. [...] It was like that with the Winter of Discontent. I don't really think we bottomed it out, so we all left it with different experiences. I know for a long time it was like a badge of honour to say, 'The unions were right.' Rodney [Bickerstaffe] was

---

[78] (Lord) Tom McNally, interview by author, November 2006.
[79] Rodney Bickerstaffe, interview by author, May 2006.
[80] Rodney Bickerstaffe, interview by author, June 2007.

in this camp. I personally did not think that this was the right thing to do. I thought it was better to say, 'We all made a mistake, and we all have to take the blame, if there was any blame.'[81]

During the 1980s, Sawyer became a key 'modernizer' in the Labour Party, heading the enquiry into the expulsion of Militant, which became a pivotal act in curtailing the influence of the hard Left in the Labour Party. Not only did his work have a profound effect on the wider shift in the Labour Party, it also had far-reaching political and personal reverberations for Sawyer himself because of what he believed was the victimization of NUPE members in Liverpool at the hands of Militant:

> It was a big thing to go through for me. I was unwell. I became ill through it because it was so frighteningly horrible to see. I didn't think people did this. I didn't believe it was being done. I didn't think people's lives would be destroyed because they were in the wrong union. I had fallen out with a lot of friends that hadn't seen what I had seen.[82]

Sawyer later became the General Secretary for the Labour Party and was in that position when Tony Blair and New Labour came into office in 1997. His work for New Labour was eventually awarded with a peerage in the House of Lords. Sawyer detailed the intensity of his work with the Labour Party:

> My detractors would say that I swung to the Right. You know that's what they would say. I don't mind. That's alright. That's ok. That's fine. I know what I did. And it wasn't Left or Right. It was about what I had to do for the members. How were we going to improve the lot of working-class people? We had tried the syndicalist route. I thought it was good to try the Parliamentary route.[83]

His response to the events of the late 1970s and early 1980s along with his commitment to supporting working people meant that his politics shifted:

> I had to do something about the problems. I couldn't just stay where I was and apply the same solutions when I thought that new solutions were required. I think you have to find your answer to your own time, and the answer comes from the working people. It comes from below. It never comes from above. So, to be good at politics, you've got to be very close to where people are. Now then, sadly, that's not always a comfortable place to be.[84]

Less high-profile changes were visible among the newly energized women of

---

[81] (Lord) Tom Sawyer, interview by author, June 2006.
[82] (Lord) Tom Sawyer, interview by author, November 2006.
[83] Sawyer, interview, November 2006.
[84] Sawyer, interview, November 2006.

the NUPE rank and file, and local and national trade union leaders. Sheila Cunnison and Jane Stageman's studies of female trade unionists during the Winter of Discontent observed significant changes in the organizational confidence of women in NUPE. For instance, they showed how a NUPE branch of school meals workers successfully created a new branch because male rubbish collectors had dominated the previous one. After the Winter of Discontent, the school meals women began to become frustrated that they were 'controlled by refuse collectors who know nothing about school kitchens.' Their ability to break away from this branch was rooted in the changes that had occurred during the Winter of Discontent. Cunnison and Stageman interviewed one school meals worker who stated that before the Winter of Discontent, 'I used to be a little grey mouse, sitting back and saying nothing. Now I will say what I have to. I'm not afraid. If I know I'm right, I'll speak up.'[85]

The school meals worker Betty Hughes echoes a comparable sense of developing self-assertion:

> Well, they [Hughes' family] were thinking I was too 'Bolshie' sort of thing. [*Laughs*] You get a reputation. You know. That used to niggle me a bit. When they used to say, 'Go to Betty, you. She'll sort it out for you.' You know. But I used to say, 'No. I can't sort out everything! I'll help.' And I used to go shopping in Asda [...] and I would get cornered! And I used to say, 'It's like having a union meeting in here! All this staff [are] moaning and groaning! Why don't you come to the meetings and then tell us what's going on?'[86]

Her reputation for being able to 'sort things out' made her an important contact within her community who neighbours turned to for help:

> Betty Hughes: And then I would be doing the tea, and somebody would ring up with a problem. 'Can you come?'
>
> Martin: Would it be a work problem?
>
> Betty Hughes: Oh yeah. It would be a work problem, but it would also be personal problems, as well. They must have thought that I was able to do everything. I couldn't get through to them that, I couldn't.

When asked why she would take on the weight of so much responsibility, Betty and Joe, her husband, both chimed in:

> Betty Hughes: Yeah, but I enjoyed it. I wouldn't say I loved it, but I enjoyed doing it. And I also enjoyed the power that I had, as well.

---

[85] Cunnison and Stageman, *Feminizing the Unions*, 95–96.
[86] Betty and Joe Hughes, interview by author, March 2007.

Martin: Really?

Joe Hughes: It brought it out!

Betty Hughes: Because I was able [...]

Joe Hughes: She could put her hand on everything! It wasn't gold. I wish it was because then I would be very rich!

These individual experiences were representative of the growing presence of the school meals workers in NUPE. When the Conservative government, for example, announced in late 1979 that school meals were to be cut by 50 per cent, NUPE school meals workers fought local authorities throughout the UK, forcing some to reconsider their plans.[87] In 1980, at the NUPE National Conference, the Executive attempted to ignore a group of school meals workers, but the women refused to remain silent and started shouting at the leaders:

Betty Hughes: That would be [nineteen] eighty [...] because that was when we [school meals workers] [...] all started to having a go.

Stuart Hill: If you think about it, it's like following on from the Winter of Discontent. I'm not saying there's a direct link, but there was the kind of feeling that the union kind of changed.[88]

The feeling that things had 'kind of changed' could definitely be seen in the trajectories of Linda Perks and Anne Gardiner. After working closely together during the Winter of Discontent, they continued to make significant inroads into NUPE. In 1983 NUPE set up a Working Women's Party, and the leadership charged Perks, Gardiner, and another Winter of Discontent veteran, Glyn Hawker, with leading this group to research and provide suggestions about how to improve the involvement of women within the union.[89] One of their most important calls was to develop Women's Advisory Committees that would specifically focus on developing leadership among the female rank-and-file majority, or, put another way, to create, 'a greenhouse to grow within the union.'[90]

On an individual basis, Gardiner and Perks made unprecedented leadership achievements for women in the union. Immediately after the Winter of Discontent, Gardiner became the first female chair of the Area Division Council, and five years later became the first woman to become Secretary

---

[87] Williams and Fryer, *Leadership & Democracy*, 379–380.
[88] Stuart Hill, Betty and Joe Hughes, interview by author, November, 2007.
[89] Cynthia Cockburn, 'Play of Power: Women, men and equality initiatives in a Trade Union,' *Anthropology of Organizations*, ed. Susan Wright (London: Routledge, 1994), 94.
[90] Glyn Hawker, interview by author, December 2011.

of her local NUPE branch. She was fast-tracked to positions of national leadership within the union. Similarly, Perks was one of three women, all of whom began their careers in NUPE during the Winter of Discontent, to be short-listed for the position of National Women's Officer in 1982.[91] Another of the three applicants, Dorothy Mae Harden, attested to the importance of the Winter of Discontent in her application. 'My employment commenced with N.U.P.E. during the so-called "Winter of Discontent," so I was thrown in the deep end, so to speak, but having made that statement I would add, one learns to swim much quicker whilst in the deep end.'[92]

The fact that women were gaining this collective presence in the union can be seen most clearly at the grassroots level. In 1981 there were only nine more female Branch Secretaries than in 1974, with men continuing to significantly outnumber women in these positions.[93] Also, by 1983, only 12 out of 180 trade union officials were women.[94] However, from 1974 to 1983, there was an 18 per cent increase in the numbers of female shop stewards, so that by 1983, 44 per cent of all shop stewards in NUPE were women.[95] Perks noted that she and Gardiner were part of a wider shift:

> I would say the difference between the achievements that were made in that period from what happened before [...] is that it was collective. That was probably a lesson from the Women's Movement. Previous to that, women were probably lone voices in a man's world. Whereas, in setting up working as a group, obviously, we were a lot stronger.[96]

Perks and Gardiner also broadened the scope of their activism and joined the Labour Party in the early 1980s.

Gardiner's political development further illustrates that NUPE women like her were part of the 'modernization' of the Labour Party. In the 1981 election of the Labour Party Deputy Leader, the NUPE Executive had a 'close affinity' with Tony Benn, yet they did not recommend a candidate to the membership. Instead, they provided members personal statements from all of the candidates. The majority of NUPE members voted for

---

[91] 'List of Applicants Short-listed for the Post of Women's Officer, Application Forms for Post of Women's Officer,' June Abdoulrahman Papers, MSS 389 Box 29, Modern Records Centre, University of Warwick, Coventry, UK.

[92] 'List of Applicants Short-listed for the Post of Women's Officer, Application Forms for Post of Women's Officer,' June Abdoulrahman Papers, MSS 389 Box 29, Modern Records Centre, University of Warwick, Coventry, UK.

[93] *Survey of Branch District Committees 1st Report, 1981*, UNISON/Rodney Bickerstaffe Papers, MSS 389 Box 5, Modern Records Centre, University of Warwick, Coventry, UK.

[94] Boston, *Women Workers and the Trade Unions*, 332.

[95] Bob Fryer and Steve Williams, *A Century of Service: An Illustrated History of the National Union of Public Employees, 1889–1993* (London: Lawrence & Wishart, 1993), 130.

[96] Linda Perks, interview by author, September, 2007.

right-leaning Healey, which 'proved decisive in securing his election.'[97] Furthermore, while Gardiner opposed much of the political moderation that came with the rise of New Labour, she became instrumental in having the Blairite Alan Milburn selected as MP when she was a local councillor in Darlington. Although it was Milburn's supposed left-wing ideas that initially attracted Gardiner to him, it was her own 'left-wing' ideas that had her labelled as a 'malcontent' in the Labour Party, and Milburn then helped to get Gardiner de-selected as a councillor. Despite such a harrowing experience after years of work for both trade unions and the Labour Party, Gardiner remained hopeful about Labour when I interviewed her in 2006:

> Martin: After all that you have gone through with the Labour Party, why do you still remain Labour? What keeps you going?
>
> Gardiner: Because the real Labour Party hasn't been elected. Has it? I mean I think that's the – I think we need the proper Labour Party elected. With Labour values. I think there's a lot of work to be done.[98]

Gardiner's assertion sheds light on the nature of memory for these working-class women. Despite the lack of avenues for expression of her politics, she continued to see that there was space for change. Larry Whitty, who became the General Secretary of the Labour Party during the 1980s and early 1990s, noted that New Labour was not 'dramatically different' from the Tories on economic policy. However, he asserted that on social policy, for instance the integration of women into leadership roles in the party, it was definitely different from that of the Conservatives.[99] The marginalization of class issues left women like Gardiner with little room for agency based on their working-class background, but openings for women in the labour movement provided them with some form of leverage. While avenues of political expression ended for left-wing men like Ian Lowes, the growth in both numbers and influence of female-dominated unions created opportunities for this fledgling leadership. Finally, despite New Labour's distanced stance from class politics, their reinvented politics have created new roles for women's political expression.[100] Even if this had had a deep effect only on a radicalized minority, it has contributed to significant and broader changes in the Labour Party and trade unions.

Similarly transformative effects could be seen amongst hospital workers

---

[97] Williams and Fryer, *Leadership & Democracy*, 384.
[98] Anne Gardiner, interview by author, November 2006.
[99] Whitty, interview, June 2010.
[100] For an account of the development of New Labour, especially the party's evolving policies on women's leadership, see: Meg Russell, *Building New Labour: The Politics of Party Organisation* (New York: Palgrave MacMillan, 2005).

who were active during the Winter of Discontent. At the NUPE Branch at Whiston Hospital in Prescott, the Winter of Discontent sparked a new feeling and form of militancy among the rank and file. NUPE shop steward and soon-to-be-elected Branch Secretary Mike Donovan described this changing mood:

> [The Winter of Discontent] made us more militant. It made us more pro-union, if that was possible. We were pro-union anyway. I think it made us more determined. You know. We could see so much injustice, not just with us in the health service, but to our friends, relatives, neighbours in the community.[101]

This transformation was especially apparent in the shifting position of women in NUPE. After the Winter of Discontent, the women who took a leading part in the strikes began to assume leadership roles in the union. Hospital cleaner Celia Newman and porter Mike Donovan agreed that many shop stewards elected soon after 1979 were motivated to become active in the union '[...] because of the Winter of Discontent, really.'[102] One such woman was Lorraine Donovan. After almost a decade of being an inactive NUPE member, Lorraine Donovan joined the likes of Newman and was elected shop steward in 1980.[103]

In addition to an increased numeric presence, there were more subtle indications that a shift in power towards the female membership in NUPE had occurred. For example, employers began to recognize that these women were becoming more powerful leaders among the rank and file, which some regarded as a potential threat. Soon after the Winter of Discontent, Celia Newman was offered a promotion. As shop steward Stuart Hill from the north east of England pointed out, 'The two ways of getting rid of a good shop steward was to promote them or to sack them.'[104] Newman observed in 2006:

> Oh yeah! I even had an offer of a brilliant job to get me off the union, and it was after – it was awhile after the big strike [Winter of Discontent]. But because, after that strike, I sort of thought, 'Hmm. I like doing this. I like being sort of a spokesperson for people. I don't like people shouting down at me. I can shout back at them. I've got people behind me now.'[105]

As Newman noted, her role in the Winter of Discontent earned her not only more respect among her co-workers, but her employers also observed

---

[101] Mike and Lorraine Donovan, and Celia Newman, interview by author, October 2006.
[102] Mike and Lorraine Donovan, and Newman, interview.
[103] Mike and Lorraine Donovan, and Newman, interview.
[104] Anne Gardiner and Stuart Hill, interview by author, March 2007.
[105] Mike and Lorraine Donovan and Newman, interview.

this transformation and sought to neutralize what they observed as a threat. However, her rejection of this promotion indicates that her commitment to the union was not fleeting, and was actually deepened by involvement in the disputes of 1979.

The changes could also be seen in hospitals in London. Part of this overall shift was a change in the role women were beginning to play in the union. NUPE steward Jonathan Neale noted the change in leadership in London while organizing collections and support for strikes in 1976 and then in 1982. He observed that in 1976 most of the union leaders were men, but in 1982 they continued to be men though 'about half the people who could actually get things done were women.'[106]

The momentum these women had created in NUPE soon spilled into their activism in the local Labour Party. Soon after the Winter of Discontent, Celia Newman, Lorraine and Mike Donovan all joined the local constituency Labour Party.[107] As a result of this activism, initially ignited during the Winter of Discontent, the two women made significant inroads into the Labour Party. Lorraine Donovan is an especially notable example as she became the first female Vice Chair of the local Labour Constituency Party, and in 2006 she was the first female elected as the Mayor of the Labour Party Group on Knowsley council.[108]

In the early 1990s, NUPE joined forces with former rivals COHSE and NALGO to form UNISON. This merger, combined with a perceived shift in UNISON's priorities, left some activists disillusioned. Bob Gregory, echoing the sentiment among many former NUPE activists, believed that the merger among the three unions was, in fact, a subtle way for NALGO to assume leadership of COHSE and NUPE. 'I think it was a takeover [by NALGO]. [...] If] you take a look at the structure of UNISON now, the majority of the people who have top jobs now are from NALGO.'[109] Others, like Newman, feel disoriented and disillusioned by the new form of militancy they believe has developed in UNISON:

> [Her branch of UNISON] is a different type of union. It's a different type of working. At the moment, I would say years ago that we were militant. We were militant – to a degree. We weren't bad militants. We weren't – we'd always sit down; we'd always listen; we'd always negotiate with management. I'm not saying we always gave in. We very, very rarely gave in, but we'd always compromise where it was needed. This regime that's

[106] Neale, *Memoirs of a Callous Picket*, 62.
[107] Mike and Lorraine Donovan and Newman, interview.
[108] Mike and Lorraine Donovan and Newman, interview.
[109] Bob Gregory, interview by author, August 2006.

come in now thinks that [they] can bring that militancy back and say, 'No. We're not having it. That's end of it!' No discussion. I'll never, ever come back into trade unions, never again.[110]

Nevertheless, she has no regrets about her involvement in the strikes of 1979.

Continued loyalty to the Labour Party assumes a similarly convoluted appearance. Gregory described the current state of the local Labour Party in 2006, which he perceived as inactive and a shell of its former self:

> I've seen the change now in the Labour movement in the seventies, eighties, into the nineties, into the year 2000. I used to go to meetings of the Labour Party in the seventies and eighties. And, don't forget, we'd have meetings in Liverpool, when they had the Winter of Discontent, from September into March, May. And I'd go to meetings in the evening, of the Labour Party, in Liverpool. You couldn't get in the door. You could not get in the door. [There would be] 75 to 80 people in that room. Now you can go to a Labour Party meeting, and you get four, you get five people.[111]

Gregory was also dismayed by the little difference he saw between the Labour and Conservative Parties. 'Is there any choice between the Tories and Labour now? You've got the most right-wing, reactionary Prime Minister we've ever had. Haven't you? He's [Blair] probably the best Tory Prime Minister we've ever seen.'[112]

For Lorraine Donovan, the changes in the Labour Party were positive, but Blair's 'appeal to middle England' was not encouraging because she had had 'high hopes for John Smith.' Nevertheless, Lorraine Donovan found the overall decline in political culture much more disheartening:

> After Labour won the second election, and there was so much apathy. We'd go out, knocking on doors, encouraging people to vote, and you found that the people that had the least, who were the poorest, who were the most downtrodden by legislation would not go out and vote because they didn't think it would make any difference. The apathy was absolutely tremendous at that point.[113]

The emergence of New Labour did not pose such a bleak future for Mike Donovan:

> Let me tell you what happened the day of the [1997] general election. [...] we went to the local pub, as you do. And they had a great big screen there, and you could see the results coming in. And it's all going red.

---

[110] Mike and Lorraine Donovan and Newman, interview.
[111] Gregory, interview.
[112] Gregory, interview.
[113] Mike and Lorraine Donovan and Newman, interview.

And you know it's really hard to take it all in, that after eighteen years of Tory battering, we'd done it. And I floated over the pub, it was probably a balance of the beer and euphoria. And the following morning, I got up. I put the television on, went over to the local shop, and I bought every paper in the shop. A copy of every paper because I wanted to read it by a different reporter. We've done it! We've won! That was a personal thing that I did.[114]

The combination of the Conservatives' efforts to 'revisit' the memory of the Winter of Discontent during general elections and the neo-liberal ascendancy in the 1980s and 1990s has lent credence to the view the Winter of Discontent supposedly embodied all the excesses of social democracy and trade unionism. The excavation of counter-memories among the participants in the Winter of Discontent, however, calls this myth into question. The memories of strikers who recall it as a series of justified actions contrasts with the version of the Winter of Discontent that has been presented by Conservative and Labour politicians and accepted by some historians.

There are different layers of memory, one dominant and prevalent in the public domain and another submerged beneath the power and influence of those who have dictated the narrative. The contrasting memories reveal how the Winter of Discontent came to be a political and cultural fulcrum in the simultaneous contraction and expansion of the sphere of political identity in the late twentieth century. The political space and legitimacy of trade union politics began to contract as that of gender expanded. For some female trade unionists, the strikes acted as important rites of passage that sparked their further involvement in the British labour movement. This gendering of labour activism in the unions has received remarkably little attention and has been drowned out in the disputes over how the Winter of Discontent is to be remembered, yet it remains in the memories of the women and men who participated.

---

[114] Mike and Lorraine Donovan and Newman, interview.

Conclusion

On September 11, 2008, the *Daily Mail* ran a story warning its readers what would happen if public sector trade unions in Scotland voted to go out on strike:

> We 'could be brought to a standstill later this month', hard men in cheap suits warn us, and we are at imminent risk of another Winter of Discontent. [...] Rubbish will rot uncollected. Grannies will loll, untended, in residential care-homes. Schools will go uncleaned. [...] And, yes, the dead will go unburied or unburned. You would not mind nearly so much if the commissars just went before the cameras and said, 'Well, we're a bunch of opportunists and we just want more money in the shameless knowledge we can bring society to a halt.' But it is the righteous preachiness that grates. They are, they sigh, 'forced into action,' there being no other way to secure a 'living wage.'[1]

Even 30 years after the fact, the myth of the Winter of Discontent remained firmly entrenched in British culture. However, I have shown that spectres of 'opportunistic' workers and bumbling Labour politicians are evocations that contrast with the multitude of motivations and experiences of those involved in the struggles and conflicts that winter of 1978–79.

For workers in Britain, the rampant inflation of the 1970s triggered a precipitous fall in real wages. So dramatic was the decline that from 1975 to 1977, '[...] the average wage earner had suffered the biggest cut in [the] standard of living since before the industrial revolution.'[2] Many of the economic gains the working class had made soon after the Second World War were dissolving under the pressure of inflation at an unprecedented rate, making a third year of wage restraint in 1978 all the more intolerable.

---

[1] 'Hostages to the Brothers in the Blinkers,' *Daily Mail*, September 11, 2008.
[2] Robert Taylor quoted in Ludlam, 'Old Labour and the Winter of Discontent,' 31.

This fall in living standards led school meals worker Maureen Groves to supplement her husband's income and prevented one gravedigger from taking his wife out for dinner more often than once every five years. My research shows this depression of real wages was affecting working people across Western industrialized nations, igniting similar acts of militancy in these countries. The Winter of Discontent was, therefore, part of a global wave of industrial militancy against the erosion of working-class living standards. The decision to strike had less to do with the 'bloody mindedness' of British workers than with responding to an assault on their livelihoods.

My research also reveals that workers' rejection of wage restraint in 1978–79 was fuelled by divergent levels of membership growth and political clout amongst trade unions. Also, the uneven effects of wage restraint exacerbated divisions between private and public sector workers. Throughout the 1970s, private sector unions based in industry and manufacturing, such as the TGWU and AEUW, continued to dominate the trade union movement politically. The loss of jobs in these two sectors of the economy was met with a simultaneous rise in low-paid service and public sector work, primarily done by a female workforce. Not only were public sector workers low paid, but since the 1960s, they experienced a disproportionate level of pressure from the government to abide by incomes' policy, while workers in the private sector had repeatedly won wage settlements in excess of these wage limits. When workers at Ford went on strike in September 1978, they triggered strikes in the public sector where workers sought to address such disparities. The Winter of Discontent was the moment where these cleavages within the British trade union movement came to a breaking point.

Although economic factors were important, shifts in political culture were also extremely significant. My interviews illustrate that although the Labour Party continued to elicit strong loyalties, new grassroots political forces were emerging. Amongst the leadership of some unions such as NUPE, ideas of participatory democracy and women's liberation transformed the trajectory of trade unionism to organize and mobilize workers previously ignored by unions. Moreover, rank-and-file workers engaged with different political ideas and refashioned them on their own terms in ways that they perceived to meet the needs of their own communities. They debated whether industrial militancy or political parties would improve working-class people's living conditions, undercutting their loyalty to Labour's imposition of wage restraint in 1978.

I further illustrate that while formal institutions such as political parties and trade unions were influential in politicizing people, the family, or the domain of the private sphere exerted an equally crucial influence on my interviewees' political identities. The politics of mothers, fathers, grandmothers reveal that for most of those involved in the Winter of

Discontent, from rank-and-file activists to Labour politicians, the influence of the family played a central role in developing their commitment to the labour movement. Furthermore, 'private' experiences such as domestic violence and divorce led people like Betty Hughes and Lorraine Donovan to seek more independent roles in their home lives, the effects of which spilled over into their trade union and Labour Party activism. Therefore, the politics that inspired people to become active in the labour movement were inextricably intertwined with 'personal' experiences that eventually played a role in sparking their activity during the winter of 1978–79.

Those immersed in these nascent political cultures of the late 1960s and 1970s were only beginning to make forays into the Labour Party power structure. The Labour Party continued to be led by Labour politicians who were shaped by a version of Labour Party ideology that was very different from the ideas circulating at the grassroots. Their loyalty was rooted in a conviction that only the Labour Party could effectively promote prosperity and social mobility in post-war Britain. This view became increasingly remote in the late 1970s as working-class opportunities contracted rather than expanded. My research reveals a gulf between the Labour leadership and working-class communities, which was evident during the Winter of Discontent.

Nevertheless, it is important to note that the Labour leadership did, indeed, face challenges beyond its control. Labour leadership's choices were certainly curtailed by the deepening global economic crisis. A hostile economic environment, combined with the restrictive IMF mandates that accompanied the loan, restricted the range of economic alternatives at their disposal. Politically too, their position was precarious, especially after the Lib-Lab pact expired in 1978.

However, James Callaghan did make several missteps. More specifically, my interviews with trade union and Labour Party leaders, combined with archival research, disclose that Callaghan showed a fatal rigidity in his dealings with the unions. Callaghan was attempting what both the Wilson and Heath governments were unable to achieve while in office in seeking to assert the authority of the central government over the trade union movement. Moreover, he began to see trade union power as an impediment to economic regeneration and believed wage restraint was central to improving the overall lives of people in Britain. Hence, Callaghan rejected wage rises in excess of 5 per cent.[3] As noted earlier in the book, in May 1978, journalist Geoffrey Goodman expressed to Callaghan the futility of maintaining the 5 per cent limit that year. Callaghan replied, 'Alright, if that is the case, then I will go over the heads of the trade union leadership and appeal directly

---

[3] Goodman, *From Bevan to Blair*, 223.

to their members – and the voters. We have to hold the line on pay or the government will fall.' However, he underestimated the restlessness of the trade union membership.

Moreover, the national trade union leadership did indeed work hard to uphold the Social Contract. The TUC's lack of support for the 1977 Fire Brigades' strike or even NUPE General Secretary's push to support the Social Contract while criticizing public expenditure cuts reveal that the national trade unions ' support for the Labour government was not flippant. Nevertheless, some leaders' willingness to 'blind through' the 5 per cent wage limit indicates their willingness to support the pay policy despite rank-and-file opposition.[4]

During the 1979 general election campaign, the Conservatives spotlighted unions' defiance of Callaghan's inflexibility with incomes' policy. It is at this point that we begin to observe the evolution of this potent myth. Images of piles of rubbish, pickets in front of hospitals, striking gravediggers, and extremely frigid weather created an overall narrative of 'siege' and 'crisis.' Thatcher offered 'harmony' to this perceived social 'discord,' and was effectively catapulted into office in May 1979.[5]

The role of the media was central during the Winter of Discontent and the general election of 1979; however, one must be careful not to overstate its role. Government reports of potential shortages of animal foodstuffs and penicillin ingredients as a result of the lorry drivers' strike, for instance, indicate that supplies were vulnerable to pressure from industrial action. Schools were shut; rubbish did go uncollected; and despite blatant media manipulation, such images did tap into a genuine feeling that a crisis was, indeed, occurring. I argue that a combination of rising political and economic discontent among working- and middle-class Britons made the images of the Winter of Discontent especially resonant. Thatcher and the Conservatives were able to 'transform [this] vague dislike of circumstances'[6] and effectively offer themselves as the logical political alternative. Labour did not effectively meet the Conservatives' media onslaught, as evidenced by Prime Minister's Callaghan's disastrous press conference upon returning from Guadeloupe and Labour's unresponsive Party Political Broadcast on January 24, 1979. As Sheila Rowbotham observes, 'In contrast to the

---

[4] Roy Hattersley, *Who Goes Home*, 107.

[5] Thatcher quoted lines from St Francis of Assisi as she entered No. 10 Downing Street: 'Where there is discord, may we bring harmony. Where there is error, may we bring truth. Where there is doubt, may we bring faith. And where there is despair, may we bring hope.' Thatcher, *The Downing Street*, 19.

[6] Bell, 'The Conservatives' Advertising Campaign,' 16.

pessimism and increasing defensiveness of the Left, the Right had a positive vision of the future they wanted to create.'[7]

Throughout the 1980s and 1990s, Margaret Thatcher, the Conservative Party, and the right-wing press continued to construct the Winter of Discontent as emblematic of the 'bad old days of socialism' and trade union excess.[8] It became a myth, which Conservatives strategically revisited during subsequent general elections. A standard narrative of flying pickets, striking gravediggers, and closed hospitals was repeated and made all the more potent by the frigid and harsh weather of 1978–79. As James Thomas observed, this 'helped [to] ideologically "structure feelings" throughout the 1980s, giving Thatcherism a negative "silent majority" in helping discredit all alternatives in the popular imagination.'[9] Within this narrative, the dismal backdrop of 1978 and 1979 made the Thatcherite changes of the 1980s and 1990s all the more legitimate. Any alternatives to Thatcherism, therefore, could easily be collapsed within this negative myth, negating a return to this 'anarchic past,' and critics would, once again, have to recognize the 'new realism' Conservatives had supposedly brought to Britain in the late twentieth century.[10] Henceforth, the Janus face of 'class warfare' the labour movement allegedly fought during the Winter of Discontent was the dawning of the new Thatcherite era of politics in which such tensions no longer existed.

The crosscurrents of memory uncovered here further reveal that the Winter of Discontent was a significant crux that propelled those closely connected in differing political directions. David Lipsey stayed with the Labour Party after 1979 and embraced New Labour's trajectory, but came to be ill at ease with New Labour's abandonment of its commitment to social equality. When I interviewed him in 2008, he saw his current role as focusing on 'micro-politics' rather than national politics.[11] Tom McNally believed that the Labour Party after 1979 was in the grip of an undemocratic trade union movement and left-wing elements. This resulted in his move to the SDP and later the Liberal Democrats. Larry Whitty, Tom Sawyer, and Judy Mallaber all saw the industrial militancy of the Winter of Discontent as a 'dead end.' They decided that the strikes, rather than

[7] Rowbotham, *A Century of Women*, 428.
[8] Thomas, 'Bound in by History,' 276.
[9] Thomas, 'Bound in by History,' 276.
[10] Term used by former Financial Secretary to the Treasury under Margaret Thatcher, Nigel Lawson. Lawson notes, '[…] The unfulfillable commitment to full employment, which had enabled the unions to hold the governments to ransom, were both essential components of the new order – and of the "new realism" which union leaders felt obliged to embrace.' *The View from No. 11* (London: Bantam Press, 1992), 437.
[11] (Baron) David Lipsey, interview by author, April 2008.

forwarding the cause of working people, were instrumental in electing Margaret Thatcher. Therefore, they became more involved in Parliamentary politics. All three were able to remake themselves politically from trade unionists and became New Labour supporters: Tom Sawyer and Larry Whitty as key Labour 'modernizers' and Judy Mallaber as a New Labour MP. In contrast, after the Winter of Discontent, both John Bohanna and Ian Lowes felt betrayed by Labour and sought out other left-wing outlets of political expression. These groups proved at times unstable or lacked the power to effect any significant political change. As 1970s working-class politics became increasingly delegitimized, no other effective and credible outlets of political expression opened up.

Although its membership and influence declined after 1979, the Winter of Discontent was a crucial entry point for some women into the British labour movement after that point. Trade unionism in the 1980s bore the visible mark of increased activism by women who were involved in the Winter of Discontent. Thatcher's free market ethos soon took hold of Britain, and in 1982, Secretary of State for Social Services Norman Fowler announced plans to have private companies take over NHS ancillary work, like catering and laundry services. These changes threatened thousands of jobs, but, in particular, the changes would affect the 70,000 West Indian and Asian women who dominated the workforce.[12] In response, West Indian and Asian women in NUPE, who made up 50 percent of the workforce at St Giles Hospital in London, joined other NUPE members across Britain in a 33-week dispute against privatization and for increased wages. One of the women working at St Giles complained: 'How can someone live on £45/47 a week? Rent is £30 and you have three children to look after, it's disgusting.'[13] Other newly energized groups of women began to be instrumental to the fights against privatization. In 1984, Asian women workers at Hillingdon Hospital in London protested against privatization of services.[14] Like the women at St Giles, they were unsuccessful in keeping private contractors from taking charge of services in their hospital. There were similar forms of resistance up north. In Prescott, Pat Corr, a hospital cleaner who became a shop steward during the Winter of Discontent, began to actively resist the efforts to contract out cleaning services at her hospital. She joined Branch Chair Mike Donovan one day when the hospital's management met with private contractors to discuss contracting out hospital ancillary

[12] Ron Ramdin, *Reimaging Britain: 500 Years of Black and Asian History* (London: Pluto Press, 1999), 227–228.
[13] Ramdin, *The Making of the Black Working Class*, 318.
[14] Jane Paul, *Where There's Muck There is Money: A Report on Cleaning in London* (Greater London Council, 1986), 67.

work. Donovan led the women with banners, forcing the private contractors out of the meeting and eventually chasing them down the motorway with placards.[15]

Trade unions' changing social composition also made them a site where ideas about gender and race equality could be debated. Tom Sawyer explained that in the case of NUPE activists, 'out of the Winter of Discontent, you got women marching on the streets who previously wouldn't have done that [...], and there was this awareness amongst the women that the union was fighting for something.' As Sawyer noted, women in NUPE began to highlight issues of equal opportunity at work and childcare, forcing the union to shift away from the 'traditional trade union agenda' of pay and conditions of to a more 'holistic approach' of serving the needs of its membership.[16] Linda Perks explains that industrial issues were no longer seen in isolation, but as connected to broader, 'community issues.'[17]

This evolving agenda was particularly visible at both local and national levels in NUPE. It meant that NUPE would take up a broader range of issues in the 1980s. For example, Betty Hughes joined other trade unionists in supporting the miners' strike. In addition to delivering parcels of food to striking miners, Hughes refused to sit as a magistrate during the miners' strikes because she believed that the miners were being arrested 'unnecessarily.'[18] In January of 1984, NUPE, along with unions such as NALGO and the NUT, campaigned to resist cuts to the Inner London Education Authority, the Greater London Council, and metropolitan councils. An NUPE school cleaner explained her motivation to join the campaign by stating that 'The whole school is the community. We all need one another [...] I think the whole country should get out and march.'[19]

Women's issues began to move up the trade union agenda as a whole. In 1979 the national TUC published the Charter *Equality for Women within Trade Unions*. The charter set out that unions should bring about greater equality by encouraging unions, among many things, to provide childcare for women members to attend union meetings and to have union publications 'be presented in non-sexist terms.'[20] In 1981, the TUC's Women's Conference passed a resolution to urge the TUC to review low pay. The TUC did a

---

[15] Pat Corr and Mike Donovan, interview by author, April 2006.
[16] (Lord) Tom Sawyer, interview by author, September 2007. Geoff Eley noted that in the 1980s, 'NUPE prioritized the minimum wage, for which industrial militants had little time, and stressed equal pay, anti-discrimination, childcare provision, and other issues for women at work [...] as well as women's public representation.' *Forging Democracy*, 393.
[17] Linda Perks, interview by author, September 2007.
[18] Betty and Joe Hughes, interview by author, March 2007.
[19] 'Save the GLC,' *Jobs for a Change* 6 (February 1984).
[20] Boston, *Women Workers and the Trade Unions*, 328–329.

review of policy and published the report *Low Pay and Women Workers* in 1984. The report not only brought a formerly peripheral issue to the foreground of the British trade union movement, but it cited goals to specifically address the issues of women workers. The document recognized, for example, that the Equal Pay Act failed to eliminate the problem of low pay among women, and one of the suggestions to remedy the situation was for unions to implement 'positive action,' or quotas, to encourage women's increased activism in unions.[21]

The continuing shift in focus on working women in the broader trade union movement would also be brought to the forefront of Labour Party policy. At the 1983 Labour Party conference NUPE General Secretary Rodney Bickerstaffe urged the Labour Party to accept the minimum wage as part of the party manifesto, 'so no employer shall force and exploit our people. And, you know, the two thirds target is no too much, but what a lift it would be for so many women.'[22] After many unsuccessful bids to convince other unions in the TUC and the Labour Party to accept the minimum wage as part of their policy, NUPE was finally successful. By 1986, both the Labour Party and the TUC had committed themselves to statutory minimum wage legislation. The following year, when the Labour Party explained its commitment to the idea of a statutory minimum wage, its Manifesto emphasized that it would be 'of particular benefit to women workers.'[23] It was eventually achieved under Tony Blair.

The themes that have emerged from this study of the Winter of Discontent have led me to consider larger historical questions. More specifically, my examination of the Winter of Discontent points to broader conclusions regarding working-class politics in the late twentieth century.

I argue that key economic and political changes can be observed emerging from the disputes of 1978–79. Once more, the power of the public sector further underlines that the industrial strength of the working class is no longer industrial; rather service and public sector work are now the sources of employment for the working class in Britain. The changing composition of the working class that can be seen in the strikes of the Winter of Discontent proved to be a long-term trend. In 2012, for the eleventh consecutive year, British women were 'more likely than male employees to be a trade union member.' Furthermore, Black British workers had overall higher rates of

---

[21] Philip Pearson, *Twilight Robbery: Low-Paid Workers in Britain Today* (London: Pluto, 1985), 101.

[22] Labour Party Conference Report quoted in Jerold L. Waltman, *Minimum Wage Policy in Great Britain and the United States* (New York, Algora, 2008), 78.

[23] Labour Party Manifesto, 1987 quoted in Waltman, *Minimum Wage*, 79.

unionization in Britain.[24] The most visible indication of this reconfiguration of the trade union movement occurred in 2013 when Frances O'Grady became the first female General Secretary of the TUC.[25]

However, these changes have occurred at an inopportune moment historically. The most viable form of working-class political formation, the labour movement, is in decline.[26] To this day, in Britain the idea of reinvigoration of class politics, and its consequent ideas of wealth distribution, continues to be summarily delegitimized by the miners' strike, over a decade of Thatcherism, and made all the more acute by the myth of the Winter of Discontent. In an article in *The Times* in 2008, the Winter of Discontent resumed its role as a foreboding bedtime story to scare Labour from moving Left, which according to the author, would inevitably presage a return to the bad old days of 'class warfare,' 'punitive taxes on the super-rich, threats of a general strike and proposals to nationalise the utility companies.' Rachael Sylvester states, 'Labour beware, the dinosaurs are not extinct.' She goes further:

> After a long period of irrelevance, the trade unions are back – and that could mean trouble for the centre-Left. It is not usually necessary to pay much attention to the Trades Union Congress. Always irrepressible, the brothers have become all but irrelevant in recent years as they threaten (yet again) to create a new 'winter of discontent.' The first gathering of the political conference season has become a quaint but rather pointless vision of the past: Jurassic Park with an Abba soundtrack, a T-Rex dressed in flares.[27]

At the heart of this article is the most pernicious legacy of the myth that has enveloped the Winter of Discontent: the undermining of any viable alternatives to the status quo. Any challenge to the neoliberal ascendancy of the 1980s and 1990s automatically ricochets off the grim and ridiculous evocations of 'general strikes,' 'nationalization,' 'Abba soundtracks,' and 'flares,' leaving us right where we started, without any political formation to resolve the underlying issues such as growing economic inequality, especially after the financial meltdown of 2008.

Two participants in the Winter of Discontent, Tom McNally and Betty Hughes, reflect on this trend in the UK today. When asked if a working-class youth in 2013 would have the same chance of being as socially mobile as in the 1960s and 1970s, Tom McNally answered:

---

[24] *Trade Union Membership, 2012, Statistical Bulletin.*
[25] 'TUC: Frances O'Grady is First Female Leader,' *BBC News* online, accessed September 3, 2013.
[26] *Trade Union Membership, 2012, Statistical Bulletin.*
[27] 'Labour Beware, the Dinosaurs are not Extinct,' *The Times*, September 9, 2008.

> The sad answer is 'no.' I was lucky. I went to a state school, a university with state funding, both in maintenance and tuition. I paid nothing for my education and neither did my parents, but it was only 6 per cent of my age group that went to university. We now have about 40 per cent of the relevant age group that go to university. But in the upper echelons of almost every profession, [...] there is an entrenchment of private education, elite universities, and social background of parents.[28]

For Betty Hughes, the prospects for working-class women today are worse than when she was a young woman raising a family. According to Hughes, young women are now expected to work and raise a family, even when jobs are scarce. Hughes is especially critical of individuals who claim that these young women are poor due to having children, a social problem she believed has been made worse by cuts in state funding. She complained while at a local hospital, 'I stood on the picket line in the snow to fight for you nurses, and look what this government's done to you. They're cutting hospitals. They're cutting everything to the bone.'[29] Unfortunately, the myth of the Winter of Discontent has resigned us to this dichotomy, this disparity between the lack of viable political alternatives and the increasing need amongst people to address serious social, political, and economic problems.

As income inequality grew more rapidly in Britain than in any other rich country, alternatives or collective responses to such encroachments became all the more elusive.[30] Colin Hay laments the legacy of the Winter of Discontent and how it divested British political culture of its ability to see beyond the supposed 'new realism' of neo-liberalism that has made such inequality so severe. 'It is difficult to disguise the fact that, for government and opposition alike, there simply is no "plan B."'[31] Nick Cohen is more cutting as the upsurge in militancy of the 1970s becomes an embarrassing counterpoint to the relative docility of people today:

> I don't want riots or a crime wave, but let's face it, when establishment commentators talked of the 'crisis of the 70s', what they meant was that organised labour could restrict the powerful's freedom of movement.
>
> With organised labour now emasculated, managers and owners can reward themselves without restraint and governments can stagger from blunder to blunder without a thought for those who must suffer the consequences.
>
> Forty years on [from the beginning of 'the long crisis of 1973 to 1983']

[28] (Lord) Tom McNally, interview by author, February 2013.
[29] Betty Hughes, interview by author, September 2013.
[30] 'Income Inequality Growing Faster in UK Thank Any Other Rich Country, Says OECD' *Guardian*, December 5, 2011.
[31] Hay, 'The Winter of Discontent Thirty Years On,' 552.

and we are in a different kind of crisis. A crisis brought by the elite rather than the masses. And the most frightening thing about it is that the elite is not frightened any more.[32]

At the beginning of my study, I pointed to George Lipsitz's definition of myth as something that not only legitimizes the status quo, but 'reconciles people to the disparity between their desires and opportunities.' However, he also argues that 'History explores how things came to be, and it inevitably confronts all the blasted hopes of the past.'[33] In my excavation of the memories of participants, I have sought to use historical enquiry in order to push beyond the limitations that have solidified under the myth of the Winter of Discontent. Set free of the oppressive myth of the Winter of Discontent, the history of this series of strikes offers new possibilities. Historian Dorothy Sue Cobble takes the difficult step of envisioning something beyond the status quo:

> It will be a multi-class movement dedicated to dismantling class hierarchies whether expressed in the workplace, in access to civic and social entitlements, or around the kitchen table. [...] It will be about how to create a different kind of capitalism, how to change the balance of power in the market and in the household, and how to sustain institutions that protect the weak from the strong.[34]

Therefore, rather than nostalgically engaging with history before 1979, the implications of the Winter of Discontent direct us in a different direction. Not only must we let go of disempowering myths, but we must also boldly look at the de-mythicized past, uncomfortable present and uncertain future. As Stuart Hall emphasizes:

> Gramsci said: 'Turn your face violently towards things as they exist now.' Not as you would like them to be, not as you think they were ten years ago, not at they're written about in the sacred texts, but as they really are: the contradictory, stony ground of the present conjuncture.[35]

---

[32] Nick Cohen, 'Comment: Where Once We Were Bolshie, Now We Are Servile,' *The Observer*, December 9, 2012.

[33] Lipsitz, *Time Passages*, 217.

[34] Dorothy Sue Cobble, 'Kissing the Old Class Politics Goodbye,' *International Labor and Working Class History* 67 (Spring 2005): 61.

[35] Stuart Hall quoted in Geoff Eley, *Forging Democracy*, 49.

Bibliography

Archival Sources

John Callaghan Papers, Bodleian Library, Oxford, UK
Labour History and Archive Centre, Manchester, UK

Archives of the British Labour Party
Judith Hart, MP, Papers
Michael Foot, Papers
NEC Minutes Part 10: Apr. 1974–Dec. 1983 (Microfiche)
The Record Office for Leicestershire, Leicester and Rutland, Wigston Magna, Leicester, UK
London Metropolitan Archives, UK
Margaret Thatcher Foundation

Modern Records Centre, University of Warwick, Coventry, UK
June Abdoulrahman Papers
Low Pay Campaign Papers
Moss Evans & Ron Todd Papers
Rodney Bickerstaffe Papers

National Archives at Kew
Cabinet Office Papers, 1978–79
Prime Minister's Office: Correspondence and Papers, 1974–79

Private Collection of John Bohanna
John Bohanna, *Report on the Ford Motor Company Halewood Strike over Wages and Conditions, Commencing Thursday, September 21, 1978*. Unpublished personal account, Mimeo. Liverpool, 1979.

The Case against the Social Contract. Pamphlet, International Socialists, 1978.
The Lessons of the 1978 Strike, Ford. Pamphlet no. 3, Revolutionary Communist League of Britain.
Halewood Strike over Wages and Conditions, Commencing Thursday, September 21, 1978. Mimeo. Liverpool, 1979.
'Ford Employee Information,' Ford Motor Company, November 20, 1978.
Ford Wage Claim, 1978. Transport and General Workers' Union
Ford Workers '78, 'One in the Eye for Sunny Jim'

Working Class Movement Library, Salford, UK
GMWU Publications.
NUPE Publications.
TGWU Publications.

Newspapers/Magazines

Big Flame
BBC News Online
Daily Mail
The Daily Post (Liverpool)
Economist
Daily Mirror
Daily Telegraph
Evening Gazette (Middlesbrough)
Guardian
Labour Monthly
Liverpool Echo
Marxism Today
Northern Echo (Darlington)
The Observer
Jobs for Change
Manchester Evening News
Race Today
Radical America
Red Rag
Scottish Daily Express
Socialist Challenge
Sunday Times
The Times (Due to industrial dispute, *The Daily Telegraph* assumed the place of *The Times* from December 1, 1978 to November 12, 1979.)
Women's Voice

Multimedia Sources

BBC Motion Gallery

'Britain's Coldest Winters on Record,' *The Daily Telegraph*, Picture Gallery, accessed June 27, 2013, http://www.telegraph.co.uk/news/picturegalleries/uknews/8209333/Britains-coldest-winters-on-record-in-pictures.html.

Secret History: Winter of Discontent. Brook Lapping Productions for Channel Four, 1998.

The Clash, 'London Calling,' by Joe Strummer and Mick Jones, released December 7, 1979, *London Calling* CBS.

OHC and the Gappers, 'The Ford Strike Song,' recorded October 9, 1978, Ford UK Workers.

'Winter of Discontent: 30 Years On,' *BBC News* online, accessed May 20, 2013, http://news.bbc.co.uk/2/hi/7598647.stm.

'Winter of Discontent Party Broadcast' YouTube video, 8:36, from a Conservative Party Broadcast on January 17, 1979, posted by 'thatcheritescot,' February 4, 2012, https://www.youtube.com/watch?v=Txsslou33HQ.

Interviews by Author

Colin Barnett, May 2006; Rodney Bickerstaffe, May 2006, June 2008; John Bohanna, June 2006, October 2006; Pat Corr and Mike Donovan, June 2006; Roger Dillon, October 2007; Mike and Lorraine Donovan and Celia Newman, October 2006; Peter Doyle, December 2011; Godfrey Eastwood, May 2007; Rod Finlayson, June 2007; Robert Fryer, June 2006; Bob Gregory, May 2006, August 2006; Anne Gardiner, November 2006; Anne Gardiner and Stuart Hill, March 2007; Jeane Hall and Stuart Hill, March 2007; Glyn Hawker, December 2011; Stuart Hill and Peter Doyle, June, 2010; Stuart Hill and Linda Hoffman, November 2006; Betty Hughes, September 2013; Stuart Hill, Betty and Joe Hughes, November 2006; Stuart Hill, November 2007, September 2008; Betty and Joe Hughes, March 2007; Alfred Illingsworth and Stuart Hill, November 2006; Robert Jones, May 2013; David Lipsey (Baron), September 2007, April 2008; Ian Lowes, July 2006, October 2006; Judy Mallaber, MP, October 2006; Tom McNally (Lord), November 2006, May 2008, February 2013; Linda Perks, September 2007, June 2010; Adam Raphael, June, 2006; Tom Sawyer (Lord), June 2006, November 2006; Johnny Slowly, September 2007; Brenda Tredwell, February 2007; Brian Whattam, November 2006; Larry Whitty (Lord), September 2006, June 2010.

Interviews from Other Sources

Avery, Don. Interview in *Secret History: Winter of Discontent*. Brook Lapping Production for Channel Four, 1998.

Beach, Fred. Interview by Andy Beckett. In *When the Lights Went Out: Britain in the Seventies*. London: Faber and Faber, 2009, 484–491, 493.

Beach, Fred. Interview by Paul Smith. November 21, 1996.

Carroll, Roger. Interview in *Secret History: Winter of Discontent*. Brook Lapping Productions for Channel Four, 1998.

Dolton, Duncan. Interview in *Secret History: Winter of Discontent*. Brook Lapping Productions for Channel Four, 1998.

Hattersley, Roy. Interview in *Secret History: Winter of Discontent*. Brook Lapping Productions for Channel Four, 1998.

Jameson, Derek. Interview in *Secret History: Winter of Discontent*. Brook Lapping Productions for Channel Four, 1998.

McNally, Tom (Lord). Interview in *Secret History: Winter of Discontent*. Brook Lapping Productions for Channel Four, 1998.

Morris, Jamie. Interview in *Secret History: Winter of Discontent*. Brook Lapping Productions for Channel Four, 1998.

Roberts, Terry. Interview in *Secret History: Winter of Discontent*. Brook Lapping Productions for Channel Four, 1998.

Rodgers, William. Interview and transcription by Mike Greenwood, *The History of Parliament* website, http://www.historyofparliamentonline.org/volume/oral-history/member/rodgers-william-1928.

Published Sources

Abrams, M., R. Rose, and R. Hinden. *Must Labour Lose?* Harmondsworth: Penguin, 1960.

Aldcroft, Derek. *The European Economy: 1914–1990*. 3rd ed. London: Routledge, 1989.

Arblaster, Anthony. 'Anthony Crosland: Labour's Last "Revisionist"?' *Political Quarterly* 48 (1977): 416–428

Arnold, David. *Famine: Social Crisis and Historical Change*. Oxford: Basil West Blackwell, 1988.

Bacon, Robert, and Walter Eltis. *Britain's Economic Problem: Too Few Producers*. London: MacMillan, 1976.

Bailey, Beth. 'She Can Bring Home the Bacon.' In *American in the 1970s*, edited by Beth Bailey and David Farber, 107–128. Lawrence: University of Kansas Press, 2004.

Barnett, Joel. *Inside the Treasury*. London: André Deutsch, 1982.

Baron, Ava. 'Gender and Labor History: Learning from the Past, Looking to the Future.' In *Work Engendered: Towards a New History of American Labor*, edited by Ava Baron, 1–46. Ithaca: Cornell University Press, 1991.

Beale, Jenny. *Getting It Together: Women as Trade Unionists*. London: Pluto Press, 1982.

Beaumont, Phil B. *Public Sector Industrial Relations*. London: Routledge, 1992.

Beckett, Andy. *When the Lights Went Out: Britain in the Seventies.* London: Faber and Faber, 2009.

Beer, Samuel. *Britain against Itself: The Political Contradictions of Collectivism.* New York; London: Norton, 1982.

Bell, Patrick. *The Labour Party in Opposition: 1970–1974.* London: Routledge, 2004.

Bell, Tim. 'The Conservatives' Advertising Campaign.' In *Political Communication: The General Election Campaign of 1979*, edited by Robert Worcester and Martin Harrop, 10–26. London: George, Allen, & Unwin, 1982.

Benn, Tony. *Conflicts of Interest: Diaries 1977–80*, edited by Ruth Winston. London: Arrow Books, 1990.

Beynon, Huw. *Working for Ford.* 2nd ed. Harmondsworth: Penguin, 1984.

Black, Lawrence, and Hugh Pemberton, 'The Winter of Discontent in British Politics.' *The Political Quarterly* 80, no. 4 (October–December 2009): 553–561.

Booker, Christopher. *The Seventies: Portrait of a Decade.* London: Allen Lane, 1980.

Boris, Eileen, and Jennifer Klein. *Caring for America: Home Health Care Workers in the Shadow of the Welfare State.* New York: Oxford University Press, 2012.

Bosanquet, Nicholas. 'The Search for a System.' In *Industrial Relations in the NHS: The Search for a System*, edited by Nicholas Bosanquet, 1–22. London: King Edward's Hospital Fund, 1979.

Boston, Sarah. *Women Workers and the Trade Unions.* 1980. Revised edition. London: Lawrence & Wishart, 1987.

Bourke, Joanna. *Working-Class Cultures in Britain, 1890–1960: Gender, Class, and Ethnicity.* London: Routledge, 1994.

British Public Opinion: General Election 1979. Market & Opinion Research International, 1979.

Brown, Michael, and Ken Coates, eds. *What Went Wrong?: Explaining the Fall of the Labour Government.* Nottingham: Spokesman for the Institute of Workers' Control, 1979.

Brown, William. 'Industrial Relations and the Economy.' In *The Cambridge Economic History of Modern Britain*, edited by Roderick Floud and Paul Johnson, 399–423. Cambridge: Cambridge University Press, 2004.

Burk, Kathleen, and Alec Cairncross. *'Goodbye, Great Britain': The 1976 IMF Crisis.* New Haven & London: 1992.

Burke, Peter. 'History as Social Memory.' In *The Collective Memory Reader*, edited by Jeffrey K. Olick, Vered Vinitzky-Seroussi, and Daniel Levy, 188–192. Oxford: Oxford University Press, 2011.

Butler, David, and Dennis Kavanagh, eds. *The British General Election of 1979.* London: Macmillan Press Ltd., 1980.

Butler, Eamonn. *Taming the Trade Unions: A Guide to the Thatcher Government's Employment Reforms, 1980–90.* London: MacMillan, 1991.

Callaghan, James. *Time and Chance.* London: Politico's, 1987.

Callaghan, John. 'Rise and Fall of the Alternative Economic Strategy: From Internationalisation of Capital to Globalisation.' *Contemporary British History* 14, no. 3 (Autumn 2000): 105–130.

Cameron, Rondo. *A Concise Economic History of the World*. New York; Oxford: Oxford University Press, 1997.

Cantz, Hatje. *Goodbye to London: Radical Art & Politics in the 70s*, edited by Astrid Proll. Germany: Hatje Cantz Verlag, 2010.

Capie, Forrest. *The Bank of England: 1950s to 1979*. Cambridge: Cambridge University Press, 2010.

Castle, Barbara. *The Castle Diaries, 1974–76*. London: Weidenfeld and Nicolson, 1980.

Castle, Barbara. *Fighting All the Way*. London: MacMillan, 1993.

Carpenter, Mick. *Working For Health: The History of COHSE*. London: Lawrence & Wishart, 1988.

Childs, David. *Britain since 1945: A Political History*. 3rd ed. London: Routledge, 1992.

Coates, Ken, and Tony Topham. *Trade Unions and Politics*. Oxford: Basil Blackwell, 1986.

Cobble, Dorothy Sue. 'Kissing the Old Class Politics Goodbye.' *International Labor and Working Class History* 67 (Spring 2005): 54–63.

Cobble, Dorothy Sue. '"A Spontaneous Loss of Enthusiasm": Workplace Feminism and the Transformation of Women's Service Jobs in the 1970s.' *International Labor and Working Class History* 56 (Fall 1999): 23–44.

Cockburn, Cynthia. 'Play of Power: Women, men and equality initiatives in a Trade Union.' In *Anthropology of Organizations*, edited by Susan Wright, 92–112. London: Routledge, 1994.

Cohen, Paul. *History in Three Keys: The Boxers as Event, Experience, and Myth*. New York: Columbia University Press, 1997.

Cohen, Sheila. 'Equal Pay – or what? Economics, Politics, and the 1968 Ford Sewing Machinists' Strike,' *Labor History* 53, no. 1 (February 2012): 51–68.

Connerton, Paul. *How Societies Remember*. Cambridge: Cambridge University Press, 1989.

Coopey, Richard, and Nicholas Woodward. 'The British Economy in the 1970s: An Overview.' In *The British Economy in the 1970s: The Troubled Decade*, 1–33. London: University College London Press, 1996.

Coventry, Liverpool, Newcastle, N. Tyneside Trades Council. *State Intervention in Industry: A Workers' Inquiry*. Nottingham: Spokesman, 1982.

Cowie, Jefferson. *Stayin' Alive: The 1970s and the Last Days of the Working Class*. New York: The New Press, 2010.

Crewe, Ivor, Bo Sarlvik, and James Alt, 'Partisan Dealignment in Britain 1964–1974.' *British Journal of Political Science* 7, no. 2 (Apr. 1977): 129–190.

Cronin, James. *Labour and Society: 1918–1979*. 1st ed. New York: Schocken Books, 1984.

Cronin, James. *New Labour's Pasts: The Labour Party and its Discontents*. Harlow: Pearson Longman, 2004.

Crosland, C.A.R. *The Future of Socialism*. 1956. Revised edition. Westport: Greenwood Press, Publishers, 1963.

Cubitt, Geoffrey. *History and Memory*. Manchester: Manchester University Press, 2007.

Cunnison, Sheila, and Jane Stageman. *Feminizing the Unions: Challenging the Culture of Masculinity*. Aldershot: Avebury, 1995.

Curran, James, Ivor Gaber, and Julian Petley. *Culture War: The Media and the British Left*. Edinburgh: Edinburgh University Press, 2005.

Darlington, Ralph, and Dave Lyddon. *Glorious Summer: Class Struggle in Britain 1972*. London: Bookmarks, 2001.

Dell, Edmund. *A Hard Pounding: Politics and Economic Crisis, 1974–1976*. Oxford: Oxford University Press, 1991.

Donoughue, Bernard. *Downing Street Diary, Volume Two*. London: Pimlico's, 2009.

Donoughue, Bernard. *The Heat of the Kitchen: An Autobiography*. 2003. Revised edition. London: Politico's, 2004.

Donoughue, Bernard. *Prime Minister: The Conduct of Policy under Harold Wilson and James Callaghan*. London: Jonathan Cape, 1987.

Doyal, Lesley, Geoff Hunt, and Jenny Mellor, 'Your Life in their Hands: Migrant Workers in the National Health Service.' *Critical Social Policy* 1, no. 2 (1981): 54–71.

Dromey, Jack, and Graham Taylor. *Grunwick: The Workers' Story*. London: Lawrence and Wishart, 1978.

Eley, Geoff. *A Crooked Line: From Cultural History to the History of Society*. Ann Arbor: University of Michigan Press, 2005.

Eley, Geoff. *Forging Democracy: The History of the Left in Europe, 1850–2000*. Oxford: Oxford University Press, 2002.

Eley, Geoff, and Keith Nield. 'Farewell to the Working Class?' *International Labor and Working Class History* 57 (Spring 2000): 1–30.

Eley, Geoff, and Keith Nield. 'Why Does Social History Ignore Politics?' *Social History* 2, no. 2 (May 1980): 249–271.

Fentress, James, and Chris Wickham. *Social Memory: New Perspectives on the Past*. Oxford: Blackwell, 1992.

Ferguson, Niall. 'Introduction: Crisis, What Crisis?: The 1970s and the Shock of the Global.' In *The Shock of the Global: The 1970s in Perspective*, edited by Niall Ferguson, Charles S. Maier, Erez Manela, and Daniel J. Sargent, 1–21. Cambridge: The Belknap Press of Harvard University Press, 2010.

Fetzer, Thomas. 'Walking Out of the National Workplace: Industrial Disputes and Trade Union Politics at Ford in Britain and Germany in the 1970s.' In *Ford: The European History, 1903–200. Vol. 1*, edited by Steven Tolliday, Yannick Lung, and Hubert Bonin, 393–415. Paris: P.L.A.G.E., 2003.

Foot, Paul. *The Vote: How It Was Won and How It Was Undermined*. London: Viking, 2005.

Foucault, Michel. *Language, Counter-Memory, Practice: Selected Essays and Interviews*. Ithaca: Cornell University Press, 1977.

Frader, Laura, and Sonya O. Rose. 'Introduction: Gender and the Reconstruction of European Working Class History.' In *Gender and Class in Modern Europe*, edited by Laura Frader and Sonya O. Rose, 1–33. Ithaca: Cornell University Press, 1996.

Friedman, Henry, and Sander Meredeen. *The Dynamics of Industrial Conflict: Lessons from Ford*. London: Crom Helm, 1980.

Fryer, R.H., and Stephen Williams. *A Century of Service: An Illustrated History of the National Union of Public Employees, 1889–1993*. London: Lawrence & Wishart, 1993.

Garnett, Mark. *From Anger to Apathy: The British Experience since 1975*. London: Jonathan Cape, 2007.

Gilroy, Paul. *There Ain't No Black in the Union Jack*. 1987. Revised edition. Milton Park: Routledge, 2006.

Glasgow University Media Group. *Really Bad News*. London: Writers and Readers, 1982.

Golding, John. *Hammer of the Left: Defeating Tony Benn, Eric Heffer and Militant in the Battle for the Labour Party*, edited by Paul Farrelly. London: Politico's, 2003.

Goodman, Geoffrey. *From Bevan to Blair: Fifty Years' Reporting from the Political Front Line*. London: Pluto Press, 2003.

Gould, Phillip. *The Unfinished Revolution: How Modernisers Saved the Labour Party*. London: Little, Brown, and Company, 1998.

Halbwachs, Maurice. *On Collective Memory*, edited and translated by Lewis Coser. Chicago: The University of Chicago Press, 1992.

Ham, Christopher. *Health Policy in Britain: The Politics and Organization of the National Health Service*. 1982. 3rd ed. London: Macmillan, 1991.

Hatfield, Michael. *The House that the Left Built: Inside Labour-Policy Making, 1970–75*. London: Victor Gollancz, 1978.

Hattersley, Roy. *Who Goes Home: Scenes from a Political Life*. London: Abacus, 1995.

Hay, Colin. 'Chronicles of a Death Foretold: The Winter of Discontent and Construction of the Crisis of British Keynesianism.' *Parliamentary Affairs* 63, no. 3 (2010): 446–470.

Hay, Colin. 'Narrating Crisis: The Discursive Construction of the "Winter of Discontent."' *Sociology* 30, no. 2 (May 1996): 253–277.

Hay, Colin. 'The Winter of Discontent Thirty Years On.' *The Political Quarterly* 80, no. 4 (2009): 545–552.

Healey, Denis. *The Time of My Life*. London: Penguin Books, 1989.

Heath, Anthony, Roger Jowell, and John Curtice. *How Britain Votes*. Oxford: Pergamon Press, 1985.

Hill, David. 'The Labour Party's Strategy.' In *Political Communications: The General Election Campaign of 1992*, edited by Ivor Crewe and Brian Gosschalk, 36–40. Cambridge: Cambridge University Press, 1995.

Hobsbawm, Eric. 'The Debate on "The Forward March of Labour Halted?"' In *Politics for a Rational Left* (1981): 29–41. London: Verso, 1989.

Hobsbawm, Eric. 'The Forward March of Labour Halted? (1978)' In *Politics for a Rational Left* (1978): 9–28. London: Verso, 1989.

Hodgkin, Katherine, and Susannah Radstone, eds. Introduction to *Contested Pasts: The Politics of Memory*. London: Routledge, 2003.

Holden, Katherine. 'Family, Caring and Unpaid Work.' In *Women in Twentieth-Britain*, edited by Ina Zweiniger-Bargiclowska, 134–148. Harlow: Longman, 2001.

Holland, Stuart. *The Socialist Challenge*. London: Quartet Books, 1975.

Holmes, Martin. *The Failure of the Heath Government*. 1982. 2nd ed. London, MacMillan Press, 1997.

Hutton, Patrick. 'Recent Scholarship on Memory and History.' *The History Teacher* 33, no. 4 (August 2000): 533–561.

Hyman, Richard. Review of *Glorious Summer: Class Struggle in 1972 Britain*, by Ralph Darlington and David Lyddon, *International Labor and Working Class History* 64 (October 2003): 187–189.

Hyman, Richard. 'Trade Unions: Structure, Policies, and Politics.' In *Industrial Relations in Britain*, edited by George Sayers Bain, 3–34. Oxford: Basil Blackwell, 1983.

James, Daniel. *Doña María's Story: Life History, Memory and Political Identity*. Durham: Duke University Press, 2000.

Jefferys, Kevin. *Finest and Darkest Hours: The Decisive Events in British Politics from Churchill to Blair*. London: Atlantic Books, 2002.

Judt, Tony. *Postwar: A History of Europe since 1945*. London: Random House, 2007.

Kenney, Michael. *The First New Left: British Intellectuals after Stalin*. London: Lawrence & Wishart, 1995.

Kenwood, A.G., and A.L. Lougheed. *The Growth of the International Economy, 1820–1990: An Introductory Text*. 3rd ed. London: Routledge, 1992.

Kitson, Michael. 'Failure Followed by Success or Success followed by Failure? A Re-examination of British Economic Growth Since 1949.' In *The Cambridge Economic History of Modern Britain*, edited by Roderick Floud and Paul Johnson, 27–56. Cambridge: Cambridge University Press, 2004.

Klein, Rudolf. *The Politics of the National Health Service*. 2nd ed. London: Longman, 1989.

The Labour Party Manifesto, February 1974. *Let Us Work Together – Labour's Way Out of the Crisis*. London: The Labour Party, 1974.

Lawson, Nigel. *The View from No. 11*. London: Bantam Press, 1992.

Lewis, Jane, and Kathleen Kiernan. 'The Boundaries between Marriage, Nonmarriage, and Parenthood: Changes in Behavior and Policy in Postwar Britain.' *Journal of Family History* 27, no. 3 (July 1996): 372–387.

Lewis, Penny. *Hardhats, Hippies, and Hawks: The Vietnam Antiwar Movement at Myth and Memory*. Ithaca: ILR Press, 2013.

Linde, Charlotte. *Life Stories: The Creation of Coherence*. New York: Oxford University Press, 1993.

Lipsitz, George. *Time Passages: Collective Memory and American Popular Culture*. 1990. Reprint, Minneapolis: University of Minnesota Press, 2000.

Ludlam, Steve. 'Labourism and the Disintegration of the Postwar Consensus: Disunited Trade Union Economic Policy Responses to Public Expenditure Cuts, 1974–79.' PhD thesis, University of Sheffield, 1991.

Ludlam, Steve. '"Old" Labour and the Winter of Discontent.' *Politics Review* 9 (February 2000): 30–33.

Ludlam, Steve. 'The Gnomes of Washington: Four Myths of the 1976 IMF Crisis.' *Political Studies* XL (1992): 713–727.

Ludlam, Steve. 'Old Labour and the Winter of Discontent.' *Politics Review* 9 (2000): 30–33.

Ludlam, Steve. 'Too Much Pluralism: Not Enough Socialism: Interpreting the Unions-Party Link.' In *Interpreting the Labour Party Approaches to Labour Politics and History*, edited by John Callaghan, Steve Fielding, and Steve Ludlam, 150–161. Manchester: Manchester University Press, 2003.

Mandelson, Peter. *The Blair Revolution Revisited*. 1993. Revised edition. London: Politico's, 2002.

Marsh, David. *The New Politics of British Trade Unionism: Union Power and the Thatcher Legacy*. London: MacMillan, 1992.

Martin, R.L. 'Job Loss and the Regional Incidence of Redundancies in the Current Recession.' *Cambridge Journal of Economics* 6, no. 4 (1982): 375–395.

Matthews, John. *Ford Strike: The Workers' Story*. London: Panther, 1972.

McDowell, Linda, Sundari Anitha, and Ruth Pearson. 'Striking Images: Gender, Ethnicity, and Industrial Politics in the 1970s, Reflections On/Of Grunwick.' *Women's History Review* (forthcoming).

McIlroy, John. 'Notes on the Communist Party and Industrial Politics.' In *British Trade Unions and Industrial Politics: The High Tide of Trade Unionism, 1964–1979*, edited by John McIlroy, Nina Fishman, and Alan Campbell, 216–258. Ashgate: Aldershot, 1999.

Middleton, Roger. *The British Economy since 1945: Engaging with the Debate*. Houndmills: MacMillan Press Ltd., 2000.

Minkin, Lewis. *The Contentious Alliance: Trade Unions and the Labour Party*. Edinburgh: Edinburgh University Press, 1991.

Moran, Joe. '"Stand Up and Be Counted": Hughie Green, the 1970s and Popular

Memory.' *History Workshop Journal* 70, no. 1 (2010): 172–198. doi: 10.1093/hwj/dbq025.

Morgan, Kenneth O. *A Life of Michael Foot*. London: HarperCollins, 2007.

Morgan, Kenneth O. *Callaghan: A Life*. Oxford: Oxford University Press, 1997.

Morgan, Kenneth O. *The People's Peace: British History 1945–1989*. Oxford: Oxford University Press, 1990.

Neale, Jonathan. *Memoirs of a Callous Picket*. London: Pluto Press, 1983.

Norris, Pippa. *Electoral Change in Britain since 1945*. Oxford: Blackwell Publishers, 1997.

Norris, Pippa. 'Mobilising the "Women's Vote": The Gender-Generation Gap in Voting Behaviour.' *Parliamentary Affairs* 49, no. 2 (April 1996): 333–342.

Panitch, Leo. *Social Democracy and Industrial Militancy: The Labour Party, the Trade Unions and Incomes Policy, 1945–74*. London: Pinter Publishers, 1991.

Paul, Jane. *Where There's Muck There's Money: A Report on Cleaning in London*. Greater London Council, 1986.

Pearce, Malcom, and Geoffrey Stewart. *British Political History 1867–1990: Democracy and Decline*. London: Routledge, 1992.

Pearson, Philip. *Twilight Robbery: Low-Paid Workers in Britain Today*. London: Pluto, 1985.

Philio, Greg. 'Political Advertising, Popular Belief and the 1992 British General Election.' *Media, Culture, & Society* 15, no. 3 (July 1993): 407–418.

Phillips, Anne. *Hidden Hands: Women and Economic Policies*. London: Pluto Press, 1983.

Pilsworth, Michael. 'Balanced Broadcasting.' In *The British General Election of 1979*, edited by David Butler and Dennis Kavanagh, 200–231. London: MacMillan Press, 1980.

Portelli, Alessandro. *The Death of Luigi Trastulli and Other Stories: Form and Meaning in Oral History*. Albany: State of New York Press, 1991.

Radice, Lisanne. *Winning Women's Votes*. London: Fabian Society, October 1985.

Ramdin, Ron. *The Making of the Black Working Class in Britain*. Aldershot: Wildwood House, 1987.

Ramdin, Ron. *Reimaging Britain: 500 Years of Black and Asian History*. London: Pluto Press, 1999.

Rodgers, Bill. *Fourth among Equals*. London: Politico's, 2000.

Rodgers, William. 'Government Under Stress: Britain's Winter of Discontent.' *The Political Quarterly* 55, no. 2 (April 1984): 171–179.

Rogaly, Joe. *Grunwick*. Harmondsworth: Penguin, 1977.

Ross, Kristin. *May '68 and Its Afterlives*. Chicago: University of Chicago Press, 2002.

Rowbotham, Sheila. *A Century of Women: The History of Women in Britain and the United States in the Twentieth Century*. London: Penguin, 1997.

Rowbotham, Sheila. 'Cleaners Organizing in Britain from the 1970s: A Personal Account.' In *The Dirty Work of Neoliberalism: Cleaners in the Global Economy*, edited by Luis Aguiar and Andrew Herod, 177–194. Oxford: Basil Blackwell, 2006.

Rowbotham, Sheila. *The Past is Before Us: Feminism in Action since the 1960s.* London: Pandora Press, 1989.

Russell, Meg. *Building New Labour: The Politics of Party Organisation.* New York: Palgrave MacMillan, 2005.

Sandbrook, Dominic. *Never Had It So Good: A History of Britain from Suez to the Beatles.* London: Abacus, 2005.

Sanbrook, Dominic. *Seasons in the Sun: The Battle for Britain, 1974–79.* London: Allen Lane, 2012.

Schudson, Michael. *Watergate in American Memory: How We Remember, Forget, and Reconstruct the Past.* Revised edition. New York: Basic Books, 1993.

Schulman, Bruce. *The Seventies: The Great Shift in American Culture, Society, and Politics.* Cambridge: Da Capo Press, 2001.

Seldon, Anthony, and Kevin Hickson, eds. *London; New Labour, Old Labour: The Wilson and Callaghan Governments, 1974–1979.* New York: Routledge, 2004.

Seyd, Patrick. *The Rise and Fall of the Labour Left.* London: MacMillan Education, 1987.

Shaw, Eric. *The Labour Party since 1945.* Oxford: Blackwell Publishers, 1996.

Sheldrake, John. *Industrial Relations and Politics in Britain 1880–1989.* London: Pinter Publishers, 1991.

Sked, Alan. *Post-War Britain: A Political History.* Brighton: Harvester Press, 1979.

Smith, Paul. 'The "Winter of Discontent": The Hire and Reward Haulage Dispute, 1979.' *Historical Studies in Industrial Relations* 7 (Spring 1999): 27–54.

Smith, Paul. *Unionization & Union Leadership: The Road Haulage Industry.* London: Continuum, 2001.

Sounes, Howard. *Seventies: The Sights, Sounds, and Ideas of a Brilliant Decade.* London: Simon & Schuster, 2006.

Suddaby, John. 'The Public Sector Strike in Camden: Winter '79.' *New Left Review* 116 (July–August, 1979): 83–93.

Tabili, Laura. *'We Ask for British Justice': Workers and Racial Difference in Later Imperial Britain.* Ithaca: Cornell University Press, 1994.

Taylor, Andrew. 'The Conservative Party and the Trade Unions.' In *British Trade Unions and Industrial Politics: The High Tide of Trade Unionism, 1964–79*, edited by John McIlroy, Nina Fishman, and Alan Campbell, 151–186. Aldershot: Ashgate, 1999.

Taylor, Robert. *The Fifth Estate: Britain's Unions in the Seventies.* London: Routledge & Kegan Paul, 1978.

Taylor, Robert. 'How Democratic are the Trade Unions?' *Political Quarterly* 47 (January 1976): 29–38.

Taylor, Robert. 'The Rise and Fall of the Social Contract.' In *New Labour, Old*

Labour: The Wilson and Callaghan Governments, 1974–79, edited by Anthony Seldon and Kevin Hickson, 70–104. London: Routledge, 2004.

Taylor, Robert. *The Trade Union Question in British Politics: Government and Unions since 1945*. Oxford: Blackwell, 1993.

Taylor, Robert, and Anthony Seldon. '"The Winter of Discontent" Symposium.' *Contemporary Record* 1, no. 3 (1987): 34–43.

Thatcher, Margaret. *The Downing Street Years*. London: HarperCollins, 1993.

Thatcher, Margaret. *The Path to Power*. London: HarperCollins, 1995.

Thomas, James. '"Bound in by History": The Winter of Discontent in British Politics, 1979–2004.' *Media, Culture, & Society* 29 (2007): 263–283. doi: 10.1177/0163443707074257.

Thomas, James. *Popular Newspapers, the Labour Party, and British Politics*. New York: Routledge, 2005.

Thompson, E.P. *The Making of the English Working Class*. 1963. Reprint. New York: Vintage Books, 1966.

Tiratsoo, Nick. '"You've Never Had It So Bad": Britain in the 1970s.' In *From Blitz to Blair: A New History of Britain since 1939*, edited by Nick Tiratsoo, 189–190. London: Weidenfeld & Nicolson 1997.

Tolliday, Steven. 'The Rise of Ford in Britain: From Sales Agency to Market Leader, 1904–1980.' In *Ford: The European History, 1903–2003. Vol. 2*, edited by Hubert Bonin, Yannick Lung, and Steven Tolliday, 7–72. Paris: P.L.A.G.E., 2003.

Turner, Alwyn W. *Crisis? What Crisis?: Britain in the 1970s*. London: Aurum, Press: 2008.

Vincent, David. *Poor Citizens: The State and the Poor in Twentieth-Century Britain*. London: Longman, 1991.

Wainwright, Hilary. *Labour: A Tale of Two Parties*. London: The Hogarth Press, 1987.

Wainwright, Hilary. 'Reporting Back From Conditions Not of Our Choosing.' In *Beyond the Fragments: Feminism and the Making of Socialism*.1979. Revised edition by Sheila Rowbotham, Lynne Segal, and Hilary Wainwright, 26–64. Pontypool, UK: Merlin Press, 2013.

Waltman, Jerold L. *Minimum Wage Policy in Great Britain and the United States*. New York, Algora, 2008.

Whitehead, Phillip. *The Writing on the Wall: Britain in the Seventies*. London: Michael Joseph, 1985.

Wickham-Jones, Mark. *Economic Strategy and the Labour Party: Politics and Policy-Making, 1970–83*. New York: St. Martin's Press, 1996.

Wigham, Eric. *Strikes and the Government, 1893–1981*. London: Macmillan Press, 1982.

Williams, Stephen, and R.H. Fryer. *Leadership & Democracy: The History of the National Union of Public Employees, Vol. 2, 1928–1993*. London: Lawrence & Wishart, 2011.

Wilson, Dolly. 'A New Look at the Affluent Worker: The Good Working Mother in Post-War Britain.' *Twentieth Century British History* 17, no. 2 (2006): 206–229.

Worcester, Robert, and Martin Harrop, eds. *Political Communications: The General Election Campaign of 1979*. London: George Allen, & Unwin, 1980.

Wrigley, Chris. 'Trade Unions, Strikes and the Government.' In *Britain in the 1970s: The Troubled Decade*, edited by Richard Coopey and Nicholas Woodward, 273–291. London: University College London Press.

Wrigley, Chris. 'Women in the Labour Market and in the Unions.' In *British Trade Unions and Industrial Politics: The High Tide of Trade Unionism, 1964–1979*, edited by John McIlroy, Nina Fishman, and Alan Campbell, 43–69. Aldershot: Ashgate, 1999.

Zelizer, Barbie. *Covering the Body: The Kennedy Assassination, the Media, and the Shaping of Collective Memory*. Chicago: The University of Chicago, 1992.

Index

abortion 35, 134
Allen, Alfred 61
Alternative Economic Strategy (AES) xi, 42–4, 51, 113
Amalgamated Union of Engineering Workers (AEUW) 33, 206
Anitha, Sundari 58
Arnold, David 87, 98
Association of Scientific, Technical, and Managerial Staffs (ASTMS) 112
Association of University Teachers (AUT) 112

Bank of England 49, 183
Barbados 97, 99, 157
Barking 142
Barnett, Colin 127, 191
Barnett, Joel (Baron) 170
Baron, Ava 15, 70
Basnett, David 61, 115, 118, 190–1
 see also General and Municipal Workers' Union (GMWU)
Beach, Fred 87, 90–95, 100, 106, 108, 188, 193
Beckett, Andy 2, 35, 98, 172
Beckett, Terence (Sir) 75, 83
Bell, Tim (Baron) 18–19
Benn, Anthony Wedgewood 3, 42, 47, 51, 107, 199

Beveridge Report 153
Beynon, Huw 67–8
Bickerstaffe, Rodney 127, 132–4, 148, 192–3, 195, 212
Big Flame 72–3
Billericay (Essex) 144
Birmingham 93, 105, 142, 171, 180
Black Power movement 67, 72
Blair, Anthony (Tony) 186, 188, 193, 196, 212
Bond, David 115
Booth, Albert 51
breadwinner 43, 130, 132, 153
Bretton Woods system 29
Bristol 144
Burke, Peter 10
Butler, Eamonn 177

Cadbury Schweppes factory 105
Cahill, Bernard 57
Callaghan, James (Lord)
 1978 election 56, 61, 63, 114
 economy 183–4
 general election campaign (1979) 179–181
 IMF loan 112, 49–54
inflation 74
In Place of Strife 37
media 20, 97–8, 107
memory 110, 177, 190

Index

public expenditure 52, 183–4
Social Contract 45
sterling crisis 49–54
state of emergency 57
Strategic Arms Limitation Talks (SALT II) 97, 99
trade unions 80, 100, 115, 130, 149, 195
vote of no confidence x, 174–6
wage restraint 1, 59–60, 208
capitalism xii, 22, 41, 45, 89, 190
Carr, Robert 111
Carroll, Roger 60, 98
Castle, Barbara 36, 59, 69
Chapple, Frank 53, 131
Charlton, Susan 81
Charter for Pickets 100
  see also road haulage
Cheshire 104
child benefit 43
childcare 139, 166, 211
Chrysler 133
Civil Contingencies Unit (CCU) 92–3, 100
  see also state of emergency
Clash 26
class *see* middle-class, social class, working class
Clause Four 42
Clemens, Pam 166
Cobble, Dorothy Sue 141, 215
Cohen, Paul 10, 12, 17n42, 178
collective memory *see* memory
collective mythology *see* Hay, Colin
commemorative ceremonies 22
communism 33
  see also Communist Party of Great Britain (CPGB)
Communist Party of Great Britain (CPGB) 66, 71–3, 131, 143
Confederation of British Industry (CBI) 39, 103, 105
Confederation of Health Service Employees (COHSE) 33, 112, 118, 157, 162, 167, 169, 202
Confederation of Shipbuilding and Engineering Union (CSEU) 43
Connor, Danny (Dan) 72, 186
Conservatism xii, 117–8
Conservative Party
  electoral support 36, 182–3, 208
  media strategy 4, 11, 18–9, 87, 99, 150, 179–81, 209
  party changes ix, 2, 5, 8, 10, 13
  see also Stepping Stones, Thatcher, Margaret
consumerism 13
  see also pin money
contraception 134
Coote, Anna 42
counter-memory 13–4, 17, 109, 177–9, 181, 183, 185–7, 189, 191–3, 195, 197, 199, 201, 203
counter-myth 15, 172
Coventry 133
Cowie, Jefferson 5, 66n15, 67n21
Crewe 127
Crisis? What Crisis? 2, 97–8, 177
Crosland, Anthony 'Tony' 42, 44, 51, 89, 121, 184
Croslandite Revisionism 40–1, 44, 51, 89, 184

Daily Express 107
Daily Mail 1, 80–1, 95, 97, 106, 124, 170–1, 185, 205
Daily Mirror 20, 60, 175
Darlington (Durham) 105, 133, 136, 140, 144–6, 200
Darlington, Ralph 12
dealignment thesis 13
  see also Hobsbawm, Eric; *The Forward March of Labour Halted*
de-industrialization 2, 154–5

Dell, Edmund 49–50
democracy xi, 22, 34, 55, 71, 104, 129, 131, 137–8, 151, 159, 206
Desai, Jayaben 58
Dillon, Roger 66, 68, 73, 79, 187
Dirty Jobs Strike 111, 122–3
Dispensation Committee
　Hull 94–5
　Cleveland County 143
divorce 139–40, 156, 165, 207
Dix, Bernard 127, 130–2, 136–7, 163–4, 172
docks 65, 154, 160–1
Dolton, Dr. Duncan 124–5
domestic violence 35, 139, 207
Domestic Violence and Matrimonial Proceedings Act 47
Donoughue, Bernard 56, 190
Donovan, Lorraine 155–9, 168, 201–3, 207
Donovan, Mike 154, 159, 165, 169, 171, 201–3, 210
Donovan Report 36, 65
Doyle, Peter 42
Drain, Geoffrey 59, 61
Durbin, Evan 89
Durham Trades Council 145
Durham University 135
Dutschke, Rudi 34

Economic Policy and the Cost of Living 44
　see also Social Contract
Economist 31, 53, 63, 82, 86, 92, 94, 102–3
economy (post-war; inflation;) see also sterling crisis 1976
Electrical, Electronic, Telecommunications, and Plumbing Union (EEPTU) 53, 131
Ellis, Peter 154
employment
　industrial 29, 154
　men 29, 129
　public sector 29 -30, 129
　service sector 29–30
　women 30–2, 129, 139, 141, 155
Employment Protection Act 46
Ennals, David (Baron) 170–1, 173
Equal Pay Act 69–70, 111, 212
Equal Pay Strike 69–70
European Economic Community (EEC) 90
Evans, Moss 61, 74, 81–2, 96, 115
Evening Gazette 143

Fallowfield 105
feminism xi, 34–5
　see also socialist feminism
Ferguson, Niall 177
Filth and the Fury 9
Financial Times 80, 86, 95
Finlayson, Rod 67–8, 72–3, 76, 78, 186
Fire Brigades' Strike 57, 208
Fisher, Alan 53, 110, 112, 115, 127, 130–2, 136, 171–2, 190
flying pickets 95, 104–5, 185, 209
Food Manufacturers' Federation 103
Foot, Michael 51, 174
Ford Combine 73, 76–7, 79–80
Ford Motor Company
　Asian workers 66–8
　Bosch plant 80
　Cologne plant 80
　Dagenham plant 65–7, 71–2, 76–80, 114, 186–7
　Equal Pay strike 69–70
　Halewood plant 63–65, 67–70, 72, 75–77, 80, 84, 87, 114, 118, 125
　Leamington plant 66
　penalty clauses 70–1, 77, 84
　sanctions 84
　shopfloor activism 65, 67–8, 70, 73–4, 187
　strikes 1, 4 63, 75–85, 87, 114, 118, 186, 206

unions 64–5, 71
West Indian workers 66–68
women 69–70, 81
Ford Women's Action Group 81
The Forward March of Labour Halted see dealignment thesis; Hobsbawm, Eric
Fountain, Nigel 2, 167
Frader, Laura 16, 161
Fraud News 79
Friedman, Milton 49
Fryer, Robert 131
full employment 27–8, 41, 52, 61, 209n10
The Future of Socialism see Crosland, Anthony (Tony)

Gardiner, Anne 140–2, 144–7, 152, 198–9, 200
gender 3,5, 15–17, 27, 30n33, 31, 36, 58–9, 70, 81, 132, 134–38, 142, 178, 194, 204, 211
General and Municipal Workers' Union (GMWU) 33, 53, 61, 110–1, 115, 117–124,126–8, 135, 143, 157, 159, 162, 169, 177, 190–2, 194
general election campaigns
 (1970) 37
 (Feb 1974) 36, 40, 46
 (Oct 1974) 36, 46
 (1979) 11, 17–8, 20, 56, 113–114, 150, 175–6, 178–80, 184, 187, 189, 208
 (1983) 21
 (1987) 21, 185
 (1992) 3, 22, 185
 (1997) 23, 179, 179, 186, 193, 196, 203
 (2001) 23
General Electric Company 138
Gilroy, Paul 16
Glorious Summer: Class Struggle in 1972 Britain 13
 see also Darlington, Ralph; Lyddon, David
Goodman, Geoffrey 20, 60, 175, 207
Gouriet, John 35, 59
Goya, Francisco 24
Gramsci, Antonio 33, 215
grassroots activism
 left-wing 5, 72–3, 131, 134
 rank-and-file 34,67–8, 118
 right-wing 35
 trade union 6–7, 65, 90, 108, 120, 134, 146 176, 204, 207
 women 81, 130, 135–40, 142, 199, 202, 210 212
gravediggers' strike
 Guildford 128
 Liverpool 5, 110, 117, 119–20, 122–6
 memory 2, 9, 20–1, 24, 110, 177, 182, 185, 189–91, 208–9
 Plymouth 128
 Tameside 127, 191–2
 Woking 128
Gregory, Robert (Bob) 124, 154, 158–60, 167, 169, 202–3
Groves, Maureen 142–3, 206
Grunwick strike 58–9
Guardian 22, 80, 86, 95–6, 104, 107, 131, 148, 162, 166

Halbwachs, Maurice 8, 178
Hailsham Lord (Quintin McGarel Hogg, Baron) 20, 125
Hall, Jeane 135
Haringey 147
Harris, Wendy 105
Harroway, Sid 72
Hattersley, Roy (Lord) 59, 87, 191
Hay, Colin 10–12, 108, 182–3, 214
Hayek, Friedrich 55
Hayward, Ted 171
Healey, Denis (Lord)
 budgets 46
 IMF loan 112, 49–54

inflation 60
memory 190
party leadership 200
public expenditure 48, 52, 112, 183–4
sterling crisis 49–54
trade unions 58, 74, 110, 116
Health and Safety at Work Act 46
Heath, Edward "Ted" (Sir) 37–40, 40, 44, 53–4, 71, 74, 117, 164, 207
Hibbins, Penny 165
Hill, Stuart 135, 143, 173, 198, 201
Hobsbawm, Eric 13
  see also dealignment thesis; Hobsbawm, Eric
Holland, Stuart 41
  see also The Socialist Challenge
Hoskyns, John 19, 55
Huff, Frank 8
Hughes, Betty 138, 140, 143–4, 197–8, 207, 211, 213–4
Hughes, Joe 140, 144, 198, 211
Hull 87, 93–5, 105–7, 115
Humberside 103
Hungarian revolution 33
Hunt, Kay

Illingsworth, Alfred (Alf) 147
In Place of Strife 36–8, 45
Indian Workers' Association (IWA) 67, 72
incomes policy 28, 38–9, 44, 54–60, 73–76, 80, 8, 116, 206, 208
industrial action *see* strikes
industrial democracy 33, 43–4, 77
Industrial Relations Act 38–9, 44, 46, 71
inflation ix, xi, xii, 1, 3, 23, 27–29, 35–39, 47–49, 5, 54–61, 74, 82, 104, 11, 164, 170, 183, 205
Institute of Workers' Control 33
International Marxist Group 67, 73

International Metal Workers' Federation 80
International Monetary Fund (IMF) 35, 49–56, 112, 164, 183, 207
International Socialists 67, 74
Iranian Revolution 29
Italy 31, 34, 72

Jamaica 66, 156
James, Daniel 14
Jameson, Derek 107
Jarratt, Alex (Sir) 20
Jefferys, Kevin 11
Johnson, Lyndon B. 29
Joint Production Committee 33
Jones, Jack 33, 54, 71, 73–4, 80, 88, 149
Jones, Mick 26
Jones, Robert 173
Jones, Steve 9
Joseph, Keith (Lord) 56, 162

Kelly, Mary 134
Keynesian economics 183
Knowsley 89, 202

Labben, Derek 115, 121, 123
labour movement *see* Labour Party; trade unions
Labour Party
  activists x, 34, 61, 65–6, 71–3, 82, 88, 102, 131, 137, 141, 147, 158–9–60, 186–7, 195, 199–200, 202–3
  Conferences 115, 117, 212
  electoral support 36, 40, 46, 56, 181–2
  ideological division 40–56, 114, 117, 184
  leadership 3–5, 159, 170, 189–90, 194, 196
  media strategy 21–2, 82, 157, 176
  memory 3, 179
Labour-TUC Liaison Committee 44

Index

Lamb, Larry (Sir) 2, 19, 21
Lawson, Nigel (Baron) 56, 209n10
legend *see* myth
Leicester Square 9, 48
Liberal Party 46, 56, 188, 194
Lib-Lab Pact 56, 113, 207
Linde, Charlotte 14
Lipsey, David (Lord) 44, 115, 121, 123–4, 209
Lipsitz, George 9, 13–14, 24, 278, 215
Liverpool Echo 124, 167
local authorities 56, 112, 122, 129, 142, 198
London 9, 26, 65–67, 147–8, 163–6, 210–1
lone motherhood 139, 152, 156
lorry drivers *see* road haulage
Lotta Continua 72
low pay 31, 45, 53, 58, 90, 112–115, 117, 119–20, 162, 165–6, 191–2
  women 129, 134, 142, 143, 211–12, 206
Lowes, Ian 120–23, 125–7, 189, 192–3, 200, 210
Lucas Aerospace Alternative Plan xi, 43
Lyddon, David 13
Lydon, John 9

MacMillan, Harold (Earl) 28
magistrate courts 140, 211
Mallaber, Judy 137–8, 209–10
Manchester 7, 80, 96, 105, 110, 127, 146, 150, 167, 191–2
Manchester Evening News 7, 31, 104, 139
Mandelson, Peter 23, 190
manufacturing xi, 29, 41, 43, 154–155, 160, 206
Marxism 33–34, 67, 73, 131
Matthews, Patricia 157
McDowell, Linda 58

McNally, Tom (Lord) 97–8, 114, 159, 170, 194–5, 209, 213
media
  Ford strike 80, 82–3
  general election (1979) 18–21, 179–81
  gravediggers' strike 110, 124–8
  local authority strikes 146–52
  memory ix, 2, 9, 11–12, 181–2, 184–6, 205, 208–9
  NHS strikes 162–4, 169–73
  road haulage strikes 86–8, 94–9, 105–6
  ownership 20, 106–8
  see also Grunwick strike; Hay, Colin; Stepping Stones; Thomas, James
Melbourne Times 125
Mellish, Bob 48
Micholl, James 151
middle class 35, 182, 208
Middlesbrough 135, 138, 143
Middlesbrough Council 147
miners 9, 39–40, 155
  strike (1984–5) x, 3, 193, 211, 213
minimum wage 31, 115–6, 211n16, 212
monetarism 52, 183–4
Moran, Joe 35
Morris, Jamie 8, 172–3
Murray, Len 61, 82, 116
myth
  definition 9–10
  evolution x, xii, 17–25, 110, 171, 173, 197–86
  resonance ix, xi, 2–5, 11–12, 14, 87, 98, 177–9, 205–215
  see also counter-memory
mythologizing *see* myth

Nation Union of Teachers (NUT) 112

National and Local Government
    Officers' Association
    (NALGO) 59, 61, 112, 169,
    202, 211
National Association for Freedom
    (NAFF) 35
National Day of Action 109, 114, 121,
    166
National Enterprise Board 47
National Freight Corporation 95
National Front 72
National Health Service (NHS)
    bonus schemes 161, 164
    employment 30, 154–7
    strike (1973) 163–4
    strike (1979) 5, 63, 153, 166–173
    strike (1984) 210
    unions 53, 158–61
National Industrial Relations Court
    38–9
National Joint Negotiating
    Committee (NJNC) 70–6,
    84
National Steering Committee against
    the Cuts (NSCAC) 53, 112–2
National Union of Mineworkers
    (NUM) 39 see also mining
National Union of Public Employees
    (NUPE)
    Dirty Jobs Strike 122
    leadership 8, 33–4, 172
    low pay 53, 115, 96–210
    memory 21, 110, 190–210
    minimum wage 212
    strikes (1979) 111–4, 118, 122, 124,
        127–8, 143–76
    women 5, 129–142, 183
National Union of Students (NUS)
    80
nationalization 30, 41–42, 54, 89, 213
    see also Alternative Economic
    Strategy (AES)
Newcastle 142

neo-liberalism x, 176, 204, 213–4
New Labour
    memory x, 5, 10 23 179, 186
    politics 188–204, 209–10
New Left 5, 33–5 131
Newman, Celia 64, 156, 160–1, 168–9,
    201–2
New Statesman 106
News of the World 104
Night Cleaners' Campaign 35
Northern Echo 91, 145
nostalgia *see* counter-memory;
    memory; myth

Oakley, Russ 166
Observer 107
oil tanker drivers 1, 92–95
Operation Drumstick 93
Organization of the Petroleum
    Exporting Countries
    (OPEC) 29, 39, 49, 164
Orme, Stan 51
Oxford 93
Oxford University 89

Palin, Michael 109
parental leave 43
Parliamentary Labour Party (PLP)
    40–54
Pearce, Malcom 28
Pearson, Ruth 58
People 20
Perks, Linda 135, 145–6, 198–9,
    211
pin money 31, 130, 132
Plymouth 128
political identity 14, 133, 177–204
popular culture 9, 24
Popular Front 71
Portelli, Alessandro 14
Poynton, Betty 180
Pratt, Brenda 124
privatization xi, 210

public sector
  employment 2–32, 41, 48, 53 212
  incomes policy 28, 38, 61, 206
  strikes 1, 57, 107–9, 110–28, 129–152, 153–176, 180, 205
  unionization 33–34
public sector borrowing requirement (PSBR) 47, 50, 184

Queen Elizabeth Hospital for Children 166, 171

race 15–17, 27, 59, 68, 178 211
Race, Reg 172
Raphael, Adam 107
Reece, Gordon 19
Reed International 20
Regional Emergency Transport Subcommittee 100
Revisionism *see* Croslandite Revisionism
Revolutionary Communist League 74
Richardson, Gordon (Baron) 183
road haulage
  denationalization 8
  memory 5, 86–7, 185, 187–9
  strike (1974) 88
  strike (1978) 1, 93–109
  unionization 91
Road Haulage Association (RHA) 90, 93
Robinson, Roy 145
Rodgers, William 'Bill' (Baron) 59, 87–93, 100–3, 108, 187–8, 193
Roe, Jeanette 167
Roldán, María (Doña) 14
Rose, Sonya O. 16, 161
Ross, Kristin 184
Rowbotham, Sheila 134, 208

Saatchi & Saatchi 17, 19, 21
Sandbrook, Dominic 83n114, 179, 182–3

Sawyer, Tom (Lord) 30, 132–4, 147, 15, 190, 195–6, 209–11
Scanlon, Hugh 33, 61, 71, 74
Scargill, Arthur 3
school caretakers 130, 135–6, 142, 147–8
school meals workers 5, 129, 135, 138–142, 147, 153, 197–8, 206
Schudson, Michael 10
Scottish National Party (SNP) 174
Scotland 88, 93, 173–4, 205
seamen's strike (1967) 28
secondary picketing 24, 87, 95, 99, 102, 104, 117, 153
Sedgefield Council 127
Sefton 127
Sewill, Brendon 40
Sewing Machinist Strike '68 *see* Equal Pay Strike
Sex Discrimination Act 184
shop stewards *see* grassroots activism
Shore, Peter (Lord) 51, 126–7
single motherhood *see* lone motherhood
Skinner, Dennis 126
Slowly, Johnny 66, 68, 79
Smith, Douglas 102
social class x, 12–17, 27, 68–9, 194–204, 209, 215
Social Contract
  development 44–49, 52–54, 57–61
  Ford 73–6
  NHS 170
  public sector 112–4
  road haulage 90
  success/failure 183, 194, 208
social democracy 22, 55, 179, 185, 193, 204
Social Democratic Party (SDP) 187, 194
socialism 2, 41, 44, 51, 56, 89, 121, 134, 158, 184–187, 209

The Socialist Challenge see Holland, Stuart
socialist feminism xi – xii, 43, 134
  see also feminism
Socialist Workers' Party (SWP) 35, 42
Solihull 115
Sounes, Howard 111
Southampton 71, 81
Southport 127
Spain 71, 159
Spanswick, Albert 115
stagflation 29
state of emergency
  debate (1978–79) 99–102, 109
  Fire Brigades' strike 57
  Heath Government 39–40
  Northern Ireland 100
Stepping Stones 18–19, 55–56, 59, 99, 149
  see also Hoskyns, John; Thatcher, Margaret (Baroness); Thatcherism
Stewart, Donald 174
Stewart, Geoffrey 28
Strategic Arms Limitation Talks (SALT II) 97
Strauss, Norman 55
strike committees 20, 100, 122, 143–5
Strummer, Joe 26
Sun 2, 19–21, 80, 98, 124, 149, 181–2, 185
Sunday Express 185
Sunday Mirror 20
Sunderland 142
Sutton Manor Colliery 80
synecdoche *see* Zeilzer, Barbie

Taft-Hartley Act 38
Tameside 127, 191–2
Taylor, Robert 13, 23
TGWU RTC (Regional Transport Commercial) 91

Thatcher, Margaret (Baroness)
  ideology 55–6
  media strategy 19–21, 59, 82, 87–88, 99–100, 107–9, 150–3, 179–82
  memory x, 8–10, 22, 177–179, 184–5, 195, 208–9
  party leadership 2, 54
  vote of no confidence 174–6
Thatcherism ix, xii, 10, 193, 210
  see also Conservative Party; Thatcher, Margaret (Baroness)
Thomas, James 2, 4, 22, 182, 184, 209
Thompson, E.P. 15
Times 186, 213
Tiratsoo, Nick 9, 11, 35, 69, 182–3
Todd, Ron 75, 82–3
Trade Unions and Employers' Associations 39
Trade Unions Congress (TUC)
  Conference (1978) 60–1
  Fire Brigades' Strike 57–8, 208
  General Council Vote (1978) 82
  Industrial Relations Act 39–40
  In Place of Strife 37
  public sector unions 33, 112, 116, 131
  Social Contract 45, 47, 54, 59, 111–2
Transport and General Workers' Union (TGWU)
  Ford 63–5
  health service 157, 162
  public sector 33, 53, 111, 118, 122, 143
  road haulage 86–109
Treasury 40, 48–51, 59
Tredwell, Brenda 167
Turner, Alwyn 24

unemployment xii, 2, 17, 29, 52, 5
University of Manchester 9
University of Warwick 136
US Federal Reserve 49

Index

Valentine's Concordat 171
Vietnam War 4, 29
Vincent, David 31

wage restraint *see* incomes policy
Waltham Forest 142
Warrington 102
Warwick Report 136–7, 151
   see also Bickerstaffe, Rodney; Fryer, Robert (Bob); Mallaber, Judy; Perks, Linda; Sawyer, Tom (Lord)
Watson, Nicola 96
Weekend World 180
Westminster Hospital 172–3
West Germany 31, 86
West Indies 30, 153, 156
Whattam, Brian 146
Whiston Hospital 154, 156, 160–1, 168–9, 201
Whitelaw, William (Viscount) 150
Whitty, Larry (Lord) 115, 118, 122–3, 177–8, 189–93, 200, 209–10
Wilson, Dolly Smith 31

Wilson, Harold (Lord) 28, 45, 47, 49
Wirral 127
Woking 128
Women's Liberation Movement *see* Women's Movement
Women's Movement xi, 5, 30, 34–5, 134–8, 199
Working for Ford see Beynon, Huw
Working Women's Charter 134
working class
   politics 13, 34, 66, 72, 85, 180–1, 193, 196, 206–13
   women 16, 132–134, 138, 151, 153, 155–7, 176, 200, 214–215
Wythenshawe 7

Yom Kippur War 29
Yorkshire 103, 106
Young Communist League 67
Young Conservatives *see* Conservative Party
Young, Hugo 22

Zeilzer, Barbie 21